W   AGE?

Other books by the author

Professional Titles
Language Teaching Course Design: Trends and Issues
Syllabus Design
The Learner-Centred Curriculum
The Teacher as Curriculum Developer
Language Teaching Methodology
Understanding Language Classrooms
Designing Tasks for the Communicative Classroom
Introducing Discourse Analysis
Research Methods in Language Learning
Second Language Teaching and Learning: Grammar
Collaborative Language Learning and Teaching
Practical English Language Teaching
Task-based Language Teaching
Second Language Teacher Education (*with Jack Richards*)
The Self-Directed Teacher (*with Clarice Lamb*)
Voices from the Classroom (*with Kathi Bailey*)
Pursuing Professional Development (*with Kathi Bailey and
    Andy Curtis*)
Learners' Stories: Difference and Diversity (*with Phil Benson*)
The Cambridge Guide to TESOL (*with Ron Carter*)
Knowledge and Discourse: Towards an Ecology of Language (*with
    Colin Barron and Nigel Bruce*)
Classroom Teachers and Classroom Research (*with Dale Griffee*)
New Ways in Teaching Listening (*with L. Miller*)

Textbook Series
ATLAS
Go For It
Listen In
Speak Out
Expressions

What is This Thing Called Language?

DAVID NUNAN

First published 2007 by
PALGRAVE MACMILLAN
Houndmills, Basingstoke, Hampshire RG21 6XS and
175 Fifth Avenue, New York, N.Y. 10010
Companies and representatives throughout the world

PALGRAVE MACMILLAN is the global academic imprint of the
Palgrave Macmillan division of St. Martin's Press, LLC and of Palgrave
Macmillan Ltd. Macmillan® is a registered trademark in the United States,
United Kingdom and other countries. Palgrave is a registered trademark in
the European Union and other countries.

ISBN-13: 978–0–230–00847–2 hardback
ISBN 10: 0–230–00847–X   hardback
ISBN-13: 978–0–230–00848–9 paperback
ISBN 10: 0–230–00848–8   paperback

This book is printed on paper suitable for recycling and made
from fully managed and sustained forest sources.

A catalogue record for this book is available from the
British Library.

A catalog record for this book is available from the
Library of Congress.

10	9	8	7	6	5	4	3	2	1
16	15	14	13	12	11	10	09	08	07

Printed in China

This book is dedicated to **Ron Carter** and **Mike McCarthy**: co-authors, co-editors, co-presenters, and, above all, friends. Readers familiar with their work will recognize their influence in the pages that follow.

Contents

List of Tables and Figures

Tables

Figures

Preface

I was sitting in the Foreign Correspondents' Club in Phnom Penh watching the sun set over the river and doodling on a beer mat when I felt a hand on my shoulder. The hand belonged to Steve Maginn, Managing Director of Macmillan Asia. Steve and I have known each other longer than either of us cares to remember. He treated me to a gin and tonic and asked what the doodling was all about.

'Well, I just had this idea for a book', I replied.
'About?'
'Language.'
'How far have you got with it?'
'Well I have a title. *What is this thing called language?* That is about as far as I've got.'
'Sounds interesting. You wouldn't let us have first refusal, would you? It's about time you did a book for Macmillan.'
'Buy me another drink and I'll think about it.'

He did, I did, and the result is this book. So, at the outset, I must thank Steve for his encouragement and enthusiasm for the project.

Heartfelt thanks go to my editor Kate Wallis who was unfailingly diplomatic in her critical comments on earlier drafts of the book.

I should also like to thank the anonymous reviewers for their detailed comments and suggestions. I am aware that I have not done justice to all of their comments, and needless to say, shortcomings that remain are mine alone.

I have drawn inspiration for this book from many sources. Particular acknowledgement goes to Michael Halliday. Michael is an inspiration to all who accept the premise that language is first and foremost a tool for communication, and the fields of linguistics, language study and language education would have been very different creatures without the conceptual models he developed over many years. Also important for my own development as a language educator and applied linguist have been David Crystal, Ronald Carter and Mike McCarthy. Their influence will be evident to all who are familiar with their work.

DAVID NUNAN

Acknowledgements

The author and publishers wish to thank the following for permission to use copyright material: Cambridge University Press for a figure from David Crystal, *The Cambridge Encyclopedia of Language*, 2nd edn (1997) p. 3; Continuum International Publishing Group for a figure from S. Eggins, *An Introduction to Systemic Functional Linguistics*, Pinter (1994) p. 54; David Higham Associates Ltd on behalf of the estate of the author and New Directions Publishing Corporation for an extract from Dylan Thomas, 'In the Beginning', from *The Poems of Dylan Thomas*, copyright © 1953 by Dylan Thomas; the International Phonetic Association for extracts from the vowel chart and the list of suprasegmentals, copyright © 2005 by International Phonetic Association; Leo van Lier for tables from his book, *Introducing Language Awareness*, Penguin (1995) pp. 3, 16–17; Routledge for a box from R. Carter *et al.*, *Working with Texts: A Core Introduction to Language Analysis*, 2nd edn (2001) p. 82; Short Books for extracts from Carl Newbrook, *Ducks in a Row* (2005). Every effort has been made to trace all the copyright-holders, but if any have been inadvertently overlooked the publishers will be pleased to make the necessary arrangement at the first opportunity.

Introduction: the stuff that surrounds us

Last night, I was trying to relax in front of the television. My daughter, who was doing a magazine crossword puzzle, kept interrupting me by calling out clues that she couldn't solve. Pretty soon the television was off and we were both hunched over the crossword puzzle, a dictionary and a thesaurus at the ready. The evening ended up in yet another arm wrestling match with language.

Language has been a large part of my life. Teaching it and writing about it have provided me with a decent living. Just as importantly, it has given me countless hours of fascination. It has entertained, puzzled and at times irritated me. I am intrigued by language, and I have spent my professional life trying to make sense of it. In this book, I hope to share the intrigue and, in the process, to inform and entertain you.

Some time ago, I bought a magazine called *Wallpaper*, a self-styled design and lifestyle magazine. I was hooked by the catchy subtitle – *the stuff that surrounds us*. If I had to give a single sentence answer to the question 'What is this thing called language?' my response would be 'It's the stuff that surrounds us!' However, just as fish are unaware of water (until they're taken out of it!), we are rarely aware of the language that surrounds us. And that, in a nutshell, is the aim of this book: to raise awareness of language.

This book is intended for students, teachers and teachers in preparation who do not have specialist training in **linguistics** or language analysis. As it assumes no specialist knowledge of theoretical or applied linguistics, it should appeal to anyone with an interest in language. As all our lives are ruled by language, I hope this means that it will appeal to everyone, not just students and laypeople, but also those who have a professional interest in the subject including teachers, authors and even perhaps the occasional linguist.

While the book aims to be academically rigorous, it also reflects a personal and somewhat idiosyncratic view of language. Woven through it are stories and anecdotes to illustrate the points I wish to make. I have also drawn on an extensive repository of spoken and written language samples collected over many years in a wide range of contexts and environments. These, I hope, will breathe life into what can sometimes be seen as a rather dry subject. (Language itself is never dry, but the way it is presented sometimes leaves a little to be desired.)

The first chapter is a general one, providing an overall introduction and orientation to the subject. It is followed by three chapters that present the three subsystems of language: the system of sounds, the system of words, and the system of grammar.

The rest of the book looks at the ways in which the three basic systems are used to do things with spoken and written language: to obtain goods and services, to socialize, to amuse, to entertain and to instruct. We shall look at how language is acquired, how it is used to create humour, and how it reflects gender differences. We shall also look at the new modes of communication that have emerged as a byproduct of the technological revolution. In the final chapter, I look ahead and speculate on the future of language.

This book is an exercise in **language awareness**, which was defined over twenty years ago as 'a person's sensitivity to and conscious awareness of the nature of language and its role in human life' (Donmall, 1985: 7). Van Lier, a more recent proponent of language awareness, characterizes it as 'an understanding of the human faculty of language and its role in thinking, learning and social life' (van Lier, 1995: xi).

Van Lier (1995: 10) summarizes his approach to language awareness by making four important points:

- Language is central to what it is to be human
- Usually we are aware of language only in a subsidiary sense, but we bring it into focal awareness when there are problems, or when we need to reach higher levels of knowledge or skill
- Language awareness can be of great importance in many aspects of life, including political, educational and social contexts
- Language awareness opens up new possibilities for language education in schools and avoids the extremes of prescribed correctness and utter neglect.

A high school teacher once said to me 'If you don't know where you're going, how will you know when you get there?' Obviously, there are some trips where it's crucial to know where you're going. Others however, are voyages of discovery. In fact, some of the greatest discoveries have been made by explorers who thought they were going in one direction and ended up some place else. As I embark on the writing of this book, my destination is a vague and distant prospect. I have a general idea of where I want to go, but may well end up some place else. In any case, I trust that you will embark with me, that you will find it an enjoyable trip, that you learn something new along the way, and that you agree, on disembarking, that the ride was worth the effort.

In the next chapter, I will begin to probe a little deeper into some of the issues and themes that have been fore-grounded in this introduction. The title of the chapter echoes that of the book; namely, 'What is this thing called language'? While it will take the rest of the book to provide anything like an adequate answer to the question, we will at least make a start in Chapter 1.

(Note: Words appearing in **bold** are defined, elaborated upon and exemplified in the Glossary at the end of the book.)

I What is this thing called language?

Introduction and overview

The aim of this chapter is to set the scene for the rest of the book. Some of the themes and key concepts that will be developed in the course of the book are introduced and illustrated here. The main subsections of the chapter, presented as bullet points below, sum up the terrain to be covered in this opening chapter.

■ Language as a defining characteristic of humanity
■ Language as a tool for communication
■ An introduction to language systems
■ Human and animal communication systems
■ The origins of language
■ The design features of language.

The chapter concludes with a brief overview of the rest of the book.

Language: a defining characteristic of humanity

Language is a common commodity. Unfortunate individuals with some form of pathology, and those religious figures who have taken vows of silence aside, humanity is assailed by language. Our lives, as the American linguist Deborah Tannen (1991) once remarked, are lived as a series of conversations. With relatively few exceptions, we all manage to acquire one (and often more than one) language in the first few years of life. Having acquired it, we use it until shortly before we draw our last breath. In short, language is the phenomenon that defines us as humans.

The main thing distinguishing humans from other animals is language. Of course, many animals also communicate in quite efficient ways, as the

4

dance of the bees, the sounds of dolphins, and the concerted actions of armies of ants demonstrate. But we humans feel that language is at the very core of our existence, that it defines us and shapes our being more than any other assets we possess (actually the ant, if we had a way of listening to it, might tell us the same thing). Language builds and cements our social relationships, helps us to think and allows us to reflect, is used first to educate us and subsequently by us to educate others. Without it no war can be declared nor peace announced, and neither ships nor babies can be named. Clearly, language is a vital area of study for a better understanding of ourselves and the improvement of our situation. (van Lier, 1995: 1)

Language is ubiquitous, it is all around us and we all possess it, and yet at the same time it is the most complex of all human phenomena and its acquisition borders on the miraculous. Despite the hundreds of researchers who have devoted their professional lives to investigating language acquisition and use, we still know comparatively little about it, although we do know a lot more than we used to. So, what is this thing called language? As you will see in the pages that follow, it is many things.

Language as a tool for communication

I want to begin this chapter with a couple of anecdotes that illustrate some important perspectives on language. The first is centred on a conversation that I overheard on a recent trip to California. It took place late one afternoon on the campus of a university in San Francisco where I had just given a talk. I was wandering around the campus trying to remember where I had left my rental car, when I was overtaken by a couple of smartly dressed young students carrying books and a notebook computer. As they passed me, the girl asked *So, who is that guy?*
The following conversation then ensued:

Boy: *That's our professor.*
Girl: *That's our professor?*
Boy: *THAT'S our professor.*

Here was part of a conversation made up of identical words and grammatical structures. The only difference was in the way that the words were uttered; in the intonation patterns and word **stress** – but what a world of difference they made. Whole realms of meaning were invested in the conversation, not by the grammar, not by the vocabulary, but by the way the words were spoken.

Although I understood the words and grammar perfectly, the conversation mystified me. I knew what the couple had said, but I did not know what they meant. Then I noticed that they were looking at a middle-aged man about my own age who was dressed the way I used dress as a student over thirty years ago – scuffed boots, torn denims and a lumber jacket. His head was shaved and he wore a long, scruffy beard. Apart from the bald head and the wrinkles, he could have been a student caught in a time warp from a former generation.

Instantly, the conversation made sense to me. Or rather, I made sense of the conversation. The visual context helped me get on the inside of the conversation, and served to remind me that non-verbal, contextual information is essential when it comes to making sense of language. It was clear that the girl had a great deal of difficulty accepting that a professor could look as dishevelled as this particular individual, and she expressed her incredulity in the form of a question – which, in fact, was not a question at all. Her male friend confirmed that this was indeed their new professor by repeating the utterance but by placing most stress on the initial word 'that'.

Here is another short conversation. I overheard the conversation as I was taking the lift to my office on my home campus in Hong Kong. It took place between the Professor of Jurisprudence and the Professor of Sociology. Both, as it happened, were Westerners.

So, did you have an enjoyable Christmas? asked the Professor of Jurisprudence.
I was in Beijing, replied the Professor of Sociology.
Oh, replied her companion.

I wondered whether she'd had a good time or a dismal time. It all depended on her attitude towards Beijing. Later, I ran into her in the faculty lounge and asked her what she thought of Beijing.
My husband's family lives there, she replied. I was still none the wiser on the question of whether she enjoyed Christmas or not, and had to ask her to spell out her attitude. (Later, I found that despite the pollution she was very fond of Beijing.)

So, what do these anecdotes have to do with the theme of this book? What insights do they provide into language and its functioning? How do they help us begin to frame a response to the question 'What is this thing called language?'

First, they tell us that language as a tool for communication can often be understood only from the inside out. As we will see, a great deal of language only makes sense in context. We can only interpret the words we hear and see when we have inside knowledge of the facts and circumstances surrounding their creation, and the loves, desires and hates of those who created them. Second, they show us that while we can tease apart and examine separately the different systems of language, the grammatical system, the lexical system (or system of words) and the phonological system (or system of sounds), this will only take us a certain way in our quest to comprehend the nature of language. Ultimately, if we really want to understand this most complex phenomenon, we need to see how the different linguistic systems work together. Finally, they illustrate the fact that ultimately language is about meaning and the creation of meaning, and the various subsystems of the language must be seen as servants to the master of meaning.

Language systems

In many books on language and linguistics, you will read that there are numerous systems; for example, the sound system, the vocabulary system, the grammatical system, the semantic (or meaning) system, the communication system and so on. But what do we mean when we use the word 'system'? Here are two dictionary definitions:

system n. 1. Complex whole, set of connected things or parts, organized body of material or immaterial things. (*Concise Oxford Dictionary*)
system n. 1. an assemblage or combination of things or parts forming a complex or unitary whole. (*Macquarie Dictionary*)

Although definitions of *system* vary, most either state or imply the following:

- a system consists of a set of 'things', entities or parts
- these are interconnected and interrelated in some way
- there are rules and principles specifying how they are interconnected
- parts of a system function to do a job.

There are open and closed systems. A closed system has a finite membership. In the natural world, closed systems would include the digestive system and the solar system. Open systems admit new members from time to time. In language, some systems are relatively closed (for example, the sound system), while others such as the lexical system are relatively open.

Language is commonly seen as a complex system consisting of the following subsystems (see, for example, van Lier, 1995). Do not be concerned if some of these terms are new to you. We will deal extensively with each of them in succeeding chapters. You can also consult the Glossary at the end of the book which provides definitions and examples.

From the diagram, you can see that these subsystems constitute a hierarchy, the subsystem above being assembled from the subsystem below. So, morphemes are made up of phonemes, words are made up from morphemes, phrases are made up from words and so on. When linguists talk of one system being made up from lower order systems they talk of **constituent structure** (Brown and Miller, 1988). Using lower level elements to understand higher level ones is known as **bottom-up processing**.

The position I take in this book is that while it is possible to argue that the bottom six levels of language constitute linguistic subsystems, the final level – discourse – does not. Phonemes belong to the subsystem of sounds; morphemes and words to the subsystem of

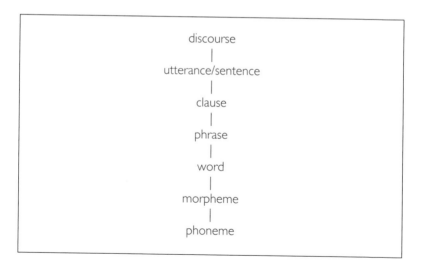

discourse
|
utterance/sentence
|
clause
|
phrase
|
word
|
morpheme
|
phoneme

FIGURE 1.1   BOTTOM-UP PROCESSING

lexicology; and phrases, clauses and utterances/sentences to the subsystem of grammar. Each has rules for determining 'well-formedness'; that is, what counts as an acceptable sound, word and sentence as well as rules for how they can be combined. As yet, however, linguists have been unable to do the same thing for discourse because discourse is a process rather than a product. This highest level of linguistic analysis has defied concerted efforts to characterize it in terms of 'well-formedness' because, although discourse is partly a linguistic phenomenon, it is also a psycholinguistic phenomenon. It exists in the mind as much as it does on the page. This does not mean that it is not systematic, nor that it does not display some of the characteristics of a system. However, the fact of the matter is that well-formedness will be determined, not by the acceptable arrangement of lower order elements, but by language users. Listeners, speakers, readers and writers draw on the lower-order subsystems, along with other sources of information, in creating discourse, but well-formedness is not determined by the selection and arrangement of these lower-order elements.

Well-formed discourse is determined by meaning. However, meaning is a psycholinguistic phenomenon that does not constitute a system. Asking where the meaning system is to be found is akin to the foreign visitor to the English city of Oxford who once asked *Nice town, but where's the University?* I am not sure what the host said in reply, but an appropriate response might have been 'You're standing in it!', because the town *is* the University. They do not exist as separate entities.

In this book, I present language as a tool for achieving ends that go beyond language itself. I will explore the ways in which the English language is constructed, and the resources it provides to do things – to order food and drink, to complain about the air-conditioning in our hotel room, to find out whether there are seats on the next shuttle flight to Barcelona, to bond with co-workers, to find out how we did on our last assignment, to make a joke, to write a poem, to cajole a friend into picking up our dry cleaning and so on.

What do I mean when I say that language is a tool for achieving ends that go beyond the language itself? In order to address this question, consider the following invented dialogue. (The great majority of language samples in this book are from real people engaged in authentic communication, but from time to time I'll throw in some examples of my own invention to illustrate a point.)

Context: In a restaurant
Waiter: *Are you ready to order?*
Customer: *Yes, I am.*
Waiter: *OK.*
Customer: *I'd like the minute steak with fries, please.*
Waiter: *That's a good choice.*
Customer: *And could I get a little salad on the side?*
Waiter: *Well done! You're obviously a master of polite requests, and you've really got modal verbs down pat!*
(Waiter departs never to be seen again.)

In this situation, while praise for facility with language might add a warm inner glow, what the customer really wants is food on the table. He is using language, not to demonstrate his linguistic acuity, but to satisfy his hunger.

In case you think this example is too fanciful to be taken seriously, here is an interaction that actually happened. It is my very first day on my very first visit to the United States and I am sitting in a restaurant trying to get served. A young man wearing a white coat and carrying a tray of glasses passes my table. I take him to be a waiter, and the following conversation ensures.

Me: *Excuse me.*
Waiter: *Yes?*
Me: *Can I get a coffee?*
Waiter: *Yes, you can.*

I catch occasional sightings of the waiter. He's busily clearing tables and pouring glasses of water. However, he doesn't come near me, and no coffee appears. Eventually he passes my table, pours me a glass of water and hurries off before I can protest that it's coffee I need right now, not water. Eventually a woman come up to me and takes my order for coffee.

I later asked an American friend about this puzzling incident. *Oh,* she said, *I guess that you were talking to the busboy. His job is to 'bus' or clear the tables. It isn't his job to take orders for food or drink. When you asked if you could order coffee in that restaurant, and he replied 'Yes', he was being perfectly truthful – you* could *order coffee there – just not from him! While you intended your utterance to be a request for coffee, he took it as a request for information because it's not his job to serve coffee.*

Human and animal communication systems

All creatures communicate with their own species, and many communicate across the species divide. The dog guarding the cemetery gate at the end of my street barked at me ferociously this morning as I passed him on my morning run. His meaning was clear and unambiguous, and I quickly crossed to the other side of the street. However, although most of us bark from time to time, human language is different from dog language, frog language, birdsong, and in fact, all non-human systems of communication. Here, I will touch on three things that make it different: in the first place it is arbitrary; second, it is creative and generative; third, as far as we know it is unique to the human species.

Before discussing these characteristics, it is worth mentioning that a great deal of human communication does not involve language. In many contexts, we convey our intentions just as animals do. We point, we grunt, we signal our attitude to circumstances and events by frowning, laughing, crying and shrugging. We also communicate through symbols and signs. Out driving, when we see a road sign consisting of an ⊕ we know that there is a crossroads ahead. When we see a ⚠, we know that there is a bend in the road.

Some symbols, such as the ⊕ and the ⚠ in the preceding paragraph, are widely used across cultures. Others are culturally specific, a fact that can sometimes cause problems. Just the other night in Hong Kong, I was having a drink in one of my favourite bars when the individual on the bar stool next to me struck up a conversation. He was on his way back to England after an unsuccessful business trip to China. *Couldn't make any headway at all,* he said, handing me his business card. I looked at his card, and thought I saw where the problem was. I pointed to the company logo, which consisted of a somewhat stylized owl, printed in the upper left-hand corner of his card.

Why do you have the owl as your logo?, I asked.
Well, my company wants to project an image of wisdom and protection, just like the owl.
Well, just so you know, I said, *in China it symbolizes deviousness and cunning! I'm not necessarily suggesting that the logo ruined your trip, but it won't have helped.*

(Some fascinating examples of intercultural communication, and miscommunication, can be found in Lustig and Koester, 1993, and similar texts on intercultural communication.)

At this point, it is pertinent to ask what it is that differentiates symbols such as a the ⚠ road sign and the owl logo from the symbols that make up languages. In the first place, the relationship between the language symbol and the thing it represents is arbitrary, whereas with the ⚠ and the owl there is a link between the symbol and the object or idea that it is trying to represent. With language, apart from onomatopoeic words such as 'Ouch!' and 'Bow-wow!' which are meant to provide some sort of direct representation between the sound and the object (although note that French dogs don't go 'Bow-wow!' – nor do Spanish dogs or Chinese dogs for that matter), the relationship is arbitrary. In the case of language, there is no direct connection or relationship between, say, the word *egg* and the object that accompanies our breakfast bacon. In fact, in French, Italian, Chinese and Arabic, it is not called *egg* at all.

Another characteristic of human language that linguists love to talk about is its generativity. This rather intimidating word (I prefer *creativity* myself) simply means that although there are finite numbers of sounds, words and structures in any language, these can be used to generate an infinite number of unique utterances. Many of the things that we say each day have never been said before and will never be said again. It is truly remarkable that with fewer than fifty sounds and (in written form) only twenty-six letters of the alphabet, the speaker of English can articulate an infinite number of ideas. These sounds and letters combine and recombine to constitute over 500,000 words, and we haven't even come close to running out of options. We even have plenty of single **syllable** options available (for example, *zug*, *wug*, *nop* are not currently part of the English lexicon but stand ready to be pressed in to service should the need arise).

Unlike symbol systems such as systems of road signs, where there is a one-to-one relationship between the symbol and the thing it represents, language is not so constrained. This is because, in the evolution of language, grammar intervened between the symbols and the entities and events that the symbols represent. Imagine that English had no grammar and its lexicon consisted of only seven words: *Betty, Bill, Ronan, tall, short, interesting, lonely*. It would only be possible to say seven things. Along comes grammar – specifically the singular form of the **verb** *to be*. We can now say twelve things. *Betty is tall, Betty is short, Betty is interesting, Betty is lonely, Bill is tall,* and so on. Add in the plural form of the verb *to be* plus the **conjunction** *and* and we can say an additional twelve things. *Betty and Bill are tall.* Add the ability to form questions by placing the verb in front of the subject, *is Ronan lonely? Are*

Betty and Bill interesting? and the generative power of language begins to make itself felt.

A further point worth noting is that, whereas symbols are used to represent objects and entities in the real world (rail crossings, stop lights and so on), language can be used to refer to things that no longer exist or that never existed. If I say *The King of France is bald*, or *The unicorn on the corner is green*, you will be able to form a mental image regardless of the fact that one of these entities no longer exists and the other, to my knowledge, never existed.

The origins of language

Where does language come from? Theories abound! Three early favourites discussed by the linguist Geoffrey Finch (2003) are the 'bow-wow' theory, 'the yo-he-ho' theory, and the 'pooh-pooh' theory. The bow-wow theory sees language as evolving from the noises made by animals as they were being hunted. The hunters imitated these sounds and turned them into human speech. According to the yo-he-ho theory, language evolved from the noises made by humans as they engaged in physical exertion. The final theory suggests that language evolved from the instinctive noises that humans make in the course of everyday life.

Finch points out that there are problems with all of these theories:

> To begin with, the first two assume that language was male in origin, since in most primitive groups it is the men who do the hunting and hauling. This seems odd because among modern humans women are generally acknowledged to have more verbal skills than men. Second and more importantly it is not immediately apparent how language offers advantages in the pursuit of any of these activities significant enough to have triggered the biological developments necessary for speech. (Finch, 2003: 11)

So, is language learned and passed down from generation to generation in the same way as other cultural knowledge and skills? Cognitive scientists think not. One such scientist, Steven Pinker (1994) is the well-known author of the best-selling book on language entitled *The Language Instinct*. He was also one of *Time* magazine's 100 most influential people in 2004 – a notable achievement for a linguist. Pinker argues that bow-wow theories and their ilk are nonsense, that language is an intrinsic characteristic of being human.

Language is not a cultural artifact that we learn the way we learn to tell the time or how the federal government works. Instead, it is a distinct piece of biological makeup of our brains. Language is a complex, specialized skill, which develops in the child spontaneously, without conscious effort or formal instruction, is deployed without awareness of its underlying logic, is qualitatively the same in every individual, and is distinct from more general abilities to process information or behave intelligently. For these reasons, some cognitive scientists have described language as a psychological faculty, a neural organ, and a computational module. But I prefer the admittedly quaint term 'instinct'. It conveys the idea that people know how to talk in more or less the same sense that spiders know how to spin webs. Web-spinning was not invented by some unsung spider genius and does not depend on having had the right education or on having an aptitude for architecture or the construction trades. Rather, spiders spin spider webs because they have spider brains, which give them the urge to spin and the competence to succeed ... Thinking of language as an instinct inverts the popular wisdom, especially as it has been passed down in the canon of the humanities and the social sciences. Language is no more a cultural invention than is upright posture. It is not a manifestation of a general capacity to use symbols: a three-year-old, we shall see, is a grammatical genius, but is quite incompetent at the visual arts, religious iconography, traffic signs, and the other staples of the semiotics curriculum. (Pinker, 1994: 18)

The claim of cognitive scientists such as Pinker that language is hard-wired into the human brain carries with it the implication that language is species specific – that it is unique to the human race, and is acquired in the same way as the spinal cord is acquired. Proponents of the hard-wiring hypothesis argue that non-human communication systems (such as the bark, yelp, or growl of a dog) have the same one-to-one correspondence as, say, road symbols. In other words, they are non-generative because they are bereft of grammar. Thus, they cannot be woven together with other sounds to create unique meanings.

This argument, however, is disputed by experts on animal communication, some of whom claim to have taught chimps languages that have the same generative and creative properties as human language. They argue that these chimps can use the symbols to create unique utterances. However, the assertion that chimps acquire language that contains all of the characteristics and attributes of human language, including generativity, can only be advanced after generations of chimps have acquired the language from their own species rather than from human beings. In other words, we need to wait and see whether parent chimps can pass on language to their offspring. (For an overview of the evolution of animal communication systems, see Noble, 1998.)

Pinker's book is brilliant, seminal even, and fully deserves the acclaim it received. Pinker himself has a compelling way with prose, and is an original and creative thinker. However, for me, there is something unsatisfactorily in the proposition that spiders spin spider webs because they have spider brains and that humans spin webs of human words because they have human brains. It's a closing-down-the-conversation kind of argument, akin to postulating the existence of God to explain the creation of the Universe. In short, it does not account for how language got there in the first place.

A comprehensive critique of Pinker's 'absolutist' position is presented by Cziko (1995). (See also Cziko, 2000; and Barron, 1996.) Cziko argues that language, along with all other human behaviour can be explained in terms of Darwinian processes of variation and selection. These arguments are quite complex, and I will not go into them here. However, I will come back to them in Chapter 7, when we look at first language acquisition and development.

Virtually all of the language samples in this book are taken from English rather than from other languages. This is because English is my own language and it is the one that I have worked in for many years. However, while the bulk of the examples are from English, the principles behind the book are applicable to all languages.

Design features of language

At this point, we can begin a tentative definition of language by looking at some of its design features. These features differentiate it from other human and non-human forms of communication. They include the fact that language is arbitrary, creative and multifunctional. (For a more elaborated list of formal and functional design features, see Finch 2003.)

Arbitrariness

Language is arbitrary in that there is no necessary connection between a word and the thing that it represents. Four legged, usually furry creatures that bark and are popular as pets around the world are called *dogs* in English speaking societies. However, they could just as well have been called *cats*, *albatrosses* or even *posts*.

Creativity

By *creativity*, I am not referring to the use of language to create poems, love songs, limericks and plays. I am referring to the fact that languages consist of a finite set of resources (Most varieties of English, for example, have around 46 sounds), and yet this finite set of resources can be used to generate an infinite number of grammatical and comprehensible utterances.

Multifunctionality

The third design feature that I want to highlight is multifunctionality. Through language, we can make statements about the world, we can obtain goods and services, we can express our attitudes and feelings, create maintain and extend human relationships, and we can use language to create connected discourse. Not only that, but we can package many of these functions into a single sentence or utterance. Consider the following utterance:

There's a fierce dog by your front gate, and I think it might bite.

In this single utterance, the speaker:

1 makes a propositional statement about an entity (*a dog*) its location (*by the front gate*) and a possible course of action (*might bite*);
2 utters a warning;
3 expresses attitudes and feeling (*fierce, might*); and
4 connects bits of the utterance to other parts of the utterance (*and, it*)

The structure of the rest of the book

One of my tasks in this book is to argue that there are three systems: the system of sounds, the system of words and the grammatical system (which are themselves made up of subsystems), and that these systems act as resources that enable us to create meaning. In the next three chapters, I will look separately at these three systems, pointing out some of their special characteristics and illustrating the characteristics in action. In doing so, I will draw on a range of language samples which I have collected over the years, or borrowed from other sources.

In the rest of the book, I will explore the ways in which we use these three linguistic systems to communicate. In Chapter 5, I will look principally at spoken communication. Chapter 6 looks at written language and compares it with spoken language. In Chapter 7, I will turn to the question of how languages are acquired in the first place. Chapter 8 is entitled *Language at play*. In this chapter, I will look at ways in which we have fun with language – using it metaphorically, creating jokes and so on. Then, in the final chapter, which is intended to bring closure to the topics and themes that emerge through the book, we will look specifically at English – at its varieties, and its future.

Summary and conclusion

In this initial chapter, I have taken a broad look at the question 'What is this thing called language?' I have argued that language consists of an interlocking set of systems and subsystems made up of sounds, words and sentences, and that these are meaning-making tools; resources through which listeners, speakers, readers and writers create, exchange and negotiate meanings, obtain and exchange goods and services and establish and maintain relationships. I have also argued that there is not a separate system of discourse, because discourse is the representation of mental processes. Rather than containing its own interlocking elements and entities, it is parasitical on the systems of sounds, words and grammar.

The chapter also looked at language as a phenomenon unique to the human species. In fact, it is the phenomenon that defines us as humans, and differs from other human and non-human communication systems in a variety of ways. The three that I highlighted in the last major subsection of the chapter are its arbitrariness, creativity and multifunctionality.

This book represents an initial foray into the world of **linguistics**. In it, you will be introduced to the study of sounds (**phonology**), words and their constituents (**lexicology** and **morphology**), the ways words are sequenced and combined (**grammar** and **syntax**), how language is used to convey meaning (**semantics**), and how it is used to get things done (**pragmatics**).

In summary, then:

■ Language is both content and process: that is, it is a body of content that can be memorized, pulled apart and put back together again, but it is also a resource for communicating
■ Language consists of three interlocking systems: the system of sounds, the system of words and the system of grammar
■ Ultimately language can only be adequately understood in context
■ Language is a unique human phenomenon displaying the characteristics of arbitrariness, creativity and multifunctionality
■ Taken together, these design features mark language as fundamentally different from the communication systems of other species.

Questions and tasks

1 How many different functions can you think of for the following utterances (as a warning, a request, an invitation and so on)? Which one is the most obvious? Which is the least obvious? Think of a context for the least obvious function.

The window is open.
I have two tickets for the movies.
It's Mum's birthday tomorrow.
I only have a few coins.

2 How does Speaker B reveal his/her feelings and attitudes in the following exchanges?

A: *I like your dress, Jenny.*
B: *It's Nancy, actually.*

A: *Think it'll rain?*
B: *It COULD do, but somehow I kind of think it won't.*

A: *That's my car over there.*
B: *THAT old wreck's your car?*

A: *Could I have more coffee?*
B: *You COULD, but well, we're just making a fresh pot. Mind waiting?*

Further reading

Bragg, M. (2003) *The Adventure of English. 500AD to 2000. The Biography of a Language* (London: Hodder & Stoughton).
Describes how a few tribal Germanic dialects evolved into the most powerful language on Earth.

Burgess, A. (1992). *A Mouthful of Air: Language and Languages Especially English* (London: Hutchinson).
An ideosyncratic survey of the evolution and nature of language.

Finch, G. (2003) *Word of Mouth: A New Introduction to Language and Communication* (Basingstoke: Palgrave Macmillan).
A clear, non-technical introduction to language.

Kuiper, K. and Allan W.S. (2004) *An Introduction to English Language: Word, Sound and Sentence*, 2nd edn (Basingstoke: Palgrave Macmillan).
This textbook has an excellent introductory chapter on the properties of human language.

2 The sound system

Introduction and overview

When you arrive in a foreign country, the first thing that assails you (often even before the customs and excise officers) is the sound of the language. First time visitors to Hong Kong often think the locals are singing to each other because of the exotic and, to those of us trying to learn it, mind-numbing variety of sing-song tones possessed by the Cantonese. The first time I went to Turkey, I thought I had landed in the middle of a major argument between everyone in earshot. I soon learned that shouting (or what, to my ears sounded like shouting) was simply normal Turkish conversation.

There are, in fact, two complementary disciplines involved in the study of speech sounds: **phonetics** and **phonology**. Phonetics is the study of speech sounds, including the mechanics of how they are formed and articulated, without any reference to meaning. Phonology is the study of the relationships between sounds and meaning in particular languages.

The study of the physiological, aerodynamic, and acoustic characteristics of speech-sounds is the central concern of phonetics. The study of how sounds are organized into systems and utilized in language is the central concern of phonology (Catford, 1988: 187).

In this chapter, the focus will be primarily on phonology. We will look at the following aspects of speech systems:

■ Sounds as a system
■ The physical mechanisms for producing sound
■ **Segmental** and **suprasegmental phonology**
■ Words and sound
■ The **International Phonetic Alphabet**
■ **Accents** and **dialects**.

Sounds as a system

Sounds constitute the first of three subsystems that all languages have for creating meaning. The second is the word system, and the third is the grammatical system. Each of these subsystems constitutes a resource for making meanings, and each exists in a hierarchical relationship: words are made up of sounds, and **sentences** are made up of words.

Firstly, to what extent do the sounds of a language constitute a system? The rather programmatic definitions in the previous chapter suggested that a system contains 'things' that are interconnected in systematic ways. In language, these 'things' are individual sounds which combine with each other in various ways. Most varieties of English contain around 46 different sounds. By combining this limited number of sounds in various ways, we can generate an infinite number of words. Think about it! Only a fraction of all possible combinations of these sounds are actually used in English, and yet they have generated hundreds of thousands of words.

Articulatory phonetics

Sounds are created when we expel air from our lungs, and at the same time, manipulate the stream of air in various ways with our lips, tongue, teeth and vocal cords. If we trap the air in our mouth, and then push it out suddenly by opening our lips, the resulting sound is the English /p/ as in *pill*. If, at the same time, we allow our vocal cords to vibrate, the sound is transformed into the English sound /b/ as in *bill*. If we open our lips slightly, place our flattened tongue against the hard palate (the roof of our mouth), and let out a puff of air, we produce the sound /t/ as in *till*. If we allow the vocal chords to vibrate, the sound will be transformed from /t/ to /d/ as in *dill*. Through these physical manipulations of puffs of air, we make tiny changes to the sound of a word that result in major changes to meaning. Single sounds that signal differences of meaning are known as **phonemes**. Variations to the pronunciation of individual sounds that do not signal difference of meaning are known as **allophones**. In English, for example, the /l/ sound is pronounced differently depending on the sounds that surround it. However, these differences do not signal differences of meaning, and are referred to as allophonic variation.

Consider a point that I made in the preceding chapter: that English only exploits a fraction of the possible combinations of sounds available to it. In the case of the *ill* combination, for example, we have *bill, dill, fill, gill, hill, ill, jill, kill, lill, mill, nill, pill, q(u)ill, rill, sill, till, will.*

However (in my dialect, at least), *aill, cill, eill,* and so on are ready and waiting to be deployed. In fact, we have used only a little over half of the possible combinations available to us.

Actually, this is something of an oversimplification. Not all word combinations are permissible. The English sound system has 'rules' prescribing certain combinations as well as the appearance of those combinations in certain positions. For example, the sound represented by /*ng*/ can appear at the end of a string of other sounds *sing, bring, acting,* but not at the beginning. Other languages, such as Thai, do allow words to be initiated with the /*ng*/ sound, and some very important words indeed are formed in this way – for example, *ngen* (money) and *ngan* (work). While native speakers of English have no difficulty pronouncing /*ng*/ when it appears in final position, they have great difficulty pronouncing it when it appears as the initial sound in a word. If you are a native speaker of English and don't speak any of the languages that deploy the /*ng*/ sound initially, try it and you will see what I mean.

The study of speech production, and the classification of sounds in different languages, is known as articulatory phonetics. Most books on this aspect of phonetics begin by describing the physical organs that are involved in the production of speech from the larynx and vocal chords, all the way through to the lips. These organs are identified in Figure 2.1.

These organs are used to produce speech through three processes: initiation, phonation and articulation. Initiation is the process of expelling air from the lungs. For English and most other languages, this airstream provides the 'fuel' for speech. Sounds are formed when air flows from the lungs past the organs of speech which manipulate it in various ways. One of these is phonation. This is the process of opening or narrowing the vocal chords as the stream of air passes through, resulting in either voiced or voiceless sounds. In a voiced sound, the process of narrowing the vocal chords causes them to vibrate together, producing sounds such as /*b*/. In contrast, leaving them open results in sounds such as /*p*/.

This difference can be significant as we saw above in the case of 'bill', which begins with a voiced consonant and 'pill' which begins with its voiceless equivalent. Articulation describes the ways in which the tongues and lips impede and manipulate the flow of air in various ways.

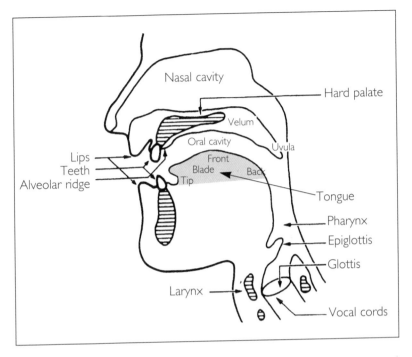

FIGURE 2.1   ORGANS OF SPEECH

Segmental and suprasegmental phonology

The academic study of the sounds in a language, and the relationship between sounds and meaning, is called phonology. There are two ways in which languages create meanings through the sound system. The first is by changing the individual sounds within words (for example, changing the sound represented by the phonetic symbol /i/ to the sound represented by the phonetic symbol /e/ turns *ship* into *sheep*. (In phonemic transcription, use of slanted brackets indicates that the word inside the brackets is a phonemic symbol, not a letter of the alphabet.) These are known as the segmental features of language, and words such as *ship* or *sheep*, which differ only in a single vowel or consonant, are known as **minimal pairs**. The second, as we saw in Chapter 1, is by changing the way that we 'sing' the words; that is, through the stress, the rhythm and the intonation of our utterances (what phonologists call the suprasegmental features of language).

As we have already seen, individual sounds in a language are known as phonemes, and are fundamental building blocks of meaning. *The President is on the ship* has a very different meaning and calls forth a very different, and some would say more appealing, mental image than *The President is on the sheep* (although a speaker whose first language is Spanish may well say the latter when he means the former!). On the other hand, *The President is on the shup* has no meaning, at least not in any dialect that is familiar to me.

Not all languages share the same phonemes. In English, the sounds represented by the letters /l/ and /r/ are phonemes because changing /l/ to /r/ changes the meaning of the word – *lock* is different from *rock*, *low* is different from *row*. In some Asian languages such as Japanese and Thai, however, these sounds are not phonemes. Not only do Japanese and Thai speakers have trouble pronouncing *lock* and *rock* so that they sound different, they have difficulty even hearing the difference. For their part, Thais have sounds that native speakers of English have trouble differentiating. For example, they have three phonemes where English speakers have only two. The /b/ /p/ distinction is a case in point. Thai has a third sound where the /p/ sound is pronounced with an additional puff of air. We can represent this sound as /ph/. So Thais have three words *bit*, *pit*, and *phit*, where English speakers have (and hear) only two.

The second way of changing the meaning of what we say is by changing the stress, rhythm or intonation of our utterance. In some languages, such as Chinese, altering the tone or intonation of a word changes the propositional meaning; that is, what the word refers to. In Chinese, the word *ma* can mean 'mother', 'hemp', 'horse' or 'to scold'. In English, the word has a single semantic meaning. We can do what we like with our vocal cords in the process in pronouncing *ma* – sing it, say it with a high tone or a low tone – but it will emerge in the ears of the listener as 'mother'. This is not to say that stress, rhythm and intonation are irrelevant to meaning in English, but they create a different kind of meaning. Changing the tone doesn't change the semantic meaning, it changes the functional meaning. Spoken with a high tone, *ma* could be a warning, *ma* spoken with a rising intonation becomes an interrogative, while *ma* uttered with a falling tone could be a remonstration.

Ma (high tone) (*Be careful, he's got a gun.*)
Ma? (rising tone) (*Is that you?*)
Ma! (falling tone) (*How could you say such a thing?*)

The fact that different language families use intonation for different purposes creates problems when first language speakers of a tonal language try to communicate in a non-tonal language and vice versa. My first opportunity to try learning a tonal language occurred when I moved to Thailand to work. At first, my struggles to speak Thai were met with blank incomprehension on the part of the local Thais. However, I persisted and my efforts gradually paid off as incomprehension was replaced by partial understanding, which was also often accompanied by helpless laughter on the part of my interlocutors.

This first time this happened was in a restaurant when I had made what I thought was a pretty simple request for some iced water (*nam khang* spoken with a rising tone as though asking a question). When the glass of water finally arrived it was tepid and had an alarming brown tinge. I waved the glass away, saying that I'd ordered iced water (*bok wah nam khang*). The waiter said nothing although his eyes began to water. He went back to the kitchen where he reported what I'd said to his co-workers. Their laughter caused all eyes to look my way. Learning and trying to use another language is an exercise in ritual humiliation – at least, in the early stages.

Later, when I asked a Thai friend what I had done wrong, she told me that I had allowed my English native-speaking tonal system, which signals attitude, to override the Thai tonal system. In Thai *nam khang*, meaning iced water, is spoken with a rising tone. However, when I had remonstrated with the waiter, I had used a falling tone, as I would have done in English (*But I asked for iced water!*). Unfortunately for me, *nam khabg*, uttered with a falling tone, means 'shin bone water' – or words to that effect.

Intonation in English is not only a tool for expressing feelings, attitudes and emotions, it also serves an important conversational management function. Ending an utterance with an upward inflection sends a signal to the listener that there's more to come. Ending with a downward inflection tells the listener that you've finished your turn and are ready to yield the floor.

Word stress works together with intonation to convey important attitudinal information. This can be illustrated by returning to the anecdote used in the introduction to the book. There, I reported the following conversation:

A: *That's our professor.*
B: *That's our professor?*
A: *THAT'S our professor.*

Each utterance in the conversation is identical in terms of what is said. The only difference is how each utterance is articulated: the second with an upward inflection, the third with the stress on the first word. These differences in pronunciation signal important differences in the meaning of the utterances. However, as we've already seen, the differences do not relate to the content of the utterances, but to the attitude of the speaker. Repeating, with an upward inflection, what someone has just said sends a signal that you have doubts about what you just heard, and would like confirmation.

Tonal languages vary in terms of the number of tones that are significant for changes in meaning. Putonghua, the official Chinese dialect of Mainland China has four tones, Central Thai dialect (used in Bangkok and the surrounding region) has five, Northern Thai has seven, and Cantonese (used in the Southern Chinese region of Guangdong as well as the Special Administrative Region of Hong Kong) has nine. The problem for first language speakers of non-tonal languages is that they can't even hear the difference between some tones, let alone produce them. Some people believe that you can get away with mis-spoken tones – *Surely they must be able to understand me, the sounds are not THAT different!)* – but that has not been my experience. To native speakers of a tonal language, changing the tone alters the word completely.

As I've already indicated, languages like English use tones, too, not to signal semantic differences, but to signal differences of attitudinal meaning. They also have a similarly rich array of tones. While experts disagree on the exact number of tones that are used by speakers of English, the consensus is that, depending on the dialect, the range is somewhere between five and eight. (Think of how many different ways you can say *Uh-huh* or *no*, and how many shades of attitudinal meaning they convey.) Here is an example from my own discourse collection.

Daughter: *Mom, can I get a belly-button ring?*
Mother: *No.* (falling tone)
Daughter: *Did you say yes?*
Mother: *No* (rising tone)
Daughter: *Well, I kinda got one today.*
Mother: *No!* (low tone)

In this interaction, the mother utters the word *no* three times, each time using a different intonation pattern. Changing the intonation alters the functional force of the utterance.

Word and syllable stress also help to highlight the bits of a conversation that are of most interest at any one point in time. Consider the following three variations of what, by now, is a well-worn utterance.

THAT'S our professor.
That's OUR professor.
That's our PROFESSOR.

Each of these places the emphasis on a different part of the message, and each would be appropriate for different communicative contexts. For example:

A: *Is that our new professor?*
B: (No) *THAT'S our professor.*

A: *Is that your boyfriend's professor?*
B: (No) *That's OUR professor.*

A: *Is that our laboratory demonstrator?*
B: (No) *That's our PROFESSOR.*

Here, stress serves to highlight that element of the utterance that is most important within the conversational context. Stress can also be significant within words as well. For example, the 'default' pronunciation of Japanese is to place the main stress on the last of the three syllables that make up the word, as in the following conversation.

A: *What's her nationality?*
B: *She's JapaNESE.*

However, English, being the extremely flexible language that it is, allows for at least one other option.

A: *She's Chinese, right?*
B: *No, she's JApanese.*

One of the themes of this book is that the three systems in language work together to enable us to create meaning. Intonation, for instance, works hand in hand with grammatical features in structures such as question tags to let the listener know how certain we are about the truth of a given proposition, as the following examples show.

She's Chinese, isn't she? (rising intonation)
We can gloss this as: I believe that she's Chinese, but I'm really not certain.

She's Chinese, isn't she? (falling intonation)
Here, the falling intonation indicates that the speaker is pretty confident that the person being talked about is Chinese, but would like the interlocutor to confirm this.

In most traditional grammar textbooks, the rule for question tags is that, if the verb in the main clause is positive, then the verb in the tag is negative, and if the verb in the main clause is negative, then the verb in the tag is positive. However, it is possible for both verbs to be positive, as in the following example:

She Chinese, is she? (rising intonation)
We can gloss this utterance as follows: 'I thought she was Japanese, but I've just received information that leads me to revise my belief.'

It is not only the sounds and the way they come out of our mouths that are important, but also the spaces between the sounds. The only difference between the next two utterances is where the pause occurs.

My brother (pause) *who lives in New York* (pause) *is visiting me in Hong Kong.*
My brother who lives in New York (pause) *is visiting me in Hong Kong.*

This tiny difference in pausing signals a considerable difference in meaning. The implication of the first utterance is that I have only one brother, while the implication of the second is that I have more than one – I'm referring to the brother who lives in New York as opposed to the ones who live in New Orleans and St Louis.

Without wishing to dwell on a point that might by now be the obvious, consider how different the following utterances are depending on where you pause for breath.

A woman without her man (pause) *is nothing.*
A woman (pause) *without her man is nothing.*

Here, the pauses turn the meaning of the utterance through 180 degrees, the first utterance implying that a woman is nothing without a man, while the second implies that a man is nothing without a woman.

Stress and intonation also help us to manage another aspect of communication that can cause severe ruts in the road to communication. This is to differentiate between information that is already shared by both speakers, or is assumed to be common knowledge, and information that is new. In the following fragment (in which the stress, rhythm, intonation and pitch can only be crudely represented by capital letters), the speakers use stress and pitch to highlight the new information.

A: *I can't find my SKIRT.*
B: *What, your BLUE skirt? The one you had on this MORNING?*
A: *No, the one I had on last NIGHT.*

In this conversation the new information is spoken strongly, and with a high pitch. This helps both participants to keep the conversation on track.

These same pronunciation features are used to signal disagreements between speakers, as in the following conversation:

A: *How much is the watch?*
B: *It's five hundred dollars.*
A: *Wow, that's EXPENSIVE.*
B: *It's NOT expensive.*
A: *It IS expensive – more than I can afford.*
B: *Well, it's not THAT expensive, not for a pre-owned Rolex.*

Here, the first speaker emphasizes *expensive*. The second speaker signals his disagreement by restating A's utterance in the negative and emphasizing *not*. A then reasserts her original proposition but this time emphasizing the verb 'to be', thus contrasting with B's prior utterance. B then softens his original claim by emphasizing *that*.

Words and sound

In the next chapter, we will look at the concept of the 'word'. You might imagine that such a concept is unproblematic, that everyone knows what a word is – that, in written language, it's a string of letters separated on either side by a white space and that, in spoken language, it's a cluster of sounds separated on either side by a pause. While this might seem a reasonable rule-of-thumb way of defining the concept, a moment's reflection will reveal that it doesn't hold up.

You only have to listen to someone speaking for a few seconds to realize that spaces do not mark the beginning or end of words in any clear-cut fashion. Here is a snatch of conversation I overheard in the foyer of my apartment block yesterday.

A: *How old is your dog?*
B: *Ten or eleven.*

The two utterances contain five and three words respectively. However, this is not what I heard. What I heard was more like:

A: *How oldzya dog?*
B: *Tenner eleven.*

When we speak, we run words together, we change the pronunciation of individual sounds to fit in with the sounds that come before and after, and we drop some sounds altogether. The two instances of *the* in the following fragment of dialogue from the movie *Suddenly Last Summer* are both pronounced differently, the difference being determined by the word that follows it.

Boy: *I'd like to get you between the sheets.*
Girl: *I'd like to get you between the eyes.*

When first encountering a foreign language, these speech characteristics make it difficult to decide how many words we are hearing, and where one word ends and another begins. Learning how to break the stream of speech into meaningful chunks is a major challenge for beginning learners. I have been living and working in Hong Kong for many years now, trying to pick up Cantonese informally through casual contact and conversation (not as easy as you might think, but that's another story.) I'm constantly discovering a chunk of language that I thought was a single word is actually two, and sometimes three, different words.

Stress timing

A major challenge for learners of English is the fact that it is what's known as a stress-timed language. In this, it contrasts with languages

THE SOUND SYSTEM **31**

such as Italian, Spanish and Japanese which have a regular rhythm or beat in which stressed syllables alternate with unstressed syllables. It is true that some English utterances conform to this alternating stressed/unstressed/stressed/unstressed pattern; for example:

*I'd **like** to see the **film**.*

Most however, have an 'irregular' rhythm. This is brought about by the fact that when unstressed syllables occur in a sequence they are uttered rapidly, the words being squashed together so that they occupy the same amount of 'air time' as a single stressed syllable. It's for this reason that English is called 'stress timed'. Try saying the following sentence and see how it sounds:

*There was a **great show** at the **Lyric last night**.*

The rhythm of normal spoken English is not a simple pattern in which, say, every second or third syllable is prominent. It is only in music and poetry that we find deliberate patterning of this kind. The rhythm of normal speech is a consequence of the words that happen to make up the utterance. (Yallop, 1995: 91–2)

For foreign learners of English, getting the hang of this irregular rhythm can be quite a challenge. In fact, some learners never quite master it, and persist with the alternating stressed/unstressed pattern of their first language when speaking English.

Unfortunately, for learners of English as a foreign language, there are very few hard and fast rules in the sound system of English (or in the lexical or grammatical systems, either, as we shall see). In fact, it is probably better to speak of 'operating principles' than 'rules'. Thus, the pronunciation of the examples above will vary according to the communicative contexts in which they are uttered. For example:

A: *Molly doesn't want to see the film.*
B: *Well, I'd like to see the film.*

The communicative functions of intonation

This last example underlines another function of stress, rhythm and intonation, which is to express attitudinal or emotional meaning. Intonation is particularly important as a vehicle for expressing attitudes, feelings and emotions. That said, making generalizations about how the system works for expressing anger, happiness, boredom or annoyance is notoriously difficult. Apart from anything else, it is the context in which an utterance is made that will have as much bearing on the listener's interpretation as the way in which the utterance is made. *How can I EVER thank you?* will be interpreted as a genuine expression of thanks or a sarcastic comment according to the actions or deeds that accompany the utterance. (For a detailed, if somewhat challenging account of the communicative value of intonation, see Brazil, 1997.)

The linguist David Crystal (1997a) suggests that intonation has six important communicative functions: emotional, grammatical, **information structure**, textual, psychological and indexical. We have already looked at examples of some of these functions. Here is how Crystal describes them:

Emotional: The most obvious function is to express a wide range of attitudinal meanings – excitement, boredom, surprise, friendliness, reserve, and many hundreds more.

Grammatical: Intonation plays an important role in the marking of grammatical contrasts. The identification of such major units as clauses and sentences depends on the way pitch contours break up an utterance; and several specific contrasts, such as question and statement, or positive and negative, may rely on intonation.

Information structure: Intonation conveys a great deal about what is new and what is already known in the meaning of an utterance – what is referred to as the 'information structure' of the utterance. If someone says *I saw a BLUE car*, with maximum intonational prominence on blue, this pronunciation presupposes that someone has previously queried the color, whereas if the emphasis is on *I*, it presupposes a previous question about which person is involved.

Textual: Intonation is not only used to mark the structure of the sentences; it is also an important element in the construction of larger stretches of discourse. [This] is well illustrated in the way paragraphs of information are given a distinctive melodic shape in radio news-reading. As the news-reader moves from one item of news to the next, the pitch level jumps up, then gradually descends, until by the end of the item the voice reaches a relatively low level.

Psychological: Intonation can help to organize language into units that are more easily perceived and memorized. Learning a long sequence of numbers, for example, proves easier if the sequence is divided into rhythmical 'chunks'.

Indexical: [These language] features also have a significant function as markers of personal identity – an 'indexical' function. In particular, they help to identify people as belonging to different social groups and occupations (such as preachers, street vendors, army sergeants).

As we have already seen, this aspect of communication is highly language specific. Different languages use intonation for different purposes. Stress and intonation patterns inherited from our first language are highly resistant to change, as I discovered through my bumbling attempts to order iced water in Thailand. Just as it is difficult for English speakers not to allow attitudinal aspects of their message to override the tones they are meant to use to express different semantic meaning, so, too, speakers of other languages have difficulty embracing the intonation system of English. In the field of **sociolinguistics**, which studies the social effects of language, there are several documented instances of Hindi speakers of English in Britain unintentionally giving offence and projecting an attitude of rudeness and arrogance, simply because they have transferred intonation patterns from their first language into English.

As the phonologist Peter Roach (1991) has pointed out, making assumptions about emotional states based on intonation takes us into tricky territory. In the first place, the expression of an emotion may be voluntary or involuntary. If you say something in a happy way, it may be because you are actually happy, or because you want to convey the impression of happiness. Additionally, the attitude that is being expressed could be directed at the listener, towards what is being said, or towards some external event or situation. Only an 'insider' analysis of the context will reveal potential ambiguities. As I have mentioned several times already, in order to understand this thing called language we need to experience, and examine, language within the communicative contexts that gave rise to it in the first place.

Roach's point about emotional states is nicely illustrated by an exchange I overheard between colleagues (call them Martha and George) at a school parent–teacher social evening:

Martha: *Hi George.*
George: *Martha. Say, I just heard about Sarah.* (Martha's daughter)
Martha: *Oh, yeah?*
George: *Yeah. Congratulations on her success – that's FANTASTIC! REALLY well done.*
Martha: *Yeah. We were thrilled.*

George: *Please give her my congratulations.*
Martha: *I will. Thanks.*

When Martha moved away to get a drink, I asked George what it was with her daughter, Sarah, that deserved such hearty congratulations. George told me that she had just been admitted to a highly prestigious and extremely selective private school. *You sounded really thrilled,* I said. *How come?* George looked at me and replied, *Well actually, I'm so envious that you wouldn't believe it. You see my daughter was also competing for a place at the school but didn't make it. It cost me a lot to congratulate Martha.*

Representing spoken language

One of the challenges in learning spoken and written English is that the relationship between the individual sounds (phonemes) and letter (**graphemes**) is indirect, or, as van Lier puts it, 'opaque'.

> It is important to realize that letter and sound are two different concepts and that, as a consequence, written and spoken language can be quite different. The less directly the written word reflects the spoken one, the more *opaque* we might call the relationship. Languages differ in terms of the degree of opacity there is between their written and spoken representations. Here is an informal ordering of some European languages:

more opaque				*less opaque*
◄ - ►				
English	*Danish*	*French*	*Spanish*	*Finnish*
|	|	|	|	|
thought	*morgen*	*deux*	*dedo*	*kukka*
|	|	|	|	|
θɔːt	**mɔːn**	**dɵ**	**deðo**	**kukːa**

(van Lier, 1995: 16–17)

As you can see from van Lier's figure, English exists at the extreme end of the 'opacity' scale. This means that the relationship between the symbols and the sounds that they represent can be extremely indirect. According to Yallop (1995: 77):

The more you study English spelling, the more you realise how indirect the relationship is between sound and spelling … there are many instances where the patterning of letters creates written forms that have only an indirect relationship.

The playwright George Bernard Shaw illustrated this point by arguing that 'fish' could be spelled as 'ghoti': 'f' as in 'tough', 'i' as in 'women' and 'sh' as in 'nation'. However, this does not mean that the language is totally chaotic, as some have asserted; merely that learners of English have more work to do when learning to read and write the language than learners of some other languages.

In order to represent spoken language more accurately in written form, the International Phonetic Alphabet was developed by the International Phonetics Association. In this alphabet, there is a one-to-one relationship between symbols and the sounds that they represent. Figure 2.2 shows the symbols for representing vowels. Figure 2.4 shows the symbols for representing suprasegmental aspects of pronunciation. These and other charts can be viewed at the IPA website (http://www.arts.gla.ac.uk/ipa/ipa.html). (See also Figure 2.3.)

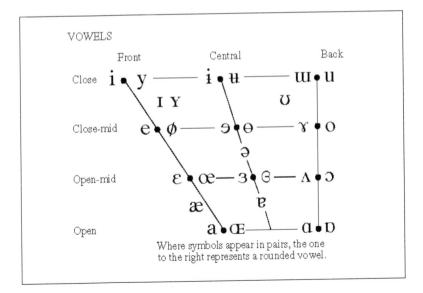

FIGURE 2.2 IPA SYMBOLS USED IN THE TRANSCRIPTION OF ENGLISH

Figure 2.2 not only shows vowel symbols, but gives a diagrammatic representation of where in the mouth the tongue is positioned when the sound is made. Imagine the head in Figure 2.1 superimposed on Figure 2.2. We would see that when the sound represented by the symbol /u/ is produced, the tongue is pushed up against the soft palate at the back of the mouth. For sounds represented by /l/, it is brought forward against the hard palate.

symbol	keyword	symbol	keyword
ɪ	bit	e	bet
æ	bat	ʌ	but
ɒ	pot	ʊ	put
ə	about		
i:	bead	ɑː	bard
ɜː	bird	ɔː	board
u:	food		
eɪ	tail	aɪ	tile
ɔɪ	toil	əʊ	coal
aʊ	cowl	ɪə	pier
eə	pear	ʊə	poor
p	pill	b	big
t	till	d	dig
k	kill	g	gig
f	fin	v	van
θ	thin	ð	than
s	sin	z	zip
ʃ	shin	ʒ	pleasure
h	hill		
m	some		
n	sun		
ŋ	sung		
tʃ	choke	dʒ	joke
l	lay	w	wet
r	ray	j	yet

FIGURE 2.3 SYMBOLS USED IN THE TRANSCRIPTION OF ENGLISH
Source: Roach, 1992: 125

Figure 2.4 illustrates symbols used to indicate suprasegmental features of speech such as stress and intonation.

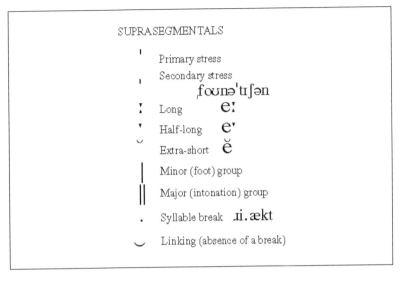

FIGURE 2.4 IPA SYMBOLS FOR REPRESENTING SUPRASEGMENTALS

Accents and dialects

One of the first things that a listener will notice (possibly even subconsciously), when they hear us speaking for the first time, is our accent. Accent refers to the ways in which we produce sounds and words.

Every time we open our mouth, the sounds that we make will lead those around us to make judgements about us. Our social standing, intelligence, and even our morals will be judged by our accent. In many social contexts and situations, how we speak is probably even more significant than what we say.

We all have prejudices when it comes to accents. When I lived in England, I frequently travelled to the north of Scotland. The further north I travelled, the more attractive the accents seemed. When I mentioned this to a friend – a fellow Antipodean, she said that for her the opposite was the case. Back in those unenlightened days I was several times refused service in London bars. When I asked why, I was told, *We don't serve Australians in here*. Several years later the Australian sit-com *Neighbours* became hugely popular in the United Kingdom, and Aussie accents were deemed 'cute'. Unfortunately for me, this came too late: I had moved on, and so had my accent.

> Differences between accents are of two main sorts: **phonetic** and **phonological**. When two accents differ from each other only phonetically, we find the same number of phonemes in both accents, but some or all of the phonemes are realised differently. There may also be differences in stress or intonation, but not such as would cause a difference of meaning ... Within the area of segmental phonology, the most obvious type of difference is where one accent has a different number of phonemes (and hence of phonemic contrasts) from another. (Roach, 1991: 188).

Accents place us as individuals both geographically and socially. This is probably why many people make judgements about others on the basis of the way they speak. Accents place a speaker geographically in terms of a region (for example, a Londoner versus a Glaswegian) or in terms of a country (a South African versus an Australian), and a listener may make judgements about the speaker on the basis of his or her prejudices about that person's place of origin.

In some countries, listeners also sometimes make judgements about a speaker's educational background and social standing on the basis of their accent. This is exemplified in Britain by what is known as Received Pronunciation (RP), also known as 'BBC English', because once upon a time, RP was a requirement for anyone wanting a job as an announcer with the BBC. Although only spoken by a tiny minority of the population, it developed and maintained its ascendancy because its users were drawn largely from the social and educational elite.

> There are clear historical reasons for the use of RP as the model accent [in the first half of the twentieth century] virtually any person qualified to teach in a university and write textbooks would have been educated at private schools. RP was (and to a considerable extent still is) mainly the accent of the privately educated ... It survives as the model accent for various reasons. Firstly, it is widely used in 'prestige' broadcasting such as newsreading. Secondly, it is claimed to belong to no particular region, being found in all parts of Britain (though in reality it is much more widespread in London and the South-East of England than anywhere else). Thirdly, it has become accepted as a common currency – an accent that (it is claimed) everyone in Britain knows and understands. (Roach, 1992: 89).

Received Pronunciation is sometimes equated with Standard English. Standard English is not synonymous with RP, although in Britain many speakers of Standard English speak it with something approximating RP. It can, in fact, be spoken with any accent. It is also not just restricted to British English. There is, for instance, Standard American English and Standard Australian English.

Standard English refers not just to accent – that is, the sounds a speaker utters – but also to grammar and vocabulary choices. Here, we need to consider dialect, and thus stray beyond the essential concern of this chapter, which is the sound systems of language. While accent refers to variations in the pronunciation patterns of particular speech communities, dialect is a broader term, encompassing differences of accent, vocabulary and grammar. The academic discipline that studies regional variations at this level is known as dialectology. Dialects, like accents, can reveal the speaker's region or country of origin, his or her social class, and whether or not he/she is a native or non-native speaker. (Richards *et al.* 1985).

According to Crystal (2004) the promotion of Standard English is a relatively recent phenomenon. We don't know what the situation was before the Middle Ages because too few written samples of language exist. As Crystal points out, we need a lot of text before the properties of a dialect begin to reveal themselves. From the Middle English period, we have a wide range of texts written by many different individuals living and working in a range of contexts and environments. From these texts, we see that standardization was not something that bothered their creators. Many even spelled their own name in different ways. Needless to say, this can lead to breakdowns in communication.

> The problem, of course, is not the writer's (or miswriter's) , but the reader's. If I am allowed to spell my words any way I want, this makes my task as a writer easier, but it makes the task for my reader more difficult. I might decide to write the word *flower, flowr, floor, flouer,* or in other ways, and I will know what I mean when I do so. But my reader has to work out what I meant ... There must have been a point, in late Middle English, when the variable ways of spelling different words began to overlap so much that ambiguity started to become a real issue. (Crystal 2004: 226)

Thus the rationale for promoting Standard English is that it ensured mutual comprehensibility in both spoken and written forms (although it is interesting to note that the problem first became apparent with the increasingly widespread use of written English in the Middle English period). Its promotion in educational contexts, however, has been controversial. Critics claim that it devalues and thereby 'disempowers' speakers of non-standard varieties. In some parts of the United States, debate has raged over whether Black Vernacular English (BVE), a variety spoken by many working class African Americans, should be allowed in schools. Proponents argue that all children have the right to be educated in their native dialect, and that to proscribe a dialect is to stigmatize and disadvantage its users.

Standardization can come about in a number of ways. It can evolve over time, out of a practical need to maintain mutual comprehension. Alternatively, it can be determined almost overnight, by fiat. The decision to impose Mandarin, or Putonghua, on all of China was made at a meeting in which Cantonese lost out by a single vote.

Attempts to proscribe non-standards forms, however, have not met with overwhelming success. Witness the spread of aspects of Black Vernacular English into non-black communities via popular culture, particularly music. Years ago it was *'ain't misbehavin'* (although *ain't* was the preferred form in the largely working class areas where I grew up, and we hadn't ever heard of Fats Waller). Today it's *Yo, Man*. It seems that, like other living entitles, languages breathe, co-habit, and mutate, and there *ain't nothin' no-one can do about it.*

Summary and conclusion

One of the major assertions presented in this book is that ultimately it makes little sense to study the individual 'bits' of language, whether these bits be isolated sounds, words, or even larger chunks such as sentences because, ultimately, these bits only make sense when considered in the context of the other bits of language that surround them, and in the context of the experiential world that gave rise to the language in the first place. Seen in this light, bits of language resonate with meaning, and that meaning expands like concentric ripples as more and more layers of language are added.

In this chapter, we have looked at some key aspects of the sound system. What I have tried do is lay out for you the ways in which we make meaning by manipulating a puff of air with vocal chords, lips, tongue and teeth. I have also demonstrated how languages differ in the way that they deploy these resources. Speakers of English create different words by changing the individual sounds that constitute a word. They indicate their attitude towards what they are saying by changing the tune of the words. When Chinese speakers change their tune, they create a whole new word.

Points covered in this chapter include the following

■ Sounds constitute the first of three language systems
■ Segmental phonology studies individual sounds in the language and how those sounds combine and change to make meaning
■ Suprasegmental phonology studies ways in which speakers use stress, rhythm and intonation to convey meaning
■ In English, suprasegmental features of language are used to convey attitudes and emotions, to emphasize particular elements of a spoken message, and to manage interactions
■ The sound system works along with the systems of words and grammar to enable us to create meaning
■ In English, the relationship between the sound of a word and how it is spelled is relatively indirect
■ Accent refers to particular ways of pronouncing a language and varies according to the geographical origin, social class and educational background of the speaker
■ Dialect refers to varieties of language that are differentiated phonologically, lexically and, to a certain extent, grammatically.

In the next chapter, I will look at that second system, the system of vocabulary. And we shall see that just as sounds are interlocked with words, so are words interlocked with the third system: the system of grammar.

Questions and tasks

1 Make a list of words you have difficulty spelling. (for example, 'harass', 'Mississippi') To what extent is the difficulty due to mismatches between spelling and pronunciation?

2 Underline the stressed words in the following responses.

Question: *Is your sister coming from Athens tonight?*
Response 1: *No, my cousin is coming from Athens.*
Response 2: *No, she's coming from Rome.*
Response 3: *No, she's coming tomorrow night.*

3 Which of the following instances of 'that' are stressed and which are unstressed? What generalization would you make about the pronunciation of 'that'?

That's my brother, over there.
John said that he'd be here by three.
The person that I'd pick for the team is John.
I'd like that piece please.
That new tie of yours is pretty garish.
Do you think that I should invite Mickey?

4 What difference in meaning is signalled by the intonation patterns in the following?

I don't lend my DVDs to any\one. (falling)
I don't lend my DVDs to any\/one. (falling-rising)

Further reading

Roach, P. (2000) *English Phonetics and Phonology*, 3rd edn (Cambridge: Cambridge University Press).
Roach provides a comprehensive and yet readable introduction to all aspects of phonetics and phonology. Practical exercises help to consolidate the concepts introduced.

Collins, B. and I. Mees (2003) *Practical Phonetics and Phonology* (London: Routledge).
A wide-ranging and accessible introduction to English phonetics and phonology.

Brazil, D. (1997) *The Communicative Value of Intonation in English* (Cambridge: Cambridge University Press).
A somewhat challenging but comprehensive treatment of how intonation works in English from a communicative perspective.

3 The lexical system

Introduction and overview

At the beginning of time the Word already was; and God had the Word abiding with him and the Word was God. At least, that's what the Gospel according to John asserts. The Old Testament is considerably less imaginative. Genesis has it that: *God, at the beginning of time, created heaven and earth.* For some reason (perhaps it's my obsession with language), the former resonates more with me. The Old Testament version is just too prosaic: a bald assertion of an event, albeit a monumental one. *God had the Word abiding with him,* on the other hand, is a metaphorical assertion of a state of affairs, and certainly puts the word on a pedestal – right up there with God.

This chapter is devoted to an exploration of this fundamental building block of language. The point of departure for the chapter is: What is a word? As you will see, the answer is less straightforward than you might think. Other concepts and issues covered in the chapter include:

- Word form and meaning
- Creating words
- Cataloguing words: dictionaries and corpora
- Word classes
- Closed and open class items
- The internal structure of words: morphology
- Personal vocabularies
- Lexical patterns in text
- **Collocations**
- **Ellipsis**.

What is a word?

In this chapter, we will look at the second of our three basic linguistic systems – the lexical system. The French linguist, Ferdinand de Saussure, sometimes referred to as the 'father' of modern linguistics, pointed out that words consist of two elements: sound (referred to as the signifier), and

43

a meaning (the signified). The relationship between the two is, as we saw in the last chapter, totally arbitrary. Saussure, by the way, was the most famous linguist never to have published. After his death, his students got together and published a slim volume summarizing his lectures. This book became one of the cornerstones of modern linguistic theory.

At first blush, the concept 'word' seems pretty straightforward. On the page, it's a string of letters separated at both ends by white space. However, this rough and ready definition doesn't work for spoken language. It doesn't work very well for written language either. The first 'word' in *We're just going for pizzas* fits the letters-bracketed-by-white-space definition, but is actually two words: *we* and *are*. And how about *basket case* as in *I was a basket case by the end of the movie*? Or *shoe-string* as in *We were living on a shoe-string*? Are we talking about one word or two? Taken singly, *basket, case, shoe and string* are all individual words. However, *basket case* and *shoe-string* refer to single entities in the world, and the words that denote them are arguably single entities as well. As you can see from these examples, the notion of 'word' is anything but straightforward.

In fact, the concept is so tricky, that most lexicologists (linguists who study words) argue that no single test is sufficient when it comes to identifying whether or not a piece of language constitutes a word. Here are several possible tests. (For further elaboration on these and other tests, see *The Cambridge Encyclopedia of Language*.)

The potential pause test
Repeat a sentence out loud very slowly with pauses. The pauses should equate to the 'white space' on the page. In other words, they should mark the word boundaries. This is a rough and ready guide. It doesn't work in the case of contractions such as *we're* and *he's*. It also fails to work with many multi-syllable words such as *nationhood*, which can be articulated as *nation hood*.

The indivisibility test
Interpolate additional words into a sentence. The interpolation points will mark word boundaries. For example, *The boy stood on the burning deck* will become *The terrified boy stood on the rapidly burning deck* not *The boterrifiedy stood on the burrapidlyning deck*.

The stand-alone test
This test was suggested by the American linguist Bloomfield, who argued that a word could be recognized by its ability to stand alone as

a complete utterance. Anthony Burgess provides a nice example of this by using individual words in the sentence *Jack's father was eating his dinner very quickly* as responses to questions.

'Whose is that cap?' '*Jack's.*'
'Can you call your father?' '*Father!*' (The speaker is calling)
'She *is* pretty, isn't she?' '*Was.*'
'What's he doing now?' '*Eating.*'
'Whose money will you steal?' '*His.*'
'What do you want?' '*Dinner.*'
'Ugly, isn't he?' '*Very.*'
'*Quickly!*' (The speaker gives an errand-goer a shove.)

It is worth noting the difference here between *Jack* and *Jack's*. Both pass the stand-alone test, and yet they are not the same. The apostrophe *'s* cannot stand alone in its own right. It can only exist glued, as it were, to *Jack*, where it transforms the meaning of *Jack*. The apostrophe *'s* is a particular form of morpheme known as a **bound morpheme** – bound because of its inability to stand on its own two legs. (Two important classes of morphemes are prefixes, which can be attached to the beginning of a word, and suffixes which can be attached to the end of a word.) It is also worth noting that the *Jack's* in *Jack's father* is different from the *Jack's* in *Jack's coming later*. The first passes the stand-alone test, the second does not.

Another problem arises in relation to variations on a word. Take the word *agree* for example. This common word spins off the following variations: *agrees, agreeing, agreement, agreements, disagreements, disagree, disagreeable, disagreed, disagreeing, disagreement, disagrees.* Does the word *agree* and its relatives consist of a single word or twelve words? To get around this problem, linguists describe groups of related words as word families. (We will look at word families and the concept of the **lexeme** in greater detail later in the chapter.)

Another lexical distinction drawn by linguists is between words as *types* and words as *tokens*. Lyons (1981: 40) explains this distinction with reference to the proverb: *He who laughs last laughs longest.*

> From one point of view [the proverb] can be said to contain six words: it is six words long. From another point of view, however, it can be said to contain only five words, since two of the words – the third and the fifth (*laughs*) – are identical: they are different tokens of the same type.

TABLE 3.1 Dimensions of speech

Word	Pronunciation	Morphology	Syntax	Meaning	Pragmatics
often	ɔfənlɔftən	two syllables stress on first	adverb, before or after verb	regularly, many times	often is less common, sounds more formal

Words can be described in terms of how they are pronounced, how they are formed, their part of speech, their meaning, and how they are used. Table 3.1 shows van Lier's (1995: 3) exemplification of these different dimensions.

Form and meaning

Word meaning is anything but transparent. Consider one of the most common verbs in the English language: *to get*. Most people would probably 'gloss' or define this word as *to obtain or secure*. In the transcript below, we see the word in action. In this brief monologue, *get* appears nineteen times.

> I have to erm **get** a confirmed date for the typescript from the author
> and then *Changes* . . . which is finally **getting** moving
> I think we've **got** spare pages
> we must allow time for things to **get**
> there and **get** into the warehouse
> we should **get** stock early July
> so that's a month to **get** to Italy
> we've **got** . . . Workbook Two film okay by the 29th of May
> we've **got** yeah film end of May again
> have you **got** costs from Tony
> about **getting** disks of things to Tony
> he's **got** Teacher's Book Two
> He hasn't **got** the bits of artwork yet
> He's **got** Workbook Two he's **got** the fonts he needed
> but he hasn't **got** the artwork
> I couldn't offer you any intelligent advice on reprints until I actually **get** it
> it would take me about three months I would think to **get** an angle on it
> but I'm not **getting** it until June. (Carter and McCarthy, 1997)

Although most of the uses of *get* in this extract embody the core meaning of *to possess*, other meanings such as *to arrive, taking delivery, to
receive, to obtain* are also evident. The various uses of *get* here illustrate
the fact that many words in English take on multiple meanings in
context, and new meanings are constantly being added. *Cool* once
meant some place between warm and cold. These days, however, by far
the most common meaning for *cool* is *trendy* or *hip*. A similar thing
happened years ago to the common verb *to go* which used to mean *to
depart*. Consider its use in the following exchange, a tantalizing fragment from a conversation that I overheard between two women in a bar
one night not so long ago.

A: *What happened between you and Johnny?*
B: *Well, I wanted to go home, but he goes, 'I want another drink'. And I
go, 'If you have another drink I'm gonna go', and he goes 'Well, you go.' So
I go, 'I will.'*
A: *And did you?*
B: *I did. I went.*

Many of our most common words have multiple meanings. This
point can be illustrated by the word *neutral*, which has a somewhat
different meaning in each of the following utterances.

Remaining neutral *during the Second World War did Switzerland no harm
at all.*
I could tell from the look on your face during the debate that you were
neutral.
Put the car into neutral *before you take your foot off the clutch.*
The neutral, *not the positive, wire goes in here.*
I find brown a pretty neutral *colour.*
Tom, could you indicate the neutral *atomic particles in the diagram?*
We need a neutral *solution, not alkali, and definitely not acid.*

Despite their differences of meaning, all of these uses of *neutral* share a
'family' resemblance in terms of their core meaning. The lexicographer
Paul Nation, who provided me with this list, suggests that the words all
share the basic meaning of 'not taking a particular side or position'
(Nation, 2003). The question remains, however, as to how many words
we are talking about here – seven, one or something in between?
    As we have seen, a single word can embody or realize a range of
different concepts or meanings. In the example above, the different

nuances of *neutral* share a common underlying meaning. Linguists refer to such words as being **polysemous**.

In English there are also many words that have the same form but completely unrelated meanings. Think, for example, of words such as *bank* (*The money is in the bank. We watched the plane bank and then go into a tailspin.*) These are called **homonyms**.

A third possibility is to have words with different forms but a common underlying meaning. Linguists refer to the underlying linguistic unit as a **lexeme**. A lexeme represents the 'base' meaning of a word. Consider the following lists. Do they each contain two words or four?

List A	List B
circus	circus
clown	circuses
juggler	clown
tent	clowns

for List A, the answer is clearly four. For List B, however, the answer is less certain. Here we have items from two different word families. The underlying meaning of the first pair is 'CIRCUS' and the underlying meaning of the second pair is 'CLOWN'. The abstract concept underlying word families is lexeme. So, while List B might be said to contain four words, it only contains two lexemes.

A somewhat more abstract illustration of the concept is provided in the following quote:

> While a word may have just one phonological form, this is not always the case. Look for example at *go* and *went*. Native speakers of English know that these are different forms of the same word. Because of cases such as this it is necessary to distinguish between the abstract item of vocabulary GO and the shapes which it can take in sound or spelling. We can think of these shapes as the abstract vocabulary item's realizations (in sound or print). Linguists term such an abstract vocabulary word a lexeme, on analogy with phonemes ... It follows that a single lexeme can have a variety of word-form realizations. You can think of this as being rather like the concept of a face and actual faces. A face has two eyes, a mouth and a nose in the middle, but an actual face 'realizes' this in particular ways. The eyes may be blue and the nose previously broken. (Kuiper and Allan, 2004: 19–20)

As we have already seen, and, as we will see repeatedly throughout this book, English is a very flexible language. In the next chapter, we'll see this flexibility manifest itself in the ways in which its grammar can be bent and twisted to serve the communicative needs of its users. This flexibility is also apparent in relation to its vocabulary. While all languages have the facility for creating new words (without which they would fossilize and die), few are more fecund than English.

Creating words

New words can be coined in a number of ways. Three common means are **compounding**, affixation and conversion. Compounding involves putting two existing words together to form a new word. There are thousands of such words in English. These include words that are now a regular part of everyday usage (such as *everyday*), to more recent additions such as *tree-hugger* – a pejorative term that conjures up images of long-haired environmentalists wearing tie-dyed shirts and sandals throwing themselves in front of logging trucks. Initially, the words co-exist as separate entities as in *compact disk*. As they move closer together they acquire the hitch of a hyphen; for example, *old-fashioned, hard-won*. Consummation (which doesn't always happen) occurs when they merge into a single entity such as *songwriter*.

Affixation, a noun created from the verb *to fix*, involves sticking a prefix to the front, or a suffix to the back, of an existing word in order to create a new word. Coinages such as *anti-Bush, pro-choice*, are so common in our language that we don't even notice them. It's also a practice that young people seem to come to quite naturally. Several moments ago, I asked my younger daughter what she was doing at my computer – I wanted to use it to work on this chapter. She replied *I won't be long. I'm just MSNing my friends*. (She was using the MSN text chat messaging service.) At the same time, in a news broadcast, the venerable BBC (British Broadcasting Service) reported on a group of conservationists who were *rewilding* Chinese tigers in Africa. Here, the adjective 'wild' is converted to a verb, and a prefix is added to form 'rewild'.

Conversion is the process of transforming one part of speech into another. For example, the creation of the terms *to out*, and *outing*, meaning to declare someone to be homosexual from the phrase *come out of the closet*, as in *The outing of public figures has become a favourite sport amongst the more homophobic members of the media*. Some of these words endure, and some get lost along the way. In the 1970s, at the height of the counter-culture movement in Western societies, an immensely popular book was published entitled *The Greening of America*. While Green Parties have flourished around the world, the verb *to green* in the sense of making people environmentally conscious, has largely disappeared along with hopes for the emergence of an alternative America. (In fact, at the present time, America, or more precisely, the United States, seems to have headed fairly determinedly in the other direction.)

If a word does not spring readily to our lips to express some inner emotion, urge or state-of-mind, we can always make one up. Many years ago I lived in London where I shared a flat with an avid football fan. One morning, my flatmate dragged himself out of bed somewhat the worse for wear after a night out celebrating a victory by his favourite football team. *Oh*, he groaned, *I'm feeling a little Wembley this morning*. I didn't need to look at him to know what he meant. Nor did I need to know that Wembley is the site of London's famous football ground, although this certainly added to the nuance. The word itself, with its aural echoes of 'wobbly' as well as its connotations of drinking excess, conveyed perfectly my erstwhile flat-mate's physical condition. Had he been a fan of American football, the coinage would have been problematic. *I'm feeling a little Rose Bowl*, simply does not resonate the way that *Wembley* does.

A friend of mine, a cranio-facial surgeon who does humanitarian work in India, provided me with the following additional example. One day he received a call at his hotel and was bemused to be told that an operation scheduled for the following week was to be *pre-poned*. In other words, the surgery was to be brought forward (rather than *postponed*, or put back).

Another amusing example was provided by, of all things, *Forbes Financial* magazine which reviewed a book on the history of the *Oxford English Dictionary*. The 'father' of the dictionary is described in this way:

> The hero (probably the only man who could have made the project work) was James Augustus Henry Murray. Born into humble circumstances in Scotland, this onetime bank clerk and schoolteacher had the amazing knowledge, perspicacity and stick-to-itiveness to organize the undertaking and push it on to an irrevocable course to completion. (*Forbes Global*, 8 February, 2004: 14).

These resources for creating new words have turned the English language into something of a lexical giant. A thousand years ago, it is estimated, the language consisted of around 100,000 words. Thanks largely to the Norman invasion, French derivatives doubled that number by the end of the Renaissance. In 1928, when the *Oxford English Dictionary* was first published, the number had more than doubled again to something in excess of 400,000 (414, 825, to be precise). The recently published online version of the *Dictionary* now contains upwards of 600,000 words. I have already discussed the fact that most **content words** have multiple meanings. Just imagine how many hundreds of thousands of words would be needed if each could only carry a single meaning.

Of all these coinages, what is the most useful single word in the English language? If you were reduced to the pitiful linguistic state of having a single word, what would it be? Writing in *The Times* newspaper on 19th June 2004, the British commentator Ben Macintyre had no doubt whatsoever. In his view, *OK* which, to Macintyre's chagrin, is sourced to the Americans, is the single most useful word, not just in English, but in numerous other languages as well.

Some of the more inventive words in English have been contributed by the most unlikely authors. Lynn Truss, a sports writer and author of a best-selling book on punctuation, has drawn attention to the verbal wordplay of golfing legend Tiger Woods. Here is one descriptive gem from Woods provided by Truss.

What do you make of the following descriptive gem?

> I played pretty good out there. I'm on this sandy lie so I'm thinking, well, I could play this ball in the water so I kind of fatted it up on the green and yipped the putt to the right. The downhill chip was greasy, but I blistered that drive. That was a high bleeder. I really hit good shots, yes, but they were not stoning. They were not kick-ins. I played safe, say a little chunk-and-run. Played a flop-shot down there to about ten feet. I squirted that one. It was a quick duck, a quacker. That drive was . . . blue.

If this extract is typical of the way that Tiger Woods talks, he should perhaps stick to playing golf rather than talking about it. Truss, however, does not have a problem with his use of language. In relation to the above quote, she notes that:

> When Tiger says he 'rips' his shots, nobody struggles with the meaning, after all. 'Fat' may not usually be taken for a transitive verb, but – as people have often pointed out to me recently – language is dynamic and must always be allowed to move on. (Truss, 2004: 2).

Cataloguing words: dictionaries and corpora

The creation of the *Oxford English Dictionary* is one of the most astonishing publishing feats of all time. The task which the fathers of the dictionary set themselves was no less than the creation an inventory of every single word in the English language. The story of the creation of the first edition of the *OED*, which took over seventy years, is brilliantly documented by Simon Winchester in his account called *The Meaning of Everything*. The result was a monumental, multi-volume work created from the labours of hundreds of volunteers who mined the written words from every conceivable source: from great works of English literature to newspapers and other forms of journalism.

Despite this richness, no dictionary, the venerable *OED* included, is fully comprehensive, incorporating all possible words and the rich variety of meanings those words carry in the language. Just yesterday, one of my better students asked me about the meaning of *bus*.

What are you talking about, Candy? I asked. *You know what a* bus *is.*
Yes, but what about to 'bus', she asked.
Oh, that's mainly used in the United States – it means to take a group of people by bus.
Yes, that's what my dictionary says, replied Candy. *But I just read a story about someone busing a table. How is this possible? Why would you want to take a table on the bus*

I then told her the story of my first restaurant encounter in the United States.

A relatively new technique in the study of words in **context** is **concordancing**. This technique draws on massive, computerized databases of authentic language (called *corpora*) to identify patterns, principles, regularities and associations between words that would not be readily apparent from a casual inspection of language samples. Earlier, we looked at a conversational extract in which the verb *to get* appeared numerous times with multiple meanings. With a concordancing program, we can instruct a computer to delve into a multi-million word corpus and pull up all instances of the verb *to get* (or its different tense forms) and to show us the linguistic company it keeps. Most concordancing programs allow you to specify how many words either side of the targeted word you want revealed.

To illustrate the way such a program presents data, here is a sampling

THE LEXICAL SYSTEM **53**

of what one concordancing program came up with when asked to carry out an analysis of the word *got*.

1	He couldn't turn the water on. And he	got	badly burned. It happened in Mar
2	anyone in the neighbourhood who	got	broken into recently? I know
3	any extra precautions since the car	got	broken into last time? Er well, I
4	he jilted her at the alter. So she	got	brought up by her grandmother
5	she's been a bit nervous ever since we	got	burgled and dark nights
6	you know of? They got burgled. They	got	burgled once. Yeah. That was a while
7	by crime that you know of. They they	got	burgled. They got burgled once. Yeah.
8	done that so I suppose I could have	got	caned. Yeah. And as you've gone
9	fool for being honest. You know he	got	called an idiot for being honest
10	it didn't seem much point. No. All	got	deported I think. Every one of them

(Carter *et al.* 2001: 161)

This pattern analysis of naturally occurring instances of a particular word in use yields interesting insights. For example, from the above data base we find that people tend to use *get* as a **passive voice** rather than **active voice** construction to describe things that happened to them personally rather than to describe what is done to impersonal things – the only inanimate object in the above sample is *the car* in line 3. This type of analysis also provides interesting links between vocabulary and grammar. Thus, we see that in the *get* passive samples, the focus is on what happened to the individuals concerned. The performers of the actions are not identified – either because the action is more important to the speaker than the doer of the action, or because the doer is unknown. Another feature of the data is that *get* appears to be associated with emotionally charged, even violent, actions and events – *burned, broken, burgled, caned, deported*. It is insights such as these that concordancing programs reveal – insights that we are unlikely to be able to generate without the assistance of technology.

Word classes

Traditional approaches to language analysis assign words to nine different classes (for definitions of each of these classes, see the glossary):

Nouns: *cat, house, intelligence*
Verbs: *run, do, think*
Adjectives: *red, beautiful, convenient*
Pronouns: *he, them, whose*
Prepositions: *on, to, with*

Conjunctions: *but, however, then*
Adverbs: *softly, now, intently*
Determiners: *a, the, this, those, her, some*
Interjections: *damn, hurrah, cool*

The problem with assigning words to classes is that many individual words can be assigned to different word classes according to the function performed in a particular sentence. Take the word *slide*, for instance. In the following sentences it acts successively as a noun, a verb and an adjective.

Just put it on the slide.
Did you see Martino slide *into second base?*
Could you pass me the slide *rule? It's on the desk.*

A great deal of humour and many jokes also depend on grammatical ambiguity as in the following example.

Question: *What's the difference between roast chicken and pea soup?*
Answer: *Anyone can roast chicken.*

Here, the humour depends on whether *roast* and *pea* are interpreted as adjectives or verbs.

In the following dialogue, *that* plays two different roles. Although they both play 'pointing' roles, the first *that* points to an individual, while the second points to a piece of information – the status of the individual in relation to the speakers.

A: That's *the new boss.*
B: *Is* that *so?*

Again, we see the central importance of context. The meaning and function of a word and the job that it has to do depend upon the company it keeps.

Closed and open class items

When looked at as a system, the vocabulary of any language consists of closed class items and open class items. Closed class members, also called **function words** or **grammar words**, are those to which no new items can be added. Prepositions, pronouns, conjunctions, **modal verbs** and **determiners** consist of finite lists of words. Open classes include and **nouns, verbs, adjectives** and **adverbs.** Members of these classes are sometimes called content words. New items are being added to these categories by the minute, if not the second. The system also has rules for creating word families, as I discussed earlier in the chapter.

Content words enable us to talk about entities, events and states-of-affairs; that is, the things that exist in and go on in the world. It is important that new content words can be added to the lexicon because otherwise the language would fossilize and we would not be able to express new realities. Sometimes the new words are 'one-offs', used only once to express a particular meaning. Recently, I heard a word that I had never heard before – in fact I don't think it had ever been uttered before, and may never be uttered again. The word was *easify*. The speaker, an educator, said *The basic function of the classroom is to easify the learning process for students.* Even though I had never heard the word before, and may never hear it again, I knew immediately what he meant.

Grammar words function to organize and relate content words to each other. They therefore carry meaning of an entirely different kind. This can be seen in the following paragraphs. The first one contains all of the grammar words from the original paragraph, while the second contains the content words.

The XXXXX between XXXXX XXXXX and XXXXX XXXXX is a XXXXX one in XXXXX XXXXX. Most XXXXX XXXXX are XXXXX XXXXX and XXXXX to the XXXXX XXXXX XXXXX XXXXX . . . XXXXX XXXXX are those XXXXX XXXXX that XXXXX to XXXXX XXXXX XXXXX. XXXXX XXXXX XXXXX that XXXXX XXXXX should be XXXXX as part of XXXXX and XXXXX XXXXX as part of XXXXX, but this is a XXXXX XXXXX XXXXX since what is XXXXX by the XXXXX of XXXXX XXXXX may be XXXXX of the XXXXX of XXXXX.

XXXXX distinction XXXXX content words XXXXX function words XXXXX XXXXX useful XXXXX XXXXX analyzing vocabulary. XXXXX vocabulary items XXXXX content words XXXXX belong XXXXX XXXXX large open word classes. Function words XXXXX XXXXX vocabulary items XXXXX belong XXXXX closed word classes. Conventional wisdom suggests XXXXX function words XXXXX XXXXX taught XXXXX XXXXX XXXXX grammar XXXXX content words XXXXX XXXXX XXXXX vocabulary, XXXXX XXXXX XXXXX XXXXX somewhat spurious distinction XXXXX XXXXX XXXXX handled XXXXX XXXXX grammar XXXXX one language XXXXX XXXXX part XXXXX XXXXX vocabulary XXXXX another.

Estimating the ratio of content words to grammar words gives a measure known as **lexical density**. The more content words, the higher the lexical density. Generally speaking, written texts display great lexical density than spoken texts.

At the beginning of this section, I referred to words as a system. Closed classes clearly constitute a system (or subsystems if you like). We know all of the members of the modal verb class, how they relate to each other and what they do. Although new members can be added to open class items, I believe that they still fit the definition. Although we cannot pre-specify all of the nouns or verbs in English, because their numbers will be growing as we try to list them, we know how they are formed, how they relate to each other and to closed class items, and what they do.

The internal structure of words: morphology

In this section, I want to take a look at the internal structure of words. The academic study of word structure is known as morphology, and it lies at the intersection of the study of words in general (lexicology) and the study of grammar. Structurally, morphology belongs to vocabulary, while functionally it belongs to grammar. The case of morphology reinforces one of the central themes of this book – that when we look at language as a resource for making meaning, we have to look at the interrelationships between the three linguistic systems and the ways in which they fit together.

What, then, is a morpheme? It is the smallest unit of meaning that resides within a word. There are two types of morpheme: 'free morphemes' and 'bound morphemes'. A free morpheme exists as a single word in its own right. *House*, *book*, *under* and *one* are examples of free morphemes. Bound morphemes, like parasites, cannot live alone, but only exist attached to other morphemes. Affixes such as *un-*, *pre-*, *-ly* and *-able* are all bound morphemes. Thus, the word *undoable* consists of three morphemes, one of which is a free morpheme and two of which are bound morphemes *un-*, *do*, *-able*.

You have to be careful here. The *-er* on the end of *runner* is a bound morpheme, the *-er* on the end of *father* is not! As Burgess (1992: 95) points out:

> 'Father' cannot be reduced to smaller elements, for though '-er' is an ending common to four nouns of family relationship, 'fath-' can no more exist on its own than 'moth-', 'broth-' or 'sist-'. If you rush to point to 'moth-' or 'broth-' as genuine nouns, I will be quick to ask you to look at the difference between the sounds.

You should be able to see now why morphology, or the study of morphemes, is partly to do with vocabulary and partly to do with grammar (and indeed, as Burgess notes, also to do with pronunciation). When we add a bound morpheme to a free morpheme we are changing the grammatical function of the word. Adding *-s* to *apartment* changes the word from a singular to a plural noun. Attaching *-ily* to *happy* transforms the word from an adjective to an adverb. Sticking *-ing* on to *read* changes the word from an action that happens in general to an action that is happening now.

However, this is not the end of the morphology story. Consider the morphological variations in irregular noun and verb forms such as *foot – feet*, *run – ran*. Here, the internal structure of the words signal differences in meaning, in one case transforming the singular to the plural, and in the other, the simple present to the simple past. However, the changes are internal to the word, and the words themselves cannot be neatly segmented into free and bound morphemes.

Personal vocabularies

How many words do you know? Most people have little idea. I have had people make guesses that range from 10,000 to 50,000 words. Most estimates, in fact, suggested that the educated native speakers know at least 20,000 word families.

Here is a simple test created by Paul Nation (2003) to give a rough estimate of how many word families you know. The words at the beginning of the list are common, those at the end extremely uncommon. Check off the words you know, and multiply that number by 500. This will give a rough estimate of the size of your word family knowledge.

TABLE 3.2 WORD FAMILY KNOWLEDGE

1 Bird	18 Monologue	35 Plainchant
2 Fell	19 Tamper	36 Astrochemistry
3 Improve	20 Acanthus	37 Nondurables
4 Barn	21 Blowout	38 Carboxyl
5 Fatigue	22 Crupper	39 Eyestalk
6 Kettle	23 Gloaming	40 Curragh
7 Combat	24 Minnesinger	41 Gunlock
8 Resent	25 Perpetuity	42 Dipole
9 Redeem	26 Riffle	43 Rigorism
10 Hurrah	27 Behindhand	44 Localist
11 Conversion	28 Embolism	45 Benchboard
12 Fixture	29 Angst	46 Stirabout
13 Accede	30 Blowhard	47 Hypothallus
14 Avocation	31 Devolute	48 Doombook
15 Calyx	32 Envoi	49 Paradiplomatic
16 Concave	33 Golliwog	50 Poroplastic
17 Hierarchy	34 Neonate	

When you completed this task, you probably came across several words where you had to ask yourself *Do I know this word?* What does it mean to know a word? You may have felt, 'Well, I know the general sense of the word, but I'd have a hard time coming up with a precise definition.' I had this experience when I went through the list. For example, I am pretty sure that *plainchant* is a kind of religious music. Does that mean I can check it off, or, in order to claim knowledge of the word, do I have to be able to produce the type of definition that can be found in a dictionary: something like 'plainsong is the unisonal liturgical music using in the Christian Church from the earliest times; Gregorian chant.'

If we happen to stray into specialist subject areas beyond our own areas of expertise, we are sure to encounter many unfamiliar words. A linguistics text, for example, is likely to contain terms such as *tagmeme*, *illocution*, *substantive*, *universal*, *pragmalinguistic* and *relexicalization*. It is the frequent appearance of words with technical meanings that can make the reading of specialist texts hard work. Mastering a new subject is, in many ways, just like learning a foreign language. Not only do we need to learn what the new words mean, we also need to learn how to use them in discourse. The junior high biology student who was repri-manded for asking *How does the fetus go to the toilet?* would have been praised has she asked *How does the fetus evacuate waste product?* Despite this, her question is, scientifically-speaking, a perfectly reasonable one, and one that reveals an inquiring mind.

It is not just fancy, foreign, or unpronounceable words that trip us up. Another challenge has to do with the fact that common words are sometimes used with uncommon or specialist meanings. For exam-ple, the language of law contains many terms that have one meaning in everyday language, and somewhat different meanings in legal texts. Take the term 'remedy' for instance, which in everyday language means a cure for some malady or ailment. In legal language, however, it means the legal procedures for enforcing a right or redressing a legal transgression. While the legal meaning can be traced back to the original meaning to 'cure', the relationship is tenu-ous, even metaphorical.

What do you do when you come across a word you don't know? You can ignore it of course. If you really want to know what a word means, you can look it up in a dictionary. If you do resort to a dictionary you will finds all sorts of information in addition to the principal meanings of the word in question. Consider the following entry:

octogenarian /oktoudze'naerian/ *adj.* Also, **octogenary** /ok'todzenari/ 1. of the age of 80 years. 2. between 80 and 90 years old. −n 3. an octo-genarian person [L. *octogenarius* containing 80 + -AN]

The entry packs a lot of information into a relatively short space. From it we learn the pronunciation of the word (assuming that we know the phonetic alphabet). We learn what kind of word it is – in this case an adjective. We are presented with its various meanings, we are provided with examples of the word in use, and we are informed of its origin – all in a few short lines.

Lexical patterns in text

Another way of enriching our knowledge is to explore the ways in which words are used in context. When it comes to exploring vocabu-lary in context, we find some really interesting things going on. In this section, I want to look at some lexical patterns in text. The extracts are taken from an unpublished piece I wrote about a few days I once spent with the British author Anthony Burgess. Consider the opening sentence to the story.

> Anthony Burgess has been called many things: that writer chappie with the wog wife (his words), a thorn in the side of the literary establishment, a pseudo intellectual. The list could go on. However, if the truth be known, he was, in fact, one of the finest writers of his generation.

Here, in a single short sentence, we have multiple references to an individual: *Anthony Burgess, that writer chappie with the wog wife, his, a thorn in the side of the literary establishment, a pseudo intellectual, he, one of the finest writers of his generation.* Notice that within the paragraph only the first reference actually identifies the individual being referred to. Outside the paragraph, *the writer chappie with the wog wife, a thorn in the side of the literary establishment, a pseudo intellectual* and *one of the finest writers of his generation* could refer to many different individuals. *His* and *he* could refer to approximately fifty per cent of the human race. The words and phrases themselves only take on an identifiable value inside the context of the sentence. Their meaning is instantiated in the text.

As we will see, the ability to make repeated references to an individual, entity or state-of-affairs is a fundamental characteristic of language. In English, various linguistic resources exist to allow us to do this. These resources are known as **cohesion**. When an exact word or phrase is used to refer to something that has already been mentioned it is known as **lexical reiteration** (see **lexical cohesion**). If the above paragraph had been written

> Anthony Burgess has been called many things: the writer chappie with a wog wife (Anthony Burgess's words), a thorn in the side of the literary establishment, a pseudo intellectual. The list could go on. However, if the truth be known, Anthony Burgess was, in fact, one of the finest writers of his generation.

the second and third occurrence of Anthony Burgess would have been an example of lexical reiteration. However, in the interests of economy and to avoid boredom, I used the pronouns *his* and *he* instead. This is an example of another type of cohesion called **anaphoric reference** or **anaphora**. The first member of the cohesive tie, in this case, Anthony Burgess, is known as the **antecedent**. (In another class of reference items, the referent comes first, for example, *He's my favourite writer, is Anthony Burgess.* This is called **cataphoric reference**.) When the writer chooses an equivalent word or phrase that is not a pronoun, it is known as lexical synonymy. In the above paragraph *the writer chappie with the wog wife, a thorn in the side of the literary establishment, a pseudo intellectual, one of the finest writers of his generation* are all synonyms for Anthony Burgess.

It is worth noting in passing that the phrases only 'stand for' Anthony Burgess within the context of this particular sentence. Outside of this sentence, any number of writers could lay claim to the titles of *a thorn in the side of the literary establishment,* and *one of the finest writers of his generation.* Some may even be happy with *the writer chappie with the wog wife,* although few of my academic acquaintances would appreciate being called *a pseudo intellectual.* When a word or a phrase is invested with a meaning, but only within the context of the sentence or text in which it appears, linguists talk of '**instantial' relationships**. The meaning is 'instantiated' or 'placed into' the word or phrase by the context in which it appears.

Here is a longer text, taken from the first volume of Burgess's autobiography. Burgess is talking about his mother and explaining why he was given her maiden name rather than his father's name.

> Burgess was the maiden name of the mother I never knew. Elizabeth Burgess, a dancer and singer, was named the Beautiful Belle Burgess on music hall posters. She married a Manchester Wilson but was right to insist that her slightly more distinguished surname get on to my baptismal certificate. There have always been too many plain Wilsons around. Of the Wilsons I belong to there are few historical records, and the family had always to rely on myth. (Burgess, 1987: 7)

Here, again, we see instantial meanings: *Elizabeth Burgess, dancer, singer, Beautiful Belle Burgess,* as well as the liberal use of pronouns: *I, she, her, my, I.* Two conceptual worlds are woven together in the paragraph. The first has to do with entertainment: (*singer, dancer, music hall*), while the second has to do with families and marriage (*maiden name, married, surname, baptismal certificate, family*). These words form what is known as **semantic networks** and they are an important aspect of the lexical patterning that all texts display, helping to create what Halliday (1985) calls **texture**.

Obviously, words such as *he, she, this* and *that* have no meaning outside of the communicative contexts in which they are used. The same is true of numerous other words. Think of *else,* as well as conjunctions such as *and, but, however, for example, therefore.* As a final example, consider the word *well,* a very common word that can serve as an adjective *You're looking well, Tony*, an adverb *You play the piano really well*, and a noun *The well dried up during the drought.* However, the word is most frequently deployed, not as an adjective, adverb or noun, but as a conversational tool to shift the focus, emphasis, or topic of the conversation. In fact, an entire thesis has been written on this use of *well.* Here are some examples from that study:

A: *It's like one little group that always stays together.*
B: *Well, that's good.*
(Marks a shift in the next turn to a comment, opinion, evaluation or explanation.)

A: *If they see me with the cane, why don't they give me the so-called right of way?*
B: *Well, they probably do, once they see it.*
(Marks a shift to a disagreement or reservation.)

You know, they gave us a room and they said well during the day the room holds forty-eight people.
(A shift by the speaker from a narrative or description to reporting what someone else said.)

He w- he had- well was twenty years old when he volunteered for the para-troopers.
(A modification, restart or **repair**.)

A: *That doesn't make sense as far a breeding goes.*
B: *Well, first of all, I happen not to have an awful lotta faith in breeding.*
(A topic opener, introducer, shifter, resumer, response.)

Well, anyway listen, I gotta do a lot of studying.
(A closing, preclosing)
(Kinsler, 1987, cited in Celce-Murcia and Olshtain, 2000)

As a final example of lexical patterns in text, notice the use of adjectives in the following text:

Recognized as one of the world's most durable hardwoods, Jarrah has an incredible natural strength and a remarkable resistance to extreme weather conditions, rot and pests, yet it is a stunningly beautiful timber with a glorious colour spectrum of rich hues, natural features and distinctive fine grain patterns. Every item in the range has been lovingly crafted and finished with quality fittings to give lasting pleasure and withstand all the tests of time. (*Home Journal*, December 2005: 189)

What type of text is it? Is it an article, an advertisement or a report? The adjectives, forming a semantic set, give it away: *durable, incredible, natural, remarkable, stunningly, glorious, rich, natural, distinctive, quality, lasting*. It could only be an advertisement.

Collocations

Words that frequently co-occur are known as collocations. English is full of collocations that are so routinely used that they have become clichés: *really great, stunning model, mountainous waves* and so on. We only notice their existence when someone violates the collocation – either trying to be funny or because they are second language speakers of the language who have not yet incorporated the collocations into their **interlanguage**. (*We were stranded in a leaky boat amid the hilly waves.*)

Regular collocations cause second language speakers a degree of difficulty, although they usually get the hang of them eventually because they occur relatively frequently and make sense. Take *mountainous waves*, or *gigantic wrestler*: *mountainous* and *gigantic* do carry with them the sense of 'extremely large'. Some collocations, however, defy logic: *terrible* to mean 'good', as in *terribly attractive*, is one that springs to mind. Another that must surely confound the non-native speaker is the use of *dead* to mean 'extremely'. This sometimes leads to unintended humour as when chef Rick Stein referred to a catch of fish as being *dead fresh*.

When we look at collocations and lexical patterns in texts, we will often find that words co-occur by virtue of the subject matter and type of text in which they occur. These lexical patterns are one of the elements that make up a particular register. Think back to the extracts in the preceding text such as the advertisement for jarrah-made furniture. Other registers belong to technical, academic or professional communication. (Consider words associated with the medical or legal professions.)

Another aspect of register that will affect vocabulary choice is the context in which the language is used and the relationships between the interlocutors. As Finch (2003: 48) observes, English contains a rich array of lexical resources that reflect borrowings from other languages.

If we are in a court of law, for instance, we might need to use the term *larceny*, which is of French origin, whereas talking with our friends we would probably use the term *theft*, which is from Anglo-Saxon, or Old English. Doctors talk about *haemorrhaging* (Greek) and *lacerations* (Latin), rather than *bleeding* and *wounds* (Anglo-Saxon). In all these cases, there is no real difference in conceptual sense between the terms used. The difference has to do with levels of formality. Part of being able to use language effectively is the ability to switch between these two levels when it is socially appropriate to do so.

Ellipsis

In this chapter, I have explored one of the fundamental building blocks of language: the word. The angle I have taken is to look at words in action and I have attempted to explain them in terms of the communicative functions they perform. When we look at the way that words are actually used, we need to consider something that at first sight might seem odd or even somewhat perverse. This is the deletion of words that can be understood from the conversational context in which they occur. The technical term for this phenomenon is **ellipsis**. Along with reference and **lexical cohesion**, ellipsis is another category of **cohesion**. Here are some examples of ellipsis (the elided words are in brackets):

A: (*It's a*) *nice party.*
B: *Yeah.* (*Do you*) *know anyone here?*
A: (*I*) *can't say I do* (*know anyone here*). *Do you* (*know anyone here*)?
B: (*No*) *I don't know anyone here.*

The litmus test for ellipsis is whether words are missing which by right should appear for the sentence or utterance to be grammatically correct.

There are, in fact, two types of ellipsis. We have just seen an example of the first kind, which involves the simple deletion of the repeated item. The second type is the **substitution** of the original words with a 'proform' such as *one/ones, so, neither, nor, not, do/does*. (In their book on cohesion, Halliday and Hasan (1976) list **substitution** as a separate category of cohesion. In their later work, however, they group the two together. My own preference is to keep them separate.)

A: *Which Porsche do you like?*
B: *I like the blue one.* (one = Porsche)

A: *Is Jo going to the Festival this year?*
B: *I think so.* (so = Jo is going to the Festival this year)

A: *I usually try and get seats for Saturday night.*
B: *I do too.* (do = try to get seats for Saturday night)

Because of the need to package the maximum amount of information into a minimum amount of space, newspaper headline writers typically deploy ellipsis. Here are some examples:

PUBLIC'S CONFIDENCE AT FIVE-YEAR HIGH
DEAL ON UNIVERSAL SUFFRAGE CLOSE
ROW BREWS OVER DISTRICT COUNCILLOR'S ELECTION BID
CLEANLINESS KING AS HOSPITALS PLAY SAFE

How about the following?

Across for up.
Across for down.

These were signs in the elevator lobby of a large and busy hotel.

Unfortunately, ellipsis often results in ambiguity. The following headlines all have at least two potential meanings depending on how we **parse** the words in the headlines, and the classes to which we assign individual words. In the case of the first headline, for example, the interpretation depends on whether the subject is *army* or *push*, and whether the main verb is *push* or *bottles up*.

ARMY PUSH BOTTLES UP TERROR SUSPECTS
CHILD'S STOOL GREAT FOR USE IN GARDEN
BALLOON RACE – SIX DROP OUT
WOMEN LAY OBSERVERS AT COUNCIL
ORGAN TROPHY LOST BY INCHES
SCHOOLGIRL IS SUSPENDED BY HEAD
THREE BATTERED IN FISH SHOP
DRUNK GETS NINE MONTHS IN VIOLIN CASE

IRAQI HEAD SEEKS ARMS
MOUNTING PROBLEMS FOR YOUNG COUPLES
FIELD MARSHALL FLIES BACK TO FRONT
QUEEN MARY MAY HAVE BOTTOM SCRAPED
(Adapted from Carter *et al.* 2001; Spiegl, 1965)

Why do we have ellipsis? In other words, what is its communicative or functional value? The answer is straightforward: economy. Why repeat something that is either stated or implied by the context? In general, we tend to leave out information that we assume the recipient of our message already knows. This can cause misunderstandings when we make erroneous assumptions about our interlocutor's state-of-knowledge.

In addition to headlines, advertisements are another interesting source of ellipsis. Consider the following text which has been taken from an advertisement for sofas:

YOU SAY: I need two new sofas, but I can only afford one.
WE SUGGEST: Buy a sofa and get another free.
Buy one, get one FREE now.

The sentence *Buy a sofa and get another free* provides an example of ellipsis. A 'complete' sentence should read *Buy a sofa and get another sofa free*. Consider the first sentence, however. Does it exemplify ellipsis or substitution? The expansion test shows that it is ellipsis. *I need two new sofas, but I can only afford one* (*sofa*). An example of substitution would be:

A: *We need a new sofa.*
B: *Let's get one at the new Furniture Mart.*

Here *one* substitutes for *a new sofa*, the most reasonable expansion being *Let's get a new sofa at the new Furniture Mart* and not *Let's get one sofa at the new Furniture Mart*.

Ellipsis, intentional and otherwise, is also sometimes deployed by shopkeepers and small businesses trying to give their firm a distinctive name. Carter *et al.* offer some additional proprietary names that attempt to be funny through ellipsis, puns and plays on words.

Hairdressers
Curl Up and Dye, Fresh Hair, Look Ahead, Kuttin' Kru, Headlines, Making Waves, Highlights

Bed salesrooms
Bedside Manor, Bedlam

Heating
Gas Flair, Power Dressing

Fur shop
Hide and Sheep

Health food shops
Open Sesame, Just Natural, In a Nutshell, Grain of Truth

Services
Diaper cleaning service: Wee Care
Chimney sweep: Clean Sweep
Drain clearing: Watershed, Blockbusters
Driving instructors: Road Train
Dry cleaners: Suits me
Plumbers: Plumbing Your Way

(Carter *et al.*, 2001: 82)

Here are two more notices where the (presumably unintentional) humor relies on misplaced lexis.

Winery notice: *Our wines leave nothing to hope for.*
Notice in a tailor's shop: *Women may have a fit upstairs.*

Summary and conclusion

I began this chapter by suggesting that the concept of 'word' was neither simple nor obvious. Our intuitive notions about what constitutes a word begin to unravel once we push and prod the concept a little. I realize that I have not come up with a definitive method of identifying or defining the 'word'. That was not my intention. I set out in this chapter to do three things. The first of these was to illustrate the richness and complexity of the English lexical system, and to show how creative we humans are with our constant additions to the lexicon. My second aim was to look at the contribution that words make as communicative tools. A third aim was to demonstrate that the study of words can be a source of endless fascination and fun.
    In this chapter, we have seen that:

- Defining the notion of the 'word' is complex, and a range of tests is needed to determine whether a particular lexical item constitutes a word
- Many words have multiple meanings and in classifying words we need to think in terms of word families and lexemes
- English has many resources for creating new words, and the English lexicon is expanding at an astonishing rate
- A useful distinction can be drawn between content words (open class items) and grammar words (closed class items)
- Dictionaries and computer-based corpora provide rich resources for exploring word form, meaning and use
- The study of the internal structure of words is known as morphology
- Exploring lexical patterns in texts can provide fascinating insights into word function and use
- Cohesion as a linguistic phenomenon sits at the intersection of lexis and grammar.

In the next chapter we will look at the third and last of the linguistic systems – grammar – from a similar perspective. We will also see that maintaining a separation between the lexical and grammatical systems is by no means easy.

Questions and tasks

1 Classify the following words into open and closed class items.

appropriate, should, thus, beauty, interesting, some, thought, linguistic, star, bungle, those, slowly, bigger.

2 To which classes can the following items belong? Tick the appropriate columns.

	NOUN	VERB	ADJECTIVE	ADVERB
hard				
snow				
fell				
great				
mixed				
black				
star				
complex				

3 Construct a word family for the word *agree*. (Hint: the family consists of 12 words in addition to the root word.)

4 Identify the individual morphemes in the following words. Which are free (can stand alone) and which are bound (must belong to another morpheme)?

newspapers, sporting, unseemly, juicy, rider, establish, childishness, hard-ship, preschool, unlearning

5 Select a concordancing program from the web. Enter a word you would like to explore and study the output from the program. What conclusions and implications can you derive from the data? What other information about a word can you retrieve from a concordancing program?

Further reading

Carter, R. (1998) *Vocabulary: Applied Linguistic Perspectives*, 2nd edn (London: Routledge).
Now in its second edition, this book provides a readable and authoritative overview of vocabulary.

Carter, R., A. Goddard, D. Reah, K. Sanger and M. Bowering (2001) *Working with Texts*, 2nd edn (London: Routledge), Unit 2 Words and things.
This unit looks at words in context based on a wide range of authentic texts.

Radford, A., M. Atkins, D. Britain, H. Clahsen and A. Spenser (1999) *Linguistics: An Introduction* (Cambridge: Cambridge University Press), Part 2 Words.
This section provides a comprehensive introduction to the study of words.

4 The grammatical system

Introduction and overview

For many people, *grammar* and *language* are synonymous. To most members of the general public, learning a language is a matter of memorizing vocabulary and learning the grammatical rules of that language. In fact, for many years, the language teaching profession also subscribed to this view. Language teachers taught grammar, plain and simple (with the occasional vocabulary and pronunciation lesson thrown in for good measure.)

In this chapter, we will look at the concept of grammar. The two key questions that I want to look at in particular are: What is grammar? And in keeping with the theme of this book: How does grammar work as a tool for creating and expressing meaning?

This chapter deals with the following concepts and issues:

- Defining grammar
- Mentalist versus functionalist approaches to grammar
- Grammar in use
- Prescriptivism versus descriptivism
- The internal workings of the sentence
- Grammar and context sensitivity.

Defining grammar

What is grammar? This question may seem relatively straightforward. However, as with sounds and words, grammar is anything but straightforward. In fact, as we shall see in this chapter, a satisfactory definition of 'grammar' is extremely elusive. Here is what some experts have had to say:

Grammar may be roughly defined as the way language manipulates and combines words (or bits of words) in order to form longer units of meaning. (Ur, 1989: 4)

[Grammar is] a description of the structure of a language and the way in which units such as words and phrases are combined to produce sentences in the language. (Richards, Platt and Weber, 1985)

[Grammar] is the way in which words change themselves and group together to make sentences. The grammar of a language is what happens to words when they become plural or negative, or what order is used when we make questions or join two clauses to make one sentence. (Harmer, 1987)

Two key threads run through these and other definitions. The first is that grammar has to do with how words are formed, and secondly, with the ways in which they are combined. The academic study of word formation is called morphology, which we looked at in the preceding chapter, while the study of ordering and combining words is called syntax. (A technical word for **grammar** that you may have already encountered is **morphosyntax**, a word created from **morphology** and **syntax**.)

Having identified the principles for word formation and sequencing, the linguist is in a position to specify rules for determining grammatical correctness. This results in linguistic formulations that are often pretty impenetrable to language learners (and, more often than not, to native speakers). Take as an example the following rule:

When making simple present declarative statements in the third person singular, it is essential that one attaches an *s* on the end of the verb.

At a practical level, the problem with this and many other such statements is that, in addition to being incomprehensible to the average native speaker (*declarative statements? third person singular?*), they are widely overlooked and ignored by second language speakers – in this case, presumably because it makes no difference to meaning whether an *s* gets attached to the end of the verb or not. *On Friday night Jose told me he love me* may be defective grammatically, but the recipient of Jose's attention almost certainly doesn't care.

Once you begin to dig beneath the surface, you will find that most grammar rules are either oversimplifications or just plain wrong. In fact, there are relatively few rules that are impervious to dispute and debate. As Finch (2003: 169) points out:

A grammar of a language consists of sets of rules for generating well-formed word sequences, whether these are phrases, clauses, or sentences. But . . . this begs the question of what counts as 'well-formed'. Who actually decides whether something is well-formed or not? People differ considerably in what they consider acceptable in a language and in many cases the rules recited to justify these differences are little more than historically, or socially acquired preferences.

Although the nature of language has been studied and written about for thousands of years, and was elevated to a high art (or was it a science?) by the Greeks, the modern, or 'scientific' study of language is less than a hundred years old. Like most other academic disciplines, no sooner had it been born, than linguists formed themselves into different factions with conflicting views on the nature of language, and how it should be investigated and described.

Mentalist versus functionalist approaches to grammar

There are many theories of language and approaches to linguistic analysis. To do justice to any one of them would take a book in itself. The purpose of this section is not to map the terrain of any one theory, but to give a brief description of two major approaches that dominate the linguistic landscape at the present time. The first consists of mentalists, the second of functionalists. Both groups have diametrically opposed views on the nature of grammar. The mentalists believe that grammar is a psychological phenomenon. The functionalists believe that it also has a social dimension. The model of language developed by the mentalists is called **transformational-generative grammar**, that of the functionalists **systemic-functional linguistics**.

For the mentalists, grammar is a highly abstract system of rules for generating correct (or 'well-formed') utterances at the level of the sentence. For them, grammar is all about form, and they reject any suggestion that there is a relationship between grammar and meaning. The ability to generate well-formed utterances is, they argue, hard-wired into the human brain. (You encountered Steven Pinker, a prominent mentalist and proponent of the hard-wired school, in Chapter 1.)

The principal architect of mentalism is Noam Chomsky (who was Pinker's teacher and mentor). He underlined the separation of grammar and meaning by pointing out that utterances can be grammatical but meaningless (something that the poet Lewis Carroll exploited in his poem *Jabberwocky* many years ago).

In Chomsky's early work, the setting aside of meaning arose from an argument that what makes a particular sequence of words in a language a grammatical sentence has nothing to do with meaningfulness or significance. *Colorless green ideas sleep furiously* and *furiously sleep ideas green colorless* are both nonsensical but the former is grammatical and the latter is not. Conversely, although there is nothing semantically wrong with *read you a book on modern music?* or *the child seems sleeping* (they are no more difficult to interpret than *have you a book on modern music?* or *the book seems interesting*) they are ungrammatical in modern standard English. Such examples suggest to Chomsky (1957:15) that 'any search for a semantically [meaning] based definition of "grammaticalness" will be futile'. (Joseph, Love and Taylor 2001: 125)

Chomsky's work has been enormously influential, particularly in North America, although he is not without his critics. (For a detailed and comprehensive critique, see Cziko, 1995; 2000 who argues that the principles of adaptation and selection can account for the evolution of language).

On the other side of the linguistic divide from the mentalists sit the functionalists. Their best-known proponent is Michael Halliday (1985). The functionalists believe passionately in the inseparability of form and meaning, thus the label for their model of grammar – systemic-functional linguistics. In fact, they argue that grammar only makes sense if it is studied as a resource for creating meaning. They point out that the existence of grammatical forms such as the passive voice *The window was broken*, as opposed to the active voice *The boy broke the window* can only be accounted for in functional terms. The passive voice, among other things, enables the speaker to emphasize the event (the breaking of the window) rather than the actor (the boy). It also enables us to talk about events where the actor is unknown or irrelevant without resorting to clumsy locutions (*Someone broke the window*).

Which model is right? Well, the fact is that they could both be correct. They could both be different ways of approaching and interpreting the most complex of human phenomena – language. While this book is solidly grounded in the functionalist school, it does not mean that I do not respect the mentalists. However, they simply don't provide me with a model of language that helps me understand and interpret the way that language systems function to facilitate communication.

Grammar in use

When native speakers use language for communication, they constantly break many of the rules set out in grammar books. You will find such violations, not just in everyday speech, but also in literary language, particularly in popular culture. And this is not a recent phenomenon. Over thirty years ago the Bee Gees waxed lyrical on the power of words to steal hearts! ('It's only words . . .')

A very common example of 'rule violation' concerns subject–verb **agreement**. In fact, as I was working on this chapter the radio in my study was tuned to the BBC World Service, and I happened to overhear the following comment.

The team were disappointed with their performance.

According to the (admittedly) very dated grammar books I studied as a young teacher, a singular noun should take a singular verb. *The team* is singular (there is only one of them) and it should therefore take the singular form of the verb *to be* (*was*) – *The team was disappointed with their performance*, a fact that even the often inaccurate and frequently irritating Microsoft Word grammar check function was able to pick up. Should we be shocked by the fact that the radio station I was tuned in to at the time was that arbiter of all things correct when it comes to the English language, the World Service of the British Broadcasting Service. If the BBC doesn't care about getting their verb tenses correct, then why should anybody else?

Many people do care, and they care passionately. Debates over language (usually revolving around the 'falling standards' issue) can generate as much heat as abortion, animal rights, legalizing marijuana, and the death penalty.

More recently, Clive James, poet, author and media personality, published an article entitled 'The Continuing Insult to the Language' in which he blamed all manner of ills in England on what he claimed is the disintegration of the English language. He is particularly upset at lack of subject–verb agreement. James argues that:

> People who have learned English as a second language rarely make the [subject–verb agreement] error because they were taught some grammar along with the vocabulary. But people who have learned English as a first language are increasingly likely to be driven to a plural verb by a plural sounding singular subject, and precisely because they have learned the language by ear, instead of by prescription. In an infinite variety of forms,

the same mistake can be seen in the feature pages of the British quality press every week. (James, 2006: 50)

How do we account for the fact that native speakers, who by definition are not supposed to make mistakes, *do* use language that violates the rules as set out in 'traditional' grammar books? Are the speakers at fault or the grammar books? The answer to this question will vary according to the nature of the error (or, rather than 'error', I guess we should say 'variations from the grammatical norms of the grammar books'). In most cases, we can find answers by taking the communicative context into consideration and looking at the piece of language containing the variation from the perspective of the speaker. In the case of the current example, the sporting commentator who said *the team were* was thinking of the team in terms of the players who made up the team. In other words, from a psychological perspective, he was thinking plural not singular, and so it was quite natural to use the plural form of the verb. If he were thinking of the team as a single entity, he would have used the singular form of the verb to be. From this example, you can see that in studying the grammatical choices that speakers make, we can go behind the words and into the minds of the speakers.

John Humphrys is a journalist, and author of *Lost for Words*, an entertaining and informative book on the mangling and manipulation of the English language by politicians, bureaucrats, academics – and others who ought to know better. In his book, he argues that grammatical errors that pass unnoticed in spoken language leap out at us in print:

> The point is that bad grammar jolts us more in written English than in spoken English. In print it can also confuse us about what is meant, even when the same words in colloquial speech do not have that effect. That's probably because we have time to think about it when we see it on a page. We can worry away at it, in the same way that the tongue keeps returning to a loose tooth. (Humphrys, 2004: 73).

Prescriptivism versus descriptivism

The foregoing discussion raises the distinction between prescriptive grammars and **descriptive grammars**. Prescriptive grammarians specify what is right and what is wrong – what people should say and what they shouldn't say (*I say, Old Chap, next time you talk about the team, please remember – singular verb!*). A descriptive grammarian, on the other hand, tries to avoid making pronouncements about correctness and focuses on describing the way people actually use language. In the case of *the team were*, the descriptive grammarian, rather than judging the utterance as incorrect, would seek an explanation such as the one I provided above, and would attempt to incorporate this explanation into his or her grammar. Luckily, contemporary grammars are overwhelmingly descriptive, and will point out the fact that plural verbs can exist quite happily alongside a singular noun phrase.

In fact, grammar is a battleground on which all kinds of conflicts are played out. Different speech communities will have their own grammars, and prescriptive grammarians have, over the years, played a part in the class warfare that is determined to impose the linguistic will of the ruling classes on the masses. I grew up in a working class environment where people said *youse* not *you* when referring to more than one person. Whenever I or my siblings used this form, our mother would castigate us, and make us repeat the correct form. She knew what was right and what was wrong, and she was going to make sure that we did too. It made no difference to her when, years later, I pointed out that the working-class pronoun *youse* is actually more sophisticated grammatically than *you* because in addition to indicating second person, it also marks the utterance for plurality. If someone says to me *Could you come over for a drink?*, I have no idea whether or not the invitation includes my mates. If they say *Could youse come over for a drink?*, it is clear that my mates are included.

In his *Encyclopedia of Language*, Crystal (1997a: 3) identifies three sources of prescriptivism as being responsible for the tension between prescriptive and descriptive approaches to grammar. The first of these is the fact that early grammars of English and other languages were based on normative rules from classical Latin and Greek. The second is the tension between spoken and written language, and the third is what he calls 'logical' analysis.

Because language is a tool for communication, and because, in the vast majority of instances, individuals use language to achieve communicative ends rather than to show how clever they are, they will, when it suits them, bend the language to their own ends. Ultimately, it is futile to try to preserve the 'purity' of language because there was nothing pure about it in the first place. Many people have pet peeves when it comes to correctness. Personally, I am quite comfortable with the use of *who* rather than *whom* in questions such as *To ___ did you give it?* (although not my grammar checker, which got so offended by the use of *who* that I had to turn it off). On the other hand, I get irrationally

	Example of a prescriptive rule	Descriptive comment
Latin and Greek The unchanging form of these languages, the high prestige they held in European education, and the undisputed brilliance of classical literature led to their adoption as models of linguistic excellence by grammarians of other languages.	You should say or write *It is I* and not *It is me*, because the verb *be* is followed by the nominative case in Latin not the accusative case.	The Latin rule is not universal. In Arabic, for example, *be* is followed by the accusative. In English, *me* is the educated informal norm; *I* is felt to be very formal. In French, only *moi* is possible (*c'est moi*, etc.)
The written language Writing is more careful, prestigious and permanent than speech, especially in the context of literature. People are therefore often told to speak as they would write.	You should say and write *whom* and not *who* in such sentences as ___ did you speak to?	*Whom* is common in writing, and in formal styles of speech, but *who* is more acceptable in informal speech. The rules which govern acceptable speech and writing are often very different.
Logic Many people feel that language should be judged insofar as it follows the principles of logic. Mathematics, from this viewpoint, is the ideal use of language.	You shouldn't say *I haven't done nothing* because two negatives make a positive.	Here, two negatives do not make a positive, but a more emphatic negative – a construction which is found in many languages (e.g. French, Russian). The example is not acceptable in standard English, but this is the result of societal factors, not the dictates of logic.

irritated when I hear someone say *different to*, not *different from*. However, I realize that on this point I am fighting a losing battle, and that I am hardly going to reverse the tide of change by pointing out the fact that *different to* is as logically offensive as *similar from*.

The internal workings of the sentence

Word order is an important aspect of grammatical correctness. In fact, grammar is often defined as a set of rules for specifying acceptable word order. In English, word order is fundamentally important to meaning. *The man bit the dog* has a very different meaning from *The dog bit the man*. *Mike loves Julie* is very different from *Julie loves Mike*. The unintended humour in *The girl was followed by a small poodle wearing jeans* has been brought about by the separation of the phrase *wearing jeans* from the presumed wearer – *the girl*. Consider also the confusion in the following newspaper headline:

DOG BREAKS WINDOW THAT HURTS WOMAN

As it stands, the headline suggests that a public spirited dog carried out a revenge attack on an offending pane of glass. Common sense suggests otherwise, but we have to read the newspaper account to confirm that the dog broke the window, and it was this that caused injury to the woman.

> A woman resting outside her restaurant in Kowloon City was injured when glass fragments rained down onto her after a dog broke a window in a flat above. (*South China Morning Post*, 14 November, 2005: 14)

We can begin to unpick some of the issues surrounding the arrangement of information within the sentence by looking at the elements that make up a simple sentence. The basic building block of the sentence is the phrase. Phrases are meaningful groups of words below the level of the sentence that cannot stand alone as sentences in their own right. A simple sentence must contain a noun phrase acting as the subject (S) and a verb phrase (V) which indicates some action or state of affairs relating to the subject. Depending on the nature of the verb, it can also contain phrases following the verb that act as **objects** (O), **complements** (C), and **adverbials** (A).

Objects are usually noun phrases that normally follow the main verb and answer the questions 'what?' or 'who(m)?'

My sister eats snails. (*What does your sister eat?*)
Tilly loves Richard. (*Who does Tilly love?*)

Some sentences may have an **indirect object** in addition to a **direct object**. In *I gave my wife some flowers*, the indirect object is *my wife* and *some flowers* is the direct object.

Complements are required to complete the meaning of certain verbs and, in simple sentences, define the subject in some way or provide addition information about it. They typically follow the verb *be* and let us know how the subject of the sentence looks, feels or seems. **Subject complements** describe or modify the subject of a sentence, while **object complements** do the same for the object of the sentence. The italic words in the following sentences are complements:

Everyone was *happy.* (Subject complement)
They made Jack *redundant.* (Object complement)
Dolores seems *a little tipsy.* (Subject complement)
I've been keeping my room *tidy.* (Object complement)

Adverbials provide additional information about how, when, where or why. In other words, they provide additional information about an event or a state of affairs. Adverbials hang out on the periphery of sentence structure. If we had a sporting team made up of these grammatical classes, the adverbials would be carrying the oranges. They are, in most sentences, optional, and can be left out without rendering the sentence ungrammatical. Like other elements, they can be moved around within the sentence to give them more or less prominence, although they have more mobility than some other elements. It is also possible to stuff a number of adverbials into a single sentence, although the usual effect of this is an unwieldy and overwritten sentence.

Suddenly, as the clock struck midnight, she rushed *quickly* from her chamber *to meet her mysterious lover.*

English is based on a small number of standard (or canonical) sentence patterns made up of the five basic phrase types described above. The most elemental pattern is Subject + Verb (S+V) as in *I cried.* Another basic pattern is Subject + Verb + Object (S+V+O) as in *I bought a ticket.* A third pattern is Subject + Verb + Object + Object (S+V+O+O) as in *I gave a bunch of flowers to my wife.* One thing worth noting about these different patterns is the important role played by the

V or verb phrase, which can consist of a single word or a group of words (as in I *had been crying*, I *am going to buy* a ticket, I *should have given* a bunch of flowers to my wife). The verbal element is significant because not all verbs can take part in all patterns. While it is permissible to say *I cried*, it is not permissible to say *I bought*: the verb *to buy* must be followed by an object. (Verbs that do not need to be followed by O, C or A are called 'intransitive', those that do are called 'transitive'.) Similarly, we can say *I bought a ticket* or *I bought a ticket for Sally*. In other words, the verb *to buy* can take part in both S+V+O and S+V+O+O patterns. The verb *to give*, however, can only take part in S+V+O+O patterns – the exception being when it is a response to a question and the indirect object which is understood from the context can be omitted. For example:

A: *What did you buy your wife?*
B: *I bought a bunch of flowers* (for my wife)
or even
B: *A bunch of flowers.*

Notice that there are two acceptable variations on this structure. We can say *I bought a bunch of flowers for my wife*, or *I bought my wife a bunch of flowers*. Looked at purely in terms of sentence-level grammar, both sentences are identical. However, from a communicative perspective, they have two different functions. In one the focus is on the flowers, in the other it is on my wife. It would be odd to answer the question *What did you buy your wife?* with *I bought the flowers for my wife*. Similarly, it would be strange to respond to the question *Who did you buy the flowers for?* with *I bought my wife a bunch of flowers*. The appropriate responses in each case are:

A: *What did you buy your wife?*
B: *I bought my wife a bunch of flowers.* (Or, more usually, *A bunch of flowers.*)
and
A: *Who did you buy the flowers for?*
B: *I bought the flowers for my wife.* (Or *My wife.*)

The preceding discussion raises a point made repeatedly in this book on the interconnectedness of the different linguistic subsystems, in this instance, grammar and lexis. As we saw above, the choice of verb will have an important bearing on grammatical acceptability. Here is an elaboration on that point, illustrating the importance of verb choice and direct and indirect object:

> Consider the following sentences (an asterisk precedes words and sentences that are ungrammatical in English):
> Beth sold the cookies to Eric.
> Beth sold Eric the cookies.
> Beth pulled the cookies to Eric.
> *Beth pulled Eric the cookies.
> From the first two sentences, it is clear that a speaker of English can use one of two different grammatical structures for sentences containing both a direct object (*the cookies*) and indirect object (*Eric*). We can put the direct object after the verb followed by *to* and the indirect object. Or we can drop the *to* and switch the positions of the two objects. But notice that although the second structure seems to work fine for the verb *sold*, it does not sound right for most speakers of English for the verb *pulled* to be used in (4), despite the fact that both verbs behave similarly in (1) and (3). (Cziko, 1995: 202)

Drawing on the work of Pinker, Cziko points out that these constraints are not arbitrary, but depend on what are often quite subtle differences in the semantics of the verbs, and the meanings of syntactic constructions. In other words, there is a close interrelationship between the lexical and the grammatical systems.

Because a grammar specifies rules for determining correctness at the level of the sentence, the traditional approach to studying grammar is restricted to the level of the sentence. However, as we have just seen, it is impossible to give a complete account of most grammatical features (in this case, word order choices) without considering the context in which the sentence occurs.

Let's now look at a somewhat idiosyncratic word order choice. Consider the following sentence:

Looking out of my window, I can see my girl walking down the street with another guy.

While we might sympathize with the author of the sentence, grammatically, it seems to be reasonably unexceptional. The words are all common, high-frequency ones, and are presented in an order that makes sense. However, here is how the words actually appeared:

I can see right out my window walking down the street my girl with another guy.

Readers of a certain age and with a certain musical taste will recognize this as the first line of the song *Here comes the night* by the sixties pop group *Them*. The words were sung by Van Morrison and, in the context of the song, the ordering does not seem strange at all. In fact, altering the order of the words gives them a rhythmic intensity that the more standard or 'canonical' word order lacks. It also provides a dramatic point of departure for the rest of the song, and allows Morrison to rhyme the first line with the second which goes:

His arms around her like it used to be with me oh it makes me want to die.

Thus, although English sentences and clauses have a standard or 'canonical' word order, for example Subject + Verb + Object as in *The boy stood on the burning deck*, it also has a great deal of malleability. *On the burning deck stood the boy*, and even *On the burning deck the boy stood* are both grammatical and unexceptional. Options such as *The burning deck stood on the boy* are grammatical but are semantically vacuous (that's another way of saying that they're nonsensical), while other combinations of words are clearly ungrammatical; for example, *Deck burning the on boy the stood*.

So, what makes certain rearrangements grammatical and not others? To answer this question, we need to look inside the sentence at the phrases that make them up. When asked to divide this sentence into two, most people slice it between *boy* and *stood*:

The boy / stood on the burning deck.

In terms of the sentence constituents described above, what they have done is to separate the subject from the rest of the sentence (in traditional terms, the predicate). When asked to make a second cut, some place the cut between *stood* and *on* while others put it between *on* and *the*. So, where should the cut be made? Does *on* belong to *stood* or to *the burning deck*?

One way to answer this question, is to apply the 'movement' test? The question here is: Which interior chunks of the sentence can we rearrange while still preserving its grammaticality? If we apply the rearrangement test in order to determine where *on* belongs, we end up with the following variants:

On the burning deck the boy stood.
The burning deck the boy stood on.

An informal poll of native speakers revealed that, while the second version was considered acceptable in some contexts, most speakers thought that the first version 'sounded better' grammatically. In other words, 'on' seemed to belong most happily to *the burning deck*, making it part of a prepositional phrase (a prepositional phrase is an adverbial that has a preposition at its head) rather than to the verb *stand* – which would make it part of what is known as a phrasal verb.

There is another test that can be applied to help us to decide how the sentence might be chunked. This is the 'question' test. A natural answer to the question *Where's the boy?* Would be *On the burning deck*. The response *The burning deck* seems incomplete. However, the question *What happened to the burning deck?* elicits a rather different response: *The boy stood on it*. So, the question test leaves us in a kind of linguistic limbo. One question suggests a prepositional phrase, the other a phrasal verb. If we aggregate results from both the 'movement' test and the 'question' test, then majority support would be for the notion that *on* is happiest attached to *the burning deck* rather than *stood*, and that the final constituent in the sentence is a prepositional phrase *on the burning deck*.

This example illustrates the flexibility and malleability of English. When pressed into service as a tool for communication, it can be bent and twisted into all kinds of shapes without breaking. In the current instance, the malleability enables us to emphasize or highlight different aspects of the message. The sentence *The boy stood on the burning deck* is about the boy. It answers the question *Who stood on the burning deck?* On the other hand, *On the burning deck, the boy stood* is about his location on the ship and answers the question *Where did the boy stand?* Yet another variant answers the question *What did the boy do?* Answer: *Stood on the burning deck, the boy did*. Each of these options is **thematizing** a different entity or event within the sentence.

In this section we have looked at possible sentence and utterance variations from the 'canonical' or 'standard' word order of Subject + Verb + Object. (for example, *The boy stood on the burning deck*, versus *On the burning deck, stood the boy*). We have seen that **discourse** considerations such as the speaker's desire to highlight one part of the message rather than another, determined the choices made by the speaker about the ordering of information within the sentence.

Another discourse consideration relates to whether the information has already been introduced into the discourse or can otherwise be assumed to be known to the listener or reader. This is known as '**given**' information. It contrasts with information that is introduced for the first time, which is known as 'new' information (see **given** informa-tion). It is important when thinking about given and new information in discourse to remember that it is the speaker or writer who decides what is assumed to be known and what is new. Speakers and writers often get it wrong, and sometimes badly so!

As a rough rule of thumb, the given information in a sentence or utterance comes first and is followed by the new information. In the utterance *The boy stood on the burning deck* it is assumed the listener is aware of the fact that the boy was standing somewhere. This principle of placing new information at the end of the sentence is known as **end focus**.

The distribution of information in certain kinds of sentences is facil-itated by the use of **existential subjects**. (These are also known as 'empty' or 'dummy' subjects.) *It* in the response to the following ques-tion is an example of an existential subject:

A: *Why are you bringing in the washing?*
B: *It's going to rain.*

Existential subjects solve the problem of how to give end focus to a piece of information in certain kinds of sentence.

Grammar and context sensitivity

This leads us to another important aspect of grammar: the context sensitivity of grammatical choices. The word and phrase order options we have discussed in this chapter allow the speaker or writer to make choices. In fact, grammar can be described as a system for allowing users to make choices, and most descriptive grammars present in great detail the various grammatical subsystems in the language that allow such choices to be made. Good grammars also show language learners how the different choices they make from the grammatical sub-systems enable them to convey meanings of increasingly subtle and sophisticated kinds.

In order to illustrate this point, let us consider the case of the article system – the use of *a/an*, *the*, or zero article. This system is often described as a simple system, and is frequently one of the first grammar items to be taught to second language learners. However, it is extremely complex; so complex, in fact, that we shall look only briefly at one aspect of the article system.

The following is typical of the kind of description that you will find if you look up 'articles' in a standard reference grammar:

> You use **a** and **an** when you are talking about a person or thing for the first time. **A** and **an** are called the **indefinite article**. You only use **a** and **an** with singular count nouns. The second time you refer to the same person or thing you use **the**.
> She picked up a book.
> The book was lying on the table.
> (Collins Cobuild English Usage, 1992: 1)

While this description is perfectly correct, it is a gross oversimplification, telling us nothing about the power of choice inherent in the article system. Consider the following responses to the question *Who is Al Gore?*

Oh, he's the former Vice-President of the United States.
Oh, he's a former Vice-President of the United States.

The responses differ only in terms of their choice of articles. However, this choice tells us a great deal about the attitude of the speaker towards the former Vice-President. In the first response, Al Gore is singled out as a unique individual (just in case you didn't know, he was a heartbeat away from being President during Bill Clinton's terms in office). Use of the indefinite article 'a' in the second response, on the other hand puts him in the position of simply being 'one among many'. Here again, we see context (in this instance, the attitude of the speaker towards the object of the conversation) driving the grammatical choices.

Summary and conclusion

In this chapter, we have looked at aspects of the grammatical system of English (with the occasional sideways look at other languages). We have seen what a subtle, complex and fantastic resource is provided by the system for creating an infinite variety of meanings. These meanings have to do, not only with expressing propositions about the world, to buy goods and services, and to socialize; they also enable us to make communicative choices and to express our feelings and attitudes towards the world. Finally, grammar is a resource that enables the speaker to escape the tyranny of the here and now. Stripped of grammar, we would be reduced to point-and-grunt, me-Tarzan-you-Jane type utterances.

Points covered in this chapter include the following:

- Grammar constitutes the third of three language systems
- From a formal perspective, grammar is a set of rules for specifying correct sentences
- From a functional perspective, grammar is a resource for making meanings
- Grammar in use is both subtle and complex: users bend and twist it in all sorts of ways to suit their communicative ends
- There are very few grammatical features that are not influenced by the communicative context in which they occur
- There are very few simple and straightforward grammatical rules.

Questions and tasks

1 Identify the different phrases in the following sentences and label them S, V, C, O, A.

The gentle giant laughed.
I'm tired.
At lunchtime, I should be seeing the dentist.
The teacher should have given me an A.
Three absurdly dressed party goers came waltzing out of the pub.
We will come to the party at around nine o'clock.
You seem to be a little upset right now.

2 Think of questions or statements to which these responses would be appropriate.

It was chocolate that I bought my girlfriend.
Chocolate it was that I bought my girlfriend.
What I bought for my girlfriend was chocolate.
My girlfriend got chocolate.
I bought chocolate for my girlfriend.
I bought my girlfriend chocolate.

3 Study the following two newspaper accounts of a particular event (these are based on two accounts in Woods, 1995: 29). The information in both texts is identical. However, the focus is very different. What grammatical resources do the writers use to achieve this difference? With what effect?

Account 1

Police searching for a man in connection with a spate of armed robberies were last night questioning a man arrested in a West London hotel.

Armed anti-terrorist squad detectives surrounded the London Visitors Hotel on Holland Road, Holland Park shortly before 6.00 p.m. after a member of the public told them that the man they were seeking was there.

Mr Nat Handsworth, 35, offered no resistance and was taken to the Paddington Green police station after his arrest under the Prevention of Terrorism Act. (*Guardian*, 18 April 1986)

Account 2

Nat Handsworth, the most wanted man in Britain, was captured last night after a dramatic swoop by armed police.

Handsworth, 35, was seized in an early evening raid in West London – nearly thirty hours after a massive police hunt was launched for him following a spate of armed robberies.

Last night, he was being questioned by senior anti-terrorist squad officers at the high security Paddington Green police station in London. (*Today*, 18 April 1986)

Further reading

Fabb, N. (2005) *Sentence Structure* (London: Routledge).
This workbook offers an inductive approach to the analysis of sentence structure.

Thompson, G. (1996) *Introducing Functional Grammar* (London: Arnold).
Although some of the discussion in this book might be challenging to readers completely new to functional grammar, in general, the first three chapters provide an accessible introduction to the subject.

Thornbury, S. (2001) *Uncovering Grammar* (London: Macmillan).
This book provides an easy-to-read, discovery oriented approach to the investigation of grammar.

5 Doing things with spoken language

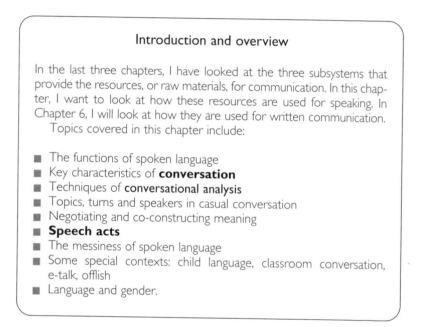

Introduction and overview

In the last three chapters, I have looked at the three subsystems that provide the resources, or raw materials, for communication. In this chapter, I want to look at how these resources are used for speaking. In Chapter 6, I will look at how they are used for written communication.
Topics covered in this chapter include:

- The functions of spoken language
- Key characteristics of **conversation**
- Techniques of **conversational analysis**
- Topics, turns and speakers in casual conversation
- Negotiating and co-constructing meaning
- **Speech acts**
- The messiness of spoken language
- Some special contexts: child language, classroom conversation, e-talk, offlish
- Language and gender.

Functions of spoken language

Just think for a minute of all the speaking tasks that you have carried out in the last twenty-four hours. Here is a selective list of some of the things I achieved through language yesterday. I:

- called a friend and reminded him about a dinner party I was having last night
- took part in a meeting at the office
- ordered a coffee in the faculty lounge
- called my travel agent to see if I was still wait-listed on an upcoming flight from Sao Paulo to Miami (I was!)

- wished my daughter good luck for her school drama audition
- over a coffee, asked a colleague about the plot of a movie she had seen the evening before
- booked my car in for a service
- ordered flowers for a colleague who is leaving
- had a Cantonese lesson (some of which was conducted in English)
- discussed a research proposal with a graduate student.

This is a somewhat random list of the kinds of things we do through language every day. Although the tasks vary, the overall functions can be reduced to just two: we use language to obtain goods (such as coffee and flowers) and services (a car service, flight information), and we socialize (wishing a daughter luck, talking with a friend about a movie). The first function (obtaining goods and services) is called the **transactional** and the second (socializing) the **interpersonal function** or meaning. Although we can separate the two for purposes of analysis, in many exchanges such as the following the two functions are woven together:

A: *Morning.*
B: *Morning.*
A: *Nice day, again.*
B: *Yep. Gonna be another good one.*
A: *What can I get you?*
B: *Oh, coffee thanks.*
A: *Regular or decaf?*
B: *Regular.*
A: *Cream and sugar?*
B: *Just a little cream.*
A: *Here you go.*
B: *Cheers.*

The interpersonal dimension of an utterance, also known as **modality**, is often signalled by specific linguistic devices such as modal verbs and adverbs.

Some of the features of language that we observed in the preceding chapter are apparent in the conversation. Note in particular the extent to which ellipsis is a feature of the conversation. If you look at the internal workings of the conversation, we see that in addition to an interweaving of the transactional and interpersonal functions, the conversation can be broken down into a series of two-utterance pairings, called **adjacency pairs**. All languages have these pairings, in which one type of utterance calls forth an expected response, for example:

Greet:	*How are you Dave?*
Greet:	*Hi Chris.*

Offer	*Would you like a coffee?*
Accept/Decline	*Thanks./No thanks.*

Apologize	*I'm sorry.*
Acknowledge	*That's OK.*

Assert	*I love Oprah.*
Agree/Disagree	*Yeah, she's great./Oh, I can't stand her.*

These are 'default' or expected pairings. When we greet someone, we expect a greeting in return. When we make an offer, we expect the other person either to accept or decline our offer. In some ways, these pairings are similar to the grammatical ordering of words in sentences. As we saw in the last chapter, the standard word order in declarative statements is subject + verb + object. (*The dog bit the man.*) A deviation from this standard order such as verb + object + subject (*Bit the man, the dog* (did).) immediately attracts our attention, and we ask ourselves *why* the speaker has chosen to shuffle the lexical cards in his linguistic deck in this way.

The same is true of conversations. As already noted, when we say *Good morning* to someone, we expect a *Good morning* in return. A reply such as *What's good about it?* is a deviation from the expected norm, and prompts us to wonder what the problem is with our conversational partner.

Key characteristics of conversation

In this section, I want to foreground some of the characteristics of spoken language that I will deal with in greater detail in the rest of the chapter. We will touch briefly on speech acts, the **negotiation of meaning**, and transactional and interpersonal interactions. (As we saw in the preceding section, transactional interactions take place when the speakers are trading goods or services. In interpersonal interactions, they are basically socializing.)

One of the challenges in learning to take part in conversations in a foreign language is knowing how to interpret and respond appropriately to speech acts that are indirect; that is, where the speakers do not mean what they say in a literal sense, and where 'inside-the-head' or **background knowledge** is required in order to determine what the speaker means. (Use of inside-the-head knowledge is known as **top-down processing** and the theory of how this works is known as **schema theory**.) This point is illustrated in following exchange which was recorded between two co-workers, A (a native speaker of English) and B a second language speaker. Here, B interprets A's utterance as an invitation rather than a formulaic farewell:

A: *See you later.*
B: *What time?*
A: *What do you mean?*

Here is a somewhat more complex piece displaying a number of features that are typical of casual conversation between intimates:

J: *It's a worry, isn't it?*
B: *What?*
J: *Your money (yes) organizing your money affairs.*
B: *'tis . . . a big worry.*
C: *Mmm.*
J: *I've got to manage my money to look after myself in my old age.*
C: *You're in it.*
J: *What?*
C: *You're in it – you're in your old age.*
J: *I might live for another ten years. Be . . .*
C: *. . . Be a bloody miracle.* (laughter)
B: *What? What did she say?*
C: *Be a miracle – after the life you've led. If you'd led a nice sedentary existence, and hadn't drunk or smoked you might've been able to look forward to a telegram from the Queen.*
B: *Be a thrill!*
J: *A big thrill!*

This is clearly an interpersonal rather than transactional interaction. It took place over afternoon tea late one afternoon between two elderly sisters, J and B, and J's daughter C. In her opening conversational gambit, J refers back to an earlier conversational topic, the financial concerns of the elderly. She makes an assertion *It's a worry, isn't it?* which would normally be followed by either an agreement or a disagreement. However, B's *What?* indicates that she is unsure of what exactly *it* refers to. J makes the topic (one's money, or lack of it) explicit, and B is able to complete the adjacency pair. Functionally, we therefore have the following sequence:

Assertion
Clarification request | Insertion sequence
Clarification |
Agreement

The *clarification request/clarification* make up what is known as an insertion sequence inside the adjacency pairing. Such insertion sequences are common in natural conversation, and can become quite complex:

A: *Peach Bellini, please.*
B: *Are you twenty-one?*
A: *Why do you want to know?*
B: *We don't serve alcohol to anyone under twenty-one.*
A: *Do I look as though I'm under twenty-one?*
B: *That's beside the point. Can I see your ID, please?*
A: *Here.*
B: *Great. Thanks. One Bellini coming up.*
A: *Thanks.*

The clarification requests illustrate an important characteristic of natural conversation: the fact that meanings don't come ready-made, but have to be negotiated between the participants in the conversation. In this regard, they are different from movie scripts and play scripts. In real life, uncertainty and misunderstandings are the norm, and interlocutors are constantly using strategies such as requesting clarification (*What did you say?*), confirming that they have heard correctly (*Did you say X?*) and checking that the other participants in the conversation have correctly understood (*Do you follow?*) in order to avoid or resolve misunderstandings and ambiguities. J's *What?* in the earlier conversation is another example of a clarification request.

The conversational fragment about money worries among the elderly illustrates how much personal and cultural knowledge is required to make sense of many casual conversations, particularly when they take place between family members and other people who are intimately related. In order to appreciate this fragment fully, we need to know:

- the relationships between J, B and C
- the fact that J is somewhat obsessed with money, or, more precisely, the fear of being bereft of money in her old age
- that B is quite hard of hearing
- that C relieves her sense of frustration with her mother by humour which borders on the sarcastic
- that the participants are citizens of a British Commonwealth country in which it was once customary to receive a telegram from the Queen of England on reaching the ripe old age of one hundred.

In contrast, many transactional encounters, such as the following telephone encounter in which the customer is making a cab booking, are devoid of any interpersonal elements, being stripped down to the bare communicative bones. The interaction consists of a string of adjacency pairs (question/answer, question/answer) in which there is no negotiation of meaning. In contrast with the interpersonal extract above, the conversation is like a form of verbal ping-pong, with no misunderstandings, and no competition for a conversational **turn**:

Tape: *Hold the line please, all our operators are currently busy.* [music]
Operator: *Cabcharge – account name?*
Customer: *Macquarie University.*
Operator: *Passenger's name?*
Customer: *Nunan*
Operator: *Pick-up address?*
Customer: *13 Finch Avenue, East Ryde.*
Operator: *Is that a private house or flat?*
Customer: *Yes.*
Operator: *Going to?*
Customer: *The airport.*
Operator: *How many passengers?*
Customer: *One.*
Operator: *Are you ready now?*
Customer: *I'd like a cab for 2:30pm, please.*
Operator: *We'll get a car to you as close to the time as we can.*
Customer: *Thank you.*

Topics, turns and speakers in casual conversation

In casual conversation, turn taking is a trickier affair, particularly in social situations where the participants don't know each other well. While not exactly a blood sport, casual conversation contains many competitive elements and involves constantly monitoring the input of the other participants, and making strategic decisions about how to fit one's own contribution into the ongoing **topic** of the conversation, as well as diverting, subverting, and even changing the topic of conversation completely.

The following conversation took place among clerical staff in the coffee room of a hospital medical records office. The topic, what one would do if one won the lottery, was stimulated by a television programme shown the previous evening, in which someone had won a great deal of money. The text is particularly interesting in terms of **topic selection and change** and speaker selection and change.

Gary: *If I won the Lotto, I'd buy six or seven catamarans up at Noosa* (a beach resort) *and sit them on the beach and hire them out and just rest there all the time.* (Everyone laughs)
Pauline: *Oh yes, and then you – you'd want something to do.*
Gary: *Yes, you would but . . .*
Bronwyn: *Mm no, look, even if I'd won the Lotto, I'd still have to come to work – I couldn't stand it.*
Gary: *No, that's right.*
Bronwyn: *I couldn't stand it.*
Pauline: *Yes, I think that um . . .*
Pat: *I'd buy my farm.*
Bronwyn: *I'd still – no, I need contact with people.*
Pauline: *Yes, that's right – I think I'd probably – if I'd paid off all my debts and wouldn't have that on my mind – I'd feel better – um but then I'd think I would like to work part time.*
Bronwyn: *Mm.*
Gary: *Mm.*
Pauline: *You know, just for . . .*
Gary: *Oh, I – I don't know.*
Pauline: *Being able to do things and then you'd still kind of . . .*
Gary: *I think I'd use the money a bit in investment.*

(Economou, 1986: 106)

In the extract, there is a considerable amount of competition between the speakers for 'airplay'. While the overall theme remains 'what I'd do if I won the lottery', each wants to provide his or her own special angle on the topic. Interestingly, all turns occur through self-selection – there are no instances of the individual currently holding the floor giving it up willingly to one of the other participants. Despite this, the interaction proceeds smoothly, with no overlaps, and only four interruptions.

At the beginning of the extract, Pauline adds to Gary's initial contribution. However, when Gary seeks to continue the exchange, Bronwyn cuts him off, and interpolates her own perspective, which she relates to Pauline's sub-theme of boredom. Her *no, look* is a discourse marker indicating that she is either going to contradict or to change the perspective on the topic. Gary's *No, that's right* is a form of **back-channelling**, letting Bronwyn know she is being listened to. Pauline tries to get the floor back with her *Yes, I think that um. . . .* However, she loses the floor to Pat. By saying *I'd buy my farm*, rather than *I'd buy a farm* (using the **definite article** rather than **indefinite article**), it is clear that Pat has talked about this dream to her colleagues before. It is part of the shared knowledge of the group. Bronwyn tries to reinstate her own sub-theme of needing contact with people, and the fact that she would continue working regardless of whether or not she needed the money (note, again, the discourse marker *no*). Pauline agrees, but turns the sub-theme back to her own perspective. Bronwyn and Gary murmur assent, but then Gary decides to dissent. He takes over the agenda, despite Pauline's bids to maintain her turn, and then caps the exchange by returning to the theme that he initiated at the beginning – that he would use the money to invest in a boat rental business in the surfing resort of Noosa. Does Gary's dominance in setting the conversational agenda and then reasserting his perspective at the end (as well as the fact that three of the four interruptions are by him) reflect a gender difference? Some discourse analysts would certainly argue that it does. Male–female differences in conversation is something that we will look at in detail later in the chapter.

What happens when one conversational partner misunderstands or misinterprets the overall functional intention of the other? Consider the following exchange:

A: *I've been smoking for 28 years and I gave up so I could travel up here.*
B: *Sorry?*
A: *I said, I've been smoking for 28 years and I gave up so I could travel up here.*
B: *So?*
A: *So, I gave up smoking.*

B: *What do you want?*
A: *I don't want anything. You know, you're the rudest person I've ever met.*

This conversation took place between an elderly male airline passenger (A) and a young female flight attendant (B). The context was the upper deck of a Cathay Pacific 747 aircraft in the days when smoking was still allowed on the lower deck, but not on the upper deck. The miscommunication occurs because the passenger attempts to initiate a social, or interpersonal conversation. (Basically, he is fishing for a compliment.) Because of her job however, the flight attendant is cued to assume that passenger-initiated interactions are transactional. They only speak to you when they want something. In this case, the passenger didn't want his glass of champagne replenished; he wanted a pat on the head. When the flight attendant misinterpreted the functional intention of his conversational gambit, he reacted negatively. This, and several of the other conversations in this book illustrate ways in which conversations can become 'unstuck' when interlocutors violate one or more maxims of the **cooperative principle** – 'be true', 'be brief', 'be relevant', 'be clear' (Grice, 1975).

Negotiating and co-constructing meaning

As the conversational extracts we have analysed demonstrate, meanings do not come ready made. Conversations can be hard work, and conversational participants have to negotiate with each other to ensure that misunderstandings are either pre-empted or quickly sorted out, as they are in the following fragments:

A: *How do I get to Kensington Road?*
B: *Well, you go down Fullarton Road . . .*
A: *. . . what down Old Belair and around . . .?*
B: *Yeah, and then you go straight . . .*
A: *. . . past the hospital?*
B: *Yeah, keep going straight, past the racecourse to the roundabout. You know the big roundabout?*
A: *Yeah.*
B: *And Kensington Road's off to the right.*
A: *What, off the roundabout?*
B: *Yeah.*
A: *Right.*

And the following:

A: *So what would you suggest?*
B: *About?*
A: *You know . . .*
B: *. . . Chasing after Lucy?*
A: *Well, I wouldn't. . . .*
B: *That's my advice.*
A: *What?*
B: *I wouldn't.*
A: *Wouldn't what?*
B: *I wouldn't do a line for Lucy.*

This interactional 'work' carried out by speakers and listeners to ensure that conversations flow smoothly is such a natural part of everyday life that we rarely even notice that we are doing it. It's a bit like driving to work on automatic pilot and, on reaching the office, not being able to recall a single aspect of the drive because our mind was on other things.

Here are some further examples of the three main strategies for negotiating meaning and keeping the conversation on track: **comprehension checks**, **confirmation requests**, and **clarification requests**.

A: *You gotta tie that thing up under there – know what I mean?*
B: *Yeah.*
(A's *know what I mean* is a comprehension check, a strategy designed to check that the listener has understood correctly.)

A: *I saw your girlfriend talking to Steve last night.*
B: *My girlfriend?*
A: *Yeah, your girlfriend. I didn't know they knew each other.*
B: *Neither did I!*
(Here, B's *my girlfriend* serves as a request for A to confirm what he just said.)

A: *Can you pass me the Phillip's Head?*
B: *The what?*
A: *The screwdriver there on the table.*
(Here, *The what?* is a request by B for A to reformulate his message more explicitly.)

The following workplace conversation between a supervisor and a worker contains a number of these conversational devices. Note that there are several errors in A's side of the conversation, because he is a second language speaker. The conversation is interesting from an intercultural perspective because he is also the supervisor.

A: *Now, uh, how do you call the . . . that special paper that fit* [sic] *in the sliding door?*
B: *In the sliding door?*
A: *Yeah, you know, the . . .*
B: *Oh, ceraphic glass.*
A: *Creaphic gla . . . they have another name. That's not Clark?*
B: *No, this one isn't, no.*
A: *No. Uh, these ones to put to install there before the third of April, meaning the Clark product.*
B: *Which Mort Adams is taking?*
A: *Mort Adams is working on it.*
B: *OK.*
A: *Mort, Mort Adams told me that he is not sure about it if he have the material or not yet. He will let me know tomorrow.*

We have seen several times that potential or actual miscommunication, far from being an aberration, is the norm in conversational encounters. We have also seen that this miscommunication has several sources: it can be cross-cultural, it can stem from imprecision or ambiguity on the part of the speaker, or it can result from an overall misapprehension of what the other person is on about – as in the case of the airline passenger and flight attendant. It can also be intentional, as is the case in the following interaction:

Henry: *I have two tickets for the theatre tonight.*
Matilda: *Good for you. What are you going to see?*
Henry: *Measure for Measure.*
Matilda: *Interesting play. Hope you enjoy it.*
Henry: *Oh, so you're busy tonight.*

In this example, which I have borrowed from Widdowson (1983), Henry initiates the conversation with what eventually turns out to be an invitation. Matilda, however, chooses to interpret it as a casual observation. For Henry, this is a transactional encounter, but Matilda interprets (or choose to interpret) it as an interpersonal interaction. Henry's indirectness is a **face-saving** device. However, it backfires when Matilda chooses to interpret it literally.

Speech acts

So far, I have talked about the things we do with language; that is, the communicative functions we perform through language, in extremely general terms, characterizing entire conversations as being basically transactional or interpersonal in nature. Now, I want to do a more fine-grained analysis, looking at the functions being performed by individual **utterances** inside a conversation. The technical term that linguists use for **functions** at this level is **speech act**. Speech acts are so interesting, and so complex, that I could have devoted the entire book to them, as several other linguists have already done. However, I will resist the temptation to turn the book into a treatise on speech acts, and restrict consideration to the example in the preceding section. Basically, the miscommunication here is at the level of the speech act: Henry intended the speech act as an invitation, whereas Matilda interpreted it as an observation.

The function of inviting is an indirect one – it is not immediately apparent in the way the utterance is formulated that Henry is inviting Matilda to the play. Why is Henry indirect when he could have avoided all ambiguity with a direct indication of his desire by saying something like *I want you to come to Measure for Measure with me,* or *How about coming to Measure for Measure?* The answer, as I indicated above, has to do with saving face. A direct invitation is risky for Henry because he faces a direct rejection. It is also risky for Matilda, because she is placed in the position, potentially, of having to say *no.* Issuing an indirect request allows for face saving on both parts (although indirectness also caries a risk for Henry; that of not actually getting what he wants – which, presumably, is Matilda.)

In her research into indirectness in conversation, Thomas (1995) argues that indirectness is risky because the potential for failure is high but that it is also costly in that an indirect utterance takes longer for the speaker to produce and longer for the listeners to process. She illustrates the risk on indirectness with the following two examples:

Example 1

B (a non-native speaker of English) has been staying with A for several weeks. He has a passion for West Side Story *and has just played the film's sound track through for the second time in one evening:*

A: Would you like to hear something else now?
B: No.

In order to avoid making a direct complaint to his guest, which could hurt his feelings, A suggests indirectly that he has had enough of *West Side Story*. However, his strategy fails; B interprets A's utterance as a genuine question and prepares to play the record for the third time.

Example 2
An American woman was visiting Israel; one evening she went to the flat of some friends and her host asked her what she would like to drink. She replied:

'Well, I've been on whisky all day.'

The American woman intended to indicate indirectly that, having been drinking whisky previously, she would prefer to stick with whisky. Unfortunately, the host misinterpreted her indirectness and thought she was saying that, as she had been on whisky all day, she didn't want any more to drink. (Thomas 1995: 120–1)

According to Thomas, indirectness is a variable quality in conversation. The degree of directness or indirectness will be governed by four factors:

- The relative power of the speaker over the hearer
- The social distance between the speaker and the hearer
- The degree to which X is rated as an imposition in culture Y
- Relative rights and obligations between the speaker and the hearer.

Speech acts were first written about by the linguistic philosopher John Austin, who pointed out that certain utterances are not meant to convey information at all but to perform an action of some kind. When a member of the clergy, or a registered marriage celebrant utters the words *I now pronounce you man and wife*, she is not making a propositional statement but is performing an act. The same is true for

I name this boat The Bonnie Bess.
I promise to pay you back tomorrow.
I apologize for my transgressions.

Because they don't state a proposition, these performatives have no 'truth' value. It therefore makes no sense to evaluate them in terms of whether they are true or false. *No you don't* would be as inappropriate a response to *I now pronounce you man and wife* as it would be to an utterance such as: *I name this boat The Bonnie Bess.*

Another philosopher, John Searle, building on the work of Austin, set out to develop a taxonomy of speech acts. Searle identified five basic speech act types:

Directives

The speaker tries to get the hearer to do something; for example, *ask, challenge, command, insist, request.* The directive may be direct ('Stack the chairs along the wall') or indirect ('Hmm, my glass appears to be empty').

Commissives

The speaker is committed, in varying degrees, to a certain course of action or refusing to act; for example, *guarantee, pledge, promise, swear, vow.* As with directives, they vary in directness and strength.

Representatives

The speaker is committed, in varying degrees, to the truth of a proposition; for example, *affirm, believe, conclude, deny, report.* Representatives can be evaluated for their truth value. The may vary in terms of how hedged they are. '"Darwin was partially correct" is obviously not as strong a statement as "Darwin was right" or "Darwin was wrong"' (Hatch, 1992: 127).

Declaratives (also called performatives)

The speaker alters the external status or condition of an object or situation solely by making the utterance; for example, *I resign, I baptize you, You're fired, Class dismissed, War is hereby declared.* Obviously the person uttering the directive must be empowered to do so.

Expressives

The speaker expresses an attitude about a state of affairs; for example, *apologize, deplore, congratulate, thank, welcome.* Expressives include compliments, statements of joy and disappointment and expressions of likes and dislikes (Searle, 1969; Hatch, 1992).

As we have already seen, indirect speech acts are common in everyday conversation. In fact, certain speech acts such as directives and invitations are almost always expressed indirectly: invitations in order to save face, and directives in order to soften the abruptness of the directive. Think of all the ways in which the directive *Give me some more wine* could be expressed indirectly.

Could you give me a little wine please?
Would you mind passing me the wine bottle?
That's an interesting looking bottle.
Hmm, my glass appears to be empty again.
This cheese would go well with a little of that wine.
Is that the delicious Chilean cabernet you were talking about?

An extreme example of indirectness was provided to me by a friend who lives in Japan. His daughter had been practicing the piano, as she did most afternoons when there was a knock on the door. He opened the door to find his elderly neighbour standing there.

Your daughter plays the piano beautifully, she said.
Thank you very much, replied my friend.

Several days later he received an official letter from the management office requesting that his daughter curtail her piano practice. The old woman had been complaining about the noise, not praising his daughter.

Speech act theorists generally distinguish between three different dimensions or orientations to an utterance. The first is the literal or propositional meaning of the utterance. Taken at face value, *That's an interesting looking bottle* is simply a comment about a bottle. This is known as the **locutionary aspect** of the utterance. The next dimension is the effect that the speaker intended the utterance to have on the listener. This is the **illocutionary force** of the utterance. The third dimension is the actual effect that the utterance has on the listener, which is called the **perlocutionary effect**. If the illocutionary force of the utterance was to get the listener to replenish the speaker's glass, and he does so, then the illocutionary force and perlocutionary effect are one and the same. However, they may not coincide. The hearer may decide that the speaker has had enough, and reply *Yes, it is, isn't it? I quite like wines from lesser known vineyards.*

The following (presumably invented) examples, provided by Hatch illustrate the mismatch between speaker intention and listener interpretation when it comes to directives issued indirectly:

A: *How many times do I have to tell you?*
B: *Five times.*

A: *We need this photocopied for the 4 o'clock meeting.*
B: *That's true.*

A: *Let's give Heidi a call.*
B: *Yes, please do.*

A: *Could you do the dishes?*
B: *Yes, I could.*

A: *Where are the matches?*
B: *In the matchbox.*

A: *What happened to the salt?*
B: *Nothing happened to the salt.*

A: *Is Pattilee there?*
B: *Yes, she is.*

A: *How would it look if you were to arrive late?*
B: *It would look beautiful.*

Like all other aspects of communication, degree of directness will be driven by contextual factors. If you are clinging by your fingertips to the edge of a precipice, you are more likely to shout *Throw me the rope* than *I say, old chap, if you're not frightfully busy right now, would you be so awfully kind as to throw me the rope?*
Familiarity with the other person will also be an important factor, as the following anecdote from Hatch (1992: 123) attests:

A colleague (not a personal friend) at another university sent me a request to collect some comparison data for him. Our universities were in different countries, and the request came at the end of the academic year when all professors are overloaded with work and the students from whom I would need to collect the data were preparing for final exams. Therefore, the ability and willingness of the addressee (me) to carry out the request was definitely in doubt. I was physically distant from the requester, but I was asked to do an action in my own territory. Yet, the request was stated in terms of imperatives: 'Follow the directions . . .' 'Return no later than . . .' This colleague was a native speaker of English. My reaction was, 'Well, of all the nerve!'

Determining the status of speech acts, even direct speech acts, can often be problematic. Following a highly disruptive strike by staff during peak holiday travel time, former British Airways chief Sir Rod Eddington, stated that he *would like to apologize*. However, his statement did not cut much ice with one inconvenienced, and obviously disgruntled journalist. Writing in the *Financial Times* (Wednesday 30 July, 2003), Michael Skapinker argued that the utterance *I would like to apologize* no more constitutes an apology than *I would like to lose weight* constitutes weight loss. In order to interpret the speech act however, we need to know what the modal *would like to* is doing. Is it expressing a wish (*I wish I could apologize, I wish I could lose weight*), or is it used as a polite form of *will*? Skapinker clearly prefers the former interpretation, although the latter is also clearly a possibility. Does *I would like to congratulate the winner* constitute a congratulation or a wish? Is the speaker saying *I wish I could congratulate the winner*, or *I congratulate the winner*? Either interpretation is a possibility, although most winners would, I think, prefer to interpret the utterance as a congratulation than a wish.

Someone who would almost certainly take issue with my claim that there are only three systems in language is the English social anthropologist Kate Fox. (The branch of sociology concerned with the analysis and interpretation of everyday spoken interaction is known as **ethnomethodology**.) Fox's insightful and sometimes hilarious book on the hidden rules of English behaviour *Watching the English* attempts to specify the speech acts that govern the social behaviour of the English. She devotes an entire section of the book to introductions, in which she points out things one shouldn't say (such as reveal one's name) but rather what one should do. She concludes her discussion of introductions by stating that:

In fact, the only rule one can identify with any certainty in all this confusion over introductions and greetings is that, to be impeccably English, one must perform these rituals *badly*. One must appear self-conscious, ill-at-ease, stiff, awkward and, above all, embarrassed. Smoothness, glibness and confidence are inappropriate and un-English. Hesitation, dithering and ineptness are, surprising as it may seem, correct behaviour.

Introductions should be performed as hurriedly as possible, but also with maximum inefficiency. If disclosed at all, names must be mumbled; hands should be tentatively half-proffered and then clumsily withdrawn; the approved greeting is something like 'Er, how, um, plstm-, er, hello.' (Fox, 2004:41)

The messiness of spoken language

In the preceding chapter, we saw that when native speakers create utterances in real time, the results often appear to be ungrammatical. Consider the following anecdote from an exchange student who was sharing her experiences of studying abroad. Hearing the student recount the incident, it doesn't seem exceptional or odd. However, the transcript reveals the student's struggle to create a coherent account of the incident.

One thing that . . . that I kinda did wrong when I was in Thailand that I wish I . . . I had paid more attention to before I did it . . . was I wore shorts, around town, and when . . . when I went with friends to, to go, um, you know, visit the museums or whatever, and we got back home . . . and they said you know you really shouldn't wear shorts around town, and I was like . . . I didn't even think about it – and, and you know, it . . . it's really kind of offending to them. Um, and the more I thought about it, you know . . . the more it made sense . . . you know women in Thailand don't wear shorts . . . I mean . . . at least where I was . . . where I was.

Here is another example, this time from a radio talk back programme.

1 <S 01> Did you hear me darling? Love a glass of water. Would kill for a glass of
2   water. Alright? Thank you. [laughs] Where would I be without Sue
3   Kelly. Ten and a half to two and John Robinson's in Lichfield. Hello John.
4 <S 02> Hello Ed.
5 <S 01> Yes.
6 <S 02> Er just the usual. I've driven over from West Bromwith to Lichfield.
7   And I'm amazed literally amazed in these weather conditions that
8   people are still driving around without lights on.
9 <S 01> You're joking.
10 <S 02> No honestly.
11 <S 01> I can't. I can't you see it is amazing to think that there is anybody left
12   in the world who can be so thick as to drive in this weather without
13   the lights on. I'd have thought the first thing you do when it gets as

14   dark and as wet and as miserable as this. You turn your lights on and I
15   don't mean the parkers. I mean the lights.
16 <S 02> It's absolutely unbelievable.
17 <S 01> But I don't understand how how can it tell me how can there be
18   anybody left in the world that hasn't heard that's what you do.
19   [laughs] Tell me.
20 <S 02> Can I . . . Can I post a question Edward? These same people drive
21   around without the window wipers going
22 <S 01> God knows. God knows. It is I don't understand it. I don't
23   understand
24 <S 02> I mean I I know you've mentioned it several times in the past but it's
25   it still doesn't seem to get through to people.
26 <S 01> I dunno. Well th th they it's none of my listeners mate. [<S 02> well]
27   There isn't one person listening to this at the moment in the car that
28   hasn't got the full lights on. Right? So we don't have to worry about
29   that.
30 <S 02> Mm. Right.
31 <S 01> But I'm worried about the others.
32 <S 02> And I am Ed.
33 <S 01> Okay matey.
34 <S 02> Okay thanks.
35 <S 01> Good luck to you. [radio jingle] Nine minutes to two. Oh Sue. I think
36   I love you. I realise that's not money in the bank but it's nice.
                                        (Carter and McCarthy, 1997: 110–11)

These two extracts illustrate the struggle that even native speakers have
in mobilizing their grammatical knowledge to construct and co-
construct messages in real time.

Some special contexts: child language, classroom conversation, e-talk, 'offlish'

Child language

In Chapter 1, brief mention was made of the species specificity of
language, the notion that language is somehow hard-wired into the
human brain. Evidence for this position comes from several sources.

For example, the way that language expands dramatically in children between the ages of 18 months and three years, and the fact that they are able to internalize grammatical systems of incredible complexity and subtlety from the 'junky', and often ungrammatical input provided to them by adults.

However, if we study language acquisition, not by making inferences about unobservable mental states and processes, but by actually looking at what children do as they acquire language, we notice some interesting phenomena. Take the following extract of a conversation between a child and her mother:

Rebecca: *Mm. Wash it.*
Mother: *Washed it – yeah, I washed the tomato.*
Rebecca: *A bump.*
Mother: *Pardon! Don't bang it – no. It'll squash.*
  You bite it. Mm
Rebecca: *Ah*
Mother: *Oh, you've still got a mouthful. Well chew it up and swallow it. Chew, chew, chew. Chew it on your molars. That's right. How are your molars, good? Oh, yeah, big aren't they. Well now, you going to have a bite of your tomato?*
Rebecca: *A bobble* (bottle)
Mother: *Drink. OK.*

The conversation begins with the child making a statement *Wash it*. Taken by itself, out of context, the most obvious interpretation of the utterance is that the child is performing a directive speech act instructing the mother to wash an unspecified object (which turns out to be a tomato). However, from the mother's utterance, we see that the child's utterance is an observation on the mother's action. What the mother does is to provide an expanded, grammatically correct version of what the child was trying to say. The mother and child are engaging in a conversation, and it is out of the conversation that the child is provided with sentence-level grammatical knowledge. In other words, the child does not acquire grammar which is then deployed to make a conversation, rather, she learns to do conversation, and it is through conversation that she is provided with the data on which to construct her grammatical knowledge.

Classroom conversation

The next two pieces of interaction begin with the identical question. *What's the last day of the month?* However, from there they develop in two very different directions.

A: *What's the last day of the month?*
B: *Friday.*
A: *The cheque should cleared by then.*
B: *OK.*

A: *What's the last day of the month?*
B: *Friday.*
A: *A complete sentence, please.*
B: *The last day of the month is Friday.*
A: *Well done!*

It isn't difficult to come up with a context for the first fragment which appears to be a business transaction of some kind. However, the second fragment seems to run right off the rails by the third exchange. What sort of a person would request that they be answered in complete sentences (using an incomplete sentence in the process)? Who evaluates their interlocutor's response? A teacher, that's who! (Parents are known to display this odd form of linguistic behaviour as well.) The extract is from a piece of classroom interaction, and the question is an artifact, a pseudo-question. In fact, it isn't really a question at all. The teacher does not really care what day of the week marks the end of the month. He wants his students to display their knowledge of certain grammatical forms.

This habit of listening to and evaluating the grammatical form of a students' response rather than the meaning can lead to unfortunate consequences as in the following extract in which the teacher is attending to form not meaning. (I am indebted to Leo van Lier, 1989: 499, for this example.)

Teacher: *How is your mother?*
Student: *She's dead.*
Teacher: *Very good.*

Here is a more extended example of classroom language, again displaying the use of questions as an elicitation device. A notable feature of such interactions is that questioners asks questions to which they already know (or think they already know) the answer. Classroom questions thus have a different function from non-classroom questions – to elicit and evaluate language rather than to obtain information.

T: *Today, er, we're going to, um, we're going to do something where, we, er, listen to a conversation and we also talk about the subject of the conversation er, in fact, we're not going to listen to one conversation. How many conversations are we going to listen to?*
S: *Three.*
T: *How do you know?*
S: *Because, er, you will need, er, three tapes and three points.*
T: *Three?*
S: *Points.*
T: *What?*
S: *Power points.*
T: *Power points, if I need three power points and three tape recorders, you correctly assume that I'm going to give you three conversations, and that's true, and all the conversations will be different, but they will all be on the same . . .?*
S: *Subject, subject.*
T: *The same . . .?*
S: *Subject, subject.*
T: *Right, they will all be on the same subject.* (Nunan 1988: 139)

e-talk

At first sight, this next example is incoherent. It appears to be either random utterances copied and pasted from different conversations, or different fragments from a party conversation. It is, in fact, an extract from an Internet text chat log; an increasingly common form of communication. I have discussed it in this chapter rather than the next one, on written language, because text chat is more like spoken than written language.

G: *December and January is when the Americans and Canadian people come to spend here in beaches like Acapulco, Cancun, etc.*
W: *Ciao F.*
A: *Yes, that's true G. I hear Americans talking about it. Ciao W, how's it going? Hi, E. how are you today?*

E: *Z, what is H.K.?*
W: *I'm stellar, thanks, and you, F?*
F: *G, we would say 'spend time', 'spend a few days', etc. Spend must have a direct object.*
E: *I'm fine thank you.*
F: *I'm a little puzzled as to why no-one's chatting here, W.*
G: *How compare you the climate with Japan, is more or less pleasant.*
F: *Where are you, E? I'm in Berkeley, California in the USA.*
Z: *H.K. means Hong Kong.*
F: *I don't like the climate in Japan. From June to October it has the most miserable, humid, hot climate. It's horrible. It ruins my brain. I can't even think.*

This new kind of electronic language reflects the important influence that the medium has on the message. In many ways, as Marshall MacLuen so famously said all those years ago, the medium *is* the message. In addition to elisions, and other devices to overcome the cumbersome effects of having to talk through the tips of our fingers (for example, many people abandon the use of upper case for proper nouns for reasons of time and economy), there is also the fact that no one is in control of the flow of language. A question asked at one point in time may be answered several minutes later, with other interweaving conversations coming in between. It will be interesting to see whether Internet text chat will survive as a form of communication, or whether it will succumb to voice chat, which is becoming increasingly common. I suspect that it will survive in some shape or form. It has an anonymity that voice chat doesn't have. And it also allows for several conversations to emerge across time as well as space. What at first sight looks like a disadvantage – the chaotic multiple and overlapping conversations with their often disparate topics – may in fact turn out to be a significant advantage that will facilitate the survival of this particular (and, at first sight, peculiar) form of discourse.

Telephone text messaging is another evolving form of discourse that has its own characteristics as well as its own advantages. In text messaging, people communicate with each other through their cell phones, not by speaking into them, but by typing messages. What are the advantages? There are many. Students in class these days commonly evaluate a lesson or make plans for what to do after school through text messaging. And, unless the teacher spots those flying fingers, it's impossible for her to intercept the notes being passed between her classroom charges.

According to researchers, the phenomenon is here to stay. Estimates have it that teens now use their phones more for messaging than for talking. I was sitting in a movie recently, when I noticed cell phones lighting up all over the place. Shortly afterwards, a bunch of younger people, who were seated in different parts of the theater, got up and left. Apparently, as the movie was in progress, they were creating their own movie review. Judging by their abrupt departure, they had given it the thumbs-down!

Again, the imperative for economy shapes the nature of the discourse. If your fingers have to do the talking, then you are unlikely to waste time with unnecessary or excessive punctuation. While even the older people now recognize shortcuts such as *cu* (*See you!*), young people commonly type messages such as the following: *ther iz a gr8 mvie shON @ d Odeon. Do U wnt 2 chek it out?* With a little mental gymnastics you probably, rightly, figured it out as *There is a great movie showing at the Odeon. Do you want to check it out?* However, it does require interpretive work, if you are not conversant with this new medium.

I have to confess that text-messages are a foreign language to me. It takes me ages to produce a text message to my daughter. When I want to chat with my kids and appear cool at the same time, I use technology: in this case the Web site (www.transl8it.com). I compose my message using the uncool punctuation and writing conventions of my generation, hit *translate* and the message is instantly transformed into the argot of my daughter's generation. *nw, isnt dat kewl?* Unfortunately, the program does not yet do back translations, so I am often forced to call my daughter to find out what on earth she meant by her response.

Offlish

A new variety of English has recently been documented. Dubbed 'offlish', it is the often incomprehensible language of the office. A recent book, *Ducks in a Row* by Carl Newbrook (2005) take a lighthearted, tongue-in-cheek look at this new mutation.

Here are some extracts from the book. The everyday meaning is provided, followed by a gloss of how the expression is used in office contexts along with a note on how, when and by whom it is used.

Bandwidth = n: *the capacity of a communication channel*
Always too small to be fully effective
Usage A vogue word from the baffling world of IT used by executives and senior managers adding an unnecessary technical gloss to a simple statement. 'We need more bandwidth to achieve top-line growth.'

CrackBerry = n: *a person who obsessively uses their BlackBerry*
An up-to-the-minute ailment
Usage Put-upon subordinates who know that their boss can issue commands from anywhere and at any time: 'He's a control freak. A CrackBerry. Doesn't he sleep? Doesn't he realize I sleep?'

Dilbert = n: *a soothsayer*
Usage Underlings reflecting on the accuracy of the Dilbert principle which states that the most ineffective managers are systematically moved to the place where they can do the least damage – management.

Drill down = v: *go into detail*
A muscular investigation
Usage Managers everywhere examining 'the numbers', but especially finance managers for whom there is no greater pleasure.

Ducks in a row = phrase: *preparedness, show of unity*
Usage A popular if somewhat obscure phrase: 'Guys, we need to get our ducks in a row on this one.' Used by anxious managers seeking to impress upon their team that no mistakes will be tolerated. It is likely that they will go on to suggest that they must be 'on the same page' with 'all the boxes ticked' and most importantly 'singing from the same hymn sheet'.

Forward, going = phrase: *in the future*
An everyday blessing
Usage A very important offlish term, a verbal flourish that is used by everyone, everywhere to foretell a brighter tomorrow. 'Going forward we will . . . [insert relevant promise here].' Variations of the phrase are 'on a going forward basis' and 'on a go-forward basis'.

J.F.D.I. = abbreviation: *Just F****** Do It*
A brash statement intending to banish confusion
Usage The transformation of Nike's vacuous Just Do It shoutline into a blunt managerial instruction is often accompanied by a ghastly 'we are all in it together' rictus. It is used by managers for whom heavy-handed irony is a way of papering over the unpalatable truth that the J.F.D.I.! principle is the foundation of corporate relationships: 'I hear you, but this isn't a debate. It's a JFDI situation.'

Miles, go the extra = phrase: *strenuous and special exertion*
A word of warning: the office can be exhausting
Usage All managers but especially Sales managers, exhorting their team to even greater efforts: 'We have to be seen to be setting the pack, guys. I need you to pull out all the stops, throw the kitchen sink at it, and go the extra mile on this one.'

Quid pro quo = n: *something given in compensation* (Latin: 'something for something')
A popular company motto.
Usage Senior managers unfamiliar with Latin, outlining the latest tactical initiative 'When all is said and done, we've had a bumpy ride recently and there is still a shortfall in the numbers. The quid pro quo is that we now have a handle on the problem'. (Translation: 'There will be no bonus this year, but there will be at least three months of unpaid overtime in order to achieve the reforecast.')

Language and gender

Once feminism began to have an impact on the way we looked at male–female relationships, it was not too long before academics began to view language through a radically different lens. Feminism dramatically altered the ways in which we looked at social and cultural phenomena, and language was no exception. One of the first items to be put under the feminist microscope was the ubiquitous male pronoun *he* used as a generic reference for both men and woman, a practice deemed sexist when used to refer to women. This criticism led to the adoption of clumsy devices such as the inclusion of both pronouns *he or she*, *he/she*, and *s/he*. Some writers even used a form of reverse sexist discrimination by embracing the female form *she* as the default pronoun reference item for both men and women. Other generic terms with a male bias were also subjected to linguistic revisionism. Thus, *chairman* because *chairperson*, *waiter* became *waitpersons* and my neighbour, Jake Chesterman began referring to himself as Jake Chesterperson.

Gender differences in language become really interesting when we look at the different conversational styles of men and women. You may not be surprised to learn that in conversation men talk more than women, they interrupt more, and that they talk about themselves more than women do. Less commonly known is that, contrary to popular wisdom, there is evidence to suggest that men gossip more than women.

Robin Lakoff (1975), one of the first linguists to investigate gender differences in language, suggested that women's language contains linguistic features that show they are excessively polite, uncertain and deferential. Such features include:

Tag questions: questions tagged onto an utterance such as **don't we? haven't you?** which are sometimes used to gain approval or confirmation.
Rising intonation: used to turn a statement into a question, so weakening the force of it.
Super polite forms: excessive use of direct speech acts in favour of indirect speech acts marked by modals.
Hedges and fillers: expressions such as *kind of* make assertions more tentative.
Expletives: women use fewer expletives than men.

Another linguist who has investigated gender differences is Deborah Tannen, whose research into the speech styles of men and women has been turned into several bestselling paperbacks including *That's Not What I Meant* and *You Just Don't Understand*. Tannen is careful to point out that while conversational styles between men and women differ, one is not necessarily superior to the other (although, most of the anecdotes in her books imply otherwise!). Here is one of them:

> I was at a dinner with faculty members from other departments in my university. To my right was a woman. As the dinner began, we introduced ourselves. After we told each other what department we were in and what subjects we taught, she asked what my research was about. We talked about my research for a little while. Then I asked her about her research and she told me about it. Finally, we discussed the ways that our research overlapped. Later, as tends to happen at dinners, we branched out to others at the table. I asked a man across the table from me what department he was in and what he did. During the next half hour, I learned a lot about his job, his research, and his background. Shortly before the dinner ended there was a lull, and he asked me what I did. When I told him I was a linguist, he became excited and told me about a research project he had conducted that was related to neurolinguistics. He was still telling me about his research when we all got up to leave the table. (Tannen, 1991: 126).

Tannen uses the anecdote to support her claims about gender differences in conversation. She says that when she tells other women about her research into language and gender, they offer their own experiences to support the patterns she describes. She finds this flattering because it puts her centre stage without her having to grab the spotlight. Men, on the other hand, tend either to give her a lecture on language, challenge her on her research finding, or change the subject to something they know more about.

According to Tannen, gender differences suffuse all aspects of communication. She tells the story of one of her informants, Zoe, a history professor, whose favourite joke is a well known doctor–patient joke. The doctor tells the patient that he has only six weeks to live. 'I want a second opinion', cries the patient. 'You want a second opinion', replies the doctor, 'OK. You're ugly, too.'

One evening, Zoe is on a date with a man she has recently met called Earl. At one point, Earl asks Zoe her favourite joke. Tannen takes up the story:

> 'Uh, my favorite joke is probably – O.K., all right. This guy goes into a doctor's office, and –'
> 'I think I know this one', interrupted Earl, eagerly. He wanted to tell it himself. 'A guy goes into a doctor's office, and the doctor tells him he's got some good news and some bad news – that one right?'
> 'I'm not sure', said Zoe, 'this might be a different version.'
> 'So, the guy says "Give me the bad news first", and the doctor says, "O.K. You've got three weeks to live." And the guy cries, "Three weeks to live! Doctor, what is the good news?" And the doctor says, "Did you see that secretary out front? I finally fucked her."'
> Zoe frowned.
> 'That's not the one you were thinking of?'
> 'No', there was accusation in her voice. 'Mine was different.'
> 'Oh', said Earl. He looked away and then back again. 'What kind of history do you teach?'

Tannen makes the following observation on this interaction:

> When Earl interrupts Zoe, it is not to support her joke but to tell her joke for her. To make matters worse, the joke he tells isn't just different, it's offensive. When he finds out that his joke was not the same as hers, he doesn't ask what her joke was. Instead he raises another topic entirely. ('What kind of history do you teach?') (Tannen, 1991: 212–13)

The psychotherapist R.D. Laing captured the linguistic knots that men and women get tied into in a series of Jack and Jill poems. Here are some selective examples:

> Jack: The trouble with you is that you are envious of me.
> Jill: The trouble with you is that's what you think.
>
> Jack: You never give me credit for anything.
>   You can't bear to admit that I've got it.

Jill: That's where you go wrong.
You can't bear to admit I don't care. (Laing, 1970: 25)

Jack: You are a pain in the neck.
To stop *you* giving me a pain in the neck
I protect my neck by tightening my neck muscles,
which gives me the pain in the neck
you are.

Jill: My head aches through trying to stop you
giving me a headache. (Ibid: 30)

Recently a curious and rather poignant story came to light. It concerned the death of the last user of a language called Nushu. Nushu is a secret written language used only by women in Hunan province in China. Females were taught the language at around the age of ten, and used it to communicate about topics that were taboo in the male dominated society. Through the language, they were able to discuss feminine feelings, concerns about arranged marriages and, of course, the shortcomings of their husbands.

Yang Huanyi, the last remaining skilled user of the language, was born in a small village in Hunan province in 1908. She died in the same village almost 100 years later. In an obituary on her life published in the *New York Times*, she is reported to have said that 'By writing in Nushu, so much suffering disappears.' Users of the language were known as 'sworn sisters'.

Linguistic connectivity in spoken discourse

In this final section, I would like to illustrate how the different linguistic features that have been discussed in the book in general, and this chapter in particular, work together to create coherent discourse. These features are also extremely important in written discourse, and we will look at them in greater detail in the next chapter.

The following is a slightly edited extract from a piece of conversational discourse. Read the extract and see how many discourse features you can identify. This conversation took place between two good friends. One of the friends owns an Apple iPod. The other had just purchased one, and was trying to figure out how to load songs from his computer to the iPod. The conversation took place in the latter's home office one wet Sunday afternoon. The two friends were filling in time while waiting for a third friend to collect them to go to a movie, and B had suggested to A that they kill time by loading A's new iPod.

The extract, which is typical of many conversations of this kind, shows how formal features of language, particularly cohesion, **clefting**, **thematization**, and the negotiation of meaning, function to enable the interaction to proceed smoothly. It also illustrates the intimate connection between discourse and the context that gave rise to it in the first place.

As you read the extract, you might like to see how many of the conversational features already discussed in the book you can identify. (My own summary follows the extract.)

1 A: *This is SO frustrating. Look, I'm clicking here but nothing's happening.*
2 B: *Here, did you say?*
3 A: *Uhuh. But nothing's happening.*
4 B: *It says here 'Insert a CD into your computer.'*
5 A: *I did – this one here. What I did was put the CD in and . . .*
6 B: *Did you put it in before you opened iTunes?*
7 A: *Yes, I did. iTunes is supposed to open automatically.*
8 B: *But it . . .*
9 A: *. . . didn't. I had to open it myself. And now I can't import. So . . .*
10 B: *You say you tried to import.*
11 A: *Uhuh. Look. I'm clicking here and nothing's happening.*
12 B: *Oh, but it's here that you're supposed to click.*
13 A: *Where?*
14 B: *Here. Look, let me do it.*
15 A: *Oh wow. It's working. I feel such an idiot. Thanks a lot!*
16 B: *For making you look like an idiot?*
17 A: *No, silly! For helping me.*
18 B: *That's OK. You should've asked me earlier.*
19 A: *Well, I was going to, but you use a MAC.*

Here is a line-by-line analysis of some of the linguistic features to be found in the extract. In keeping with the theme of the book, I have highlighted those features that have a 'discourse implication'. That is, I have documented those features that help to create a sense of **coherence**, and that can only be fully understood and explicated with reference to the broader linguistic and experiential contexts in which they are found.

Line 1

The words *this* and *here* are referring or 'pointing' up to entities in the experiential world outside of the **text**. The general term for such 'pointing' words and expressions is **deixis** (from the Greek word 'deixis' which means 'pointing'). The specific term for words that point outside the text is **exophoric reference**. Exophoric reference and other forms of **cohesion**, including substitution and ellipsis, are discussed in greater detail in the next chapter.

Line 2

Exophoric reference, deixis – *here*
Thematization: Fronting *here*
Negotiation of meaning: confirmation request: The function of the utterance is for B to check that she has understood correctly.

Line 3

'I did put it in here . . .' is not repeated by the speaker because it is assumed to be 'understood' from the context. This is an example of ellipsis.
Conjunction: *but*

Line 4

It
here

Line 5

Did is an example of verbal substitution: *did* is substituted for Insert a CD into your computer.
Exophoric reference, deixis: *this, here*
Nominal substitution: *one*
Thematization/topicalization: *What I did . . .*
Ellipsis: *in* (the computer)
Lexical repetition or **reiteration**: *CD*

Line 6

Exophoric reference: *you, you*
Reference: *it*
Ellipsis: *in* (the computer)
Conjunction: *before*
Lexical reiteration and **collocation**: *iTunes*

Line 7

Verbal substitution: *did*
Lexical reiteration and collocation: *iTunes*

Line 8

Cohesive reference: *it*
Conjunction: *But it . . .*
Conversational hatching: *But it . . .*

Line 9

Hatching: *. . . didn't*
Reference: *I, it, I, myself*
Conjunction: *And, now, so*
Ellipsis: *can't import*
Hatching: *So . . .*

Line 10

Confirmation request: *You say you tried to import*
Reference: *you, you*
Lexical reiteration: *import*

Line 11

Adjacency pair (confirming request): *Uhuh*
Discourse marker: *Look*
Reference: *I*

Lexical reiteration: *clicking*
Reference: *here*
Conjunction: *and*

Line 12

Discourse marker: *Oh*
Clefting: . . . *it's here that.* . . .
Conjunction: *but*
Reference: *you*
Lexical reiteration: *click*

Line 13

Confirmation request: *Where?*

Line 14

Deixis: *Here*
Discourse marker: *Look*
Reference: *me, it*
Verbal substitution: *do*

Line 15

Discourse marker: *Oh wow*
Reference: *It, I*
Adjacency pair – first part: *Thanks a lot!*

Line 16

Insertion sequence – first part: *For making you look like an idiot?*
Lexical reiteration: *idiot*

Line 17

Insertion sequence – second part: *No, silly! For helping me.*
Reference: *me*
Lexical collocation: *silly*

Line 18

Adjacency pair – second part: *That's OK.*
Reference: *that, you, me*
Comparative reference/ellipsis: *earlier*

Line 19

Discourse marker: *Well*
Reference: *I, you*
Ellipsis: *going to* [ask you earlier]
Conjunction: *but*
Lexical collocation: *MAC*

Summary and conclusion

In this chapter, I have taken a first, tentative step towards exploring ways in which the three subsystems of sounds, words and grammar work together to enable spoken communication to take place. We have just seen how pronouns such as *he, she, her* and *him* become exciting, even controversial, subjects of investigation when studied as tools for communication in authentic interactions. We have seen that in such interactions even the most mundane elements within the linguistic systems can become instruments of power, oppression and liberation.

The main point to emerge from the chapter is that in order fully to appreciate the intricacy of language systems, we need to explore how they are used as tools for communication. In the next chapter, we will look at how this perspective plays out in relation to written language.

Points covered in this chapter include the following:

- We communicate to exchange goods and services, to socialize, and for enjoyment
- Meaning resides in the language user not the language; it does not come ready packaged, but needs to be negotiated between speakers
- Language is a relatively imprecise tool that provides a signpost to, rather than a blueprint for, meaning
- Effective communication involves the integration of top-down and bottom-up processing
- There are three dimensions to speech acts: the locutionary act, the illocutionary force and the perlocutionary effect

- Indirectness, which is frequently a source of misunderstanding, is an important face-saving device
- When we speak, we are creating utterances in real time which results in messy, sometimes even ungrammatical, utterances
- The context has an important effect on the type of discourse produced. Context includes purpose, mode (face-to-face versus text messaging), gender (male to male, male to female, female to female), topic, speaker relationship (co-workers versus teacher/student).

Questions and tasks

1 Write your own definitions of *negotiation of meaning, speech acts* and *adjacency pairs.*

2 What is the difference between transactional and interpersonal talk?

3 What do linguists mean when they talk about 'context'? What does context include?

4 Which of the following utterances are performatives?

Shut up!
I name this vessel The Bonny Bess.
The large dog on the other side of the gate.
I promise to pay you back tomorrow.
I apologise.
I give and bequeath my stamp collection to my brother.
I bet you ten dollars it'll rain tomorrow.
I bet it will be raining before we get home.
I baptize you in the name of the Father.

5 Match the speech act types and utterances

Speech act	Utterance
Directive	*What a terrific party!*
Commissive	*I want to apologise for my behaviour last night.*
Representative	*The coffee pot is empty.*
Performative	*Don't worry, I'll be there by ten.*
Expressive	*I went to the movies on Saturday.*

Further reading

Austin, J. (1962) *How to Do Things with Words* (Oxford: Oxford University Press).
This is THE classic introduction to speech act theory.

Blakemore, D. (1992) *Understanding Utterances* (Oxford: Blackwell).
This book provides a detailed introduction to analysing and understanding utterances.

Hatch, E. (1992) *Discourse and Language Education* (Cambridge: Cambridge University Press), ch. 4 'Speech acts and speech events'.
This chapter contains a very clear description of Searle's speech act taxonomy along with examples and practice exercises.

Schiffrin, D. (1994) *Approaches to Discourse* (Oxford: Blackwell).
Provides an accessible introduction to the key frameworks, concepts and methods in discourse analysis.

6 Doing things with written language

Introduction and overview

In the first part of this chapter, I want to challenge the idea that written language is 'talk written down'. We will see that most writing differs from speaking, not only in its mode of presentation (marks on a page rather than sounds through the air), but also in its grammar, its vocabulary and the overall shape of its messages (think of the difference on the page between a love poem and a newspaper advertisement). These differences bear out one of the central themes of this book: that from a functional perspective, language looks the way it does because of the jobs it has to perform. In Halliday's words, language is what language does. Written language is the way it is because of the purposes it evolved to serve. And those purposes are reflected in the marks that people make on paper and on computer screens.

In this chapter, I plan to focus on transactional and interpersonal uses of language. There is an important third function, the aesthetic. This is the use of language for literary purposes. I must admit that, while not entirely absent, an exploration of literary language is a little underdone in this book. I'll try and redress the balance a little in Chapter 8, where I look at playful and creative uses of language.

Topics covered in this chapter include:

- Written versus spoken language
- Cohesion and coherence
- **Register**
- **Genre**.

Written language versus spoken language

Written language is a very different beast from spoken language. While there is a relationship between the two, this relationship is complex and has many different facets. At the most basic level, consider the fact that the English alphabet has only 26 letters to represent over 40 sounds. Simply trying to represent a spoken message in written form presents a considerable challenge. These days, we have more or less standardized the spelling of most words. However, the development of a consistent relationship between sounds and letters was a long and painful process. Even Shakespeare, arguably the greatest writer ever to commit sounds to print, was inconsistent in this regard, spelling his own name differently on different occasions.

Although all languages exist in spoken form, not all languages have a written form. While spoken language appears to be a defining characteristic of humanity, the same cannot be said for written language. How and why writing systems evolved remains a matter for speculation, but we can make educated guesses based on the earliest recorded samples of written language.

Another relevant point is that all humans, with the exception of those who have some form of physical or mental disability, learn to speak. However, not all learn to read and write. It would seem that writing is as unnatural a practice as speaking is a natural one. Most of us remember learning to read and write because it was a long and often painful process consuming hundreds of hours inside and outside of the classroom. However, no one I know is able to recall learning to speak.

At a very general level, written language serves the same functions as spoken language: these are the transactional (exchanging goods and services), interpersonal (socializing) and aesthetic (enjoyment/entertainment) functions. Here are some examples of the kinds of texts, or genres, that fulfil these functions:

Transactional: Public signs in the street, product labels on canned and bottled goods, instruction manuals, maps, television programs, checks, newspapers and magazines, advertisements, dictionaries, encyclopedias, post-it notes.
Interpersonal: Letters, emails, postcards, diaries.
Aesthetic: Novels, comics, movie/play scripts, poems, computer games.

The origins of written language can be dimly glimpsed in the clay tablets that have survived through to the modern day. The oldest of these go back over 3,500 years, and are purely transactional in nature, containing records of grain harvests and various types of business transactions. What they do is to preserve messages in ways that spoken language does not, and they enable the transmission of these messages across time and space. And this, purely and simply, is the reason for written language: the preservation of the message and its transportation across time and space.

While written discourse came into existence to serve similar transactional, interpersonal and aesthetic functions as spoken language, it was not simply 'talk written down'. Written and spoken language have their own typical features: for example, written language tends to have a greater percentage of content words to function words than spoken language. However, those features typically associated with written language can appear in spoken language and vice versa. In fact, it is best to think of spoken and written texts as existing on a continuum from more-like-spoken-language to more-like-written-language.

The differences between spoken and written language are illustrated in the following conversational fragment, and the written version that follows it. It is a story that I recounted one night over dinner with friends. We had all lived in interesting or unusual places. At one point, the conversation turned to experiences we had had and people we had met. When I finally managed to grab the floor (my companions that evening were a garrulous lot), I told the following story:

When I was living in Thailand you know I lived in Bangkok for like two years give or take a few months and I met this guy Paul his name was who was a foreign correspondent kind of thing and we struck up this . . . well it wasn't exactly a friendship, but kind of . . . you know we used to drink in the same bar and used to run into each other in Patpong or Soi Cowboy . . . in those days it was a very different – well not very different I guess, but anyway, struck up this kind of friendship and he said to me one night how'd you like to meet some drug smugglers. I thought drug smugglers? Yeah kind of interesting. The police had just arrested these three farang (foreign) guys . . . it was in all the newspapers and such . . . anyway these guys were into like smuggling heroin and stuff and my friend was going to interview them so this day I tagged along and it was incredible. I mean just being inside of a Bangkok prison was incredible. All of the prisoners were kind of all chained up, like they were handcuffed and they had these chains that were like hammered onto their legs, I mean really hammered, and they had this little bit of string that was tied to the chain between their legs that they had to hold up so they could walk . . . well they couldn't really walk, all they could do was kind of waddle along like ducks in a row.

A written version of the anecdote might be as follows:

When I lived in Thailand, I struck up an acquaintance with a foreign correspondent called Paul. One night over a drink, he asked me if I'd like to meet some drug smugglers. Three foreign drug smugglers had been arrested by the police and my friend had permission to interview them. So next day I accompanied him to the prison, which turned out to be an incredible experience. All of the prisoners were handcuffed and had chains struck onto their legs. In order to walk, they had to hold up the leg chains with a piece of string.

While the spoken version is fragmentary and in places even appears to be ungrammatical, the written version is coherent, consisting of complete sentences in which the facts are neatly packaged and related to one another through grammatical devices such as cohesion and **subordination** (this is the process by which one clause is subordinated to another, resulting in a sentence with a main clause and a **subordinate clause**). The end result is a text that is much 'denser' than the spoken version. In other words, it has a much greater ratio of content words to function words than the spoken text.

Cohesion and coherence

One of the concepts informing this book is that of discourse, which I have defined as language in context. Discourse analysts want to know what differentiates coherent text from random sentences. Where does the hanging-togetherness of sentences in coherent discourse come from? Linguists are divided on this question and have looked for answers in different places. Some have looked inside the language itself, and have attempted to create discourse 'grammars' – that is, rules setting out obligatory elements for determining 'well-formed' discourses – in the same way as traditional grammarians have done at the level of the sentence.

In order to pursue the hanging-togetherness issue, consider the following three sample 'texts'. Which is the most coherent, and which is the least coherent?

Sample text 1

She was congratulated and envied in equal measure. It was slated to appear in the Saturday Arts page. One of the poets announced that she had just had a piece accepted for publication by her local newspaper. We were introduced to each other by the organizer, and made polite noises to each other until the event began. The others were women. One was an overweight individual in his early thirties who had long hair and a beard and who wore a kind of caftan. The other literary hopefuls were poets with one children's author thrown in for good measure. The programme had me listed as sixth. There were eight of us, and about thirty people in the audience. The public reading took place at the Adelaide Museum and Art Gallery in a small room (clever that!) with oak panels.

Sample text 2

'I'm Mary', she said. 'Some of us are meeting for drinks at six o'clock.' Not everybody had a charitable view of Adelaide. After all these years, what I remember most vividly of the girl were her low-slung Levis and pigtails. I earned the label 'Mary's boy' from Hal Porter. Mary's invitation was kind, but I had no intention of taking her up on it. Mary was sitting with several middle-aged people. Mary asked me what I wanted to drink. I hesitated just long enough for Hal Porter to say, 'This is Mary's boy.' This character was Max Harris, a bookshop owner, author and the convener of Writers' Week.

Sample text 3

The person I was most anxious to see, if not to meet, was Anthony Burgess. I had just read *A Clockwork Orange*, and it changed the way I looked at literature. To that point, I had struggled with a disjunction between 'high culture' enshrined in the kinds of novels I had been reading, and the popular culture that suffused all other aspects of my daily life – the music, the movies and even the poetry. How was it possible to weave Led Zepplin, Levi jeans and incense into my writing in a way that made sense? How could I create convincing characters who would just as soon consume dope than fine wine, and whose dream was to sit cross-legged on a hilltop in Nepal? Looking back, I see I was naïve, and appallingly poorly read to boot. I hadn't read *Last Exit to Brooklyn* (banned in Australia at the time), and had yet to discover the Beats. But I had read *A Clockwork Orange*, and it opened all sorts of doors. Its author was a cult figure to me and to the few of my fellow literary aspirants who had read it, and now I was on my way to meet him.

All of the sentences in these extracts come from the same source – the piece I wrote on my meeting with Anthony Burgess. However, they have been constructed in different ways, and display different degrees of coherence. Most readers agree that text 3 makes most sense and that text 2 makes least sense. The sentences in text 1 seem to be about the same entities and events, and therefore the text hangs together to a certain extent. However, there is something odd about it as several sentences presuppose knowledge that the reader cannot be expected to possess.

Text 2 consists of the lead sentences from eight consecutive paragraphs. It is therefore not surprising that it does not seem to hang together; that is, that it lacks coherence. Text 1 consists of the sentences from one of the paragraphs in the story. However, they have been reversed. (Try reading the paragraph from the bottom up and you will find that it makes much more sense.)

While readers need to know the meaning of individual words and sentences in order to comprehend written texts, they also need to know how the sentences relate to one another. While most of the sentences in Texts 1 and 2 appear to be related, the arrangement is strange. In the first sentence of Text 1, for example, there is no way of deciding who *she* is.

Here are some sentences from another paragraph in the Burgess story. They are presented in random order. See whether you can figure out the original order.

(What would Burgess have made of that?).
Inside the barn, it was cool.
'This looks promising', said Burgess eyeing the victuals and rubbing his hands.
Through the gloom, I could see that at the rear of the barn, trestle tables had been set with food and wine.
A sweet, rotting smell came from the barrels.
Also in the party was an elderly member of the family whom everyone called 'Uncle Tom'.
We were taken to a massive barn where hundreds of wine barrels were stacked from floor to ceiling.
The town only had one main street and Hardy's winery was the largest enterprise in town.
These including Frank – later to be dubbed Sir Frank Hardy for his services to yachting.
Getting Burgess to the winery wasn't difficult.
We were met by numerous members of the Hardy family.

Here is how the paragraph originally appeared:

> Getting Burgess to the winery wasn't difficult. The town only had one main street and Hardy's winery was the largest enterprise in town. We were met by numerous members of the Hardy family. These including Frank – later to be dubbed Sir Frank Hardy for his services to yachting. (What would Burgess have made of that?). Also in the party was an elderly member of the family whom everyone called 'Uncle Tom'. We were taken to a massive barn where hundreds of wine barrels were stacked from floor to ceiling. Inside the barn, it was cool. A sweet, rotting smell came from the barrels. Through the gloom, I could see that at the rear of the barn trestle tables had been set with food and wine. 'This looks promising,' said Burgess eyeing the victuals and rubbing his hands.

Most people, given a little time, can come up with a reasonably accurate reconstruction of the original text. Each sentence, in fact, contains words and phrases that link it explicitly to at least one of the sentences that has preceded it.

Here is an inventory of those words and phrases:

1		winery		
2		Hardy's winery		
3		Hardy	numerous members	
4		Sir Frank Hardy	services to yachting	
5			that	
6	Also	the party	Uncle Tom	
7		massive barn	wine barrels	
8		the barn		
9			barrels	
10		the barn		food and wine
11			this	victuals

The technical name for these discourse elements is **cohesion**. We looked briefly at several types of cohesion, including reference, lexical cohesion, and **substitution** and ellipsis in the previous chapter. It is now time to look more systematically and in greater detail at these and the other features that make up cohesion.

Cohesive devices (also known as **text-forming devices**) are used to signal relationships of various kinds between individuals, entities and states-of-affairs within spoken and written discourse. In addition to substitution and **ellipsis**, English has the following categories

TABLE 6.1 DIFFERENT CATEGORIES OF COHESION

Cohesive category	Subcategory	Examples
Reference	Personal	My grandfather died last year. **He** was eighty-four.
	Demonstrative	George W. Bush wanted to be seen as tough and decisive. **This** only happened among his conservative constituents. A: Would you like this seat?
	Comparative	B: No thanks, I'd prefer **the other seats**.
Substitution	Nominal	Could you pass me another pencil? This **one** is broken.
	Verbal	A: I saw the new Scorsese video last week. B: So **did I**.
	Clausal	A: Are you going to the game on Saturday? B: I think **so**.
Ellipsis	Nominal	A: I want the white wine. B: I prefer the red.
	Verbal	A: Have you ever skied? B: Yes, I have.
	Clausal	A: Mike and Sandy are going to Bangkok for Christmas. B: Yeah? They didn't tell me.
Conjunction	Adversative	There's a typhoon on the way. **However**, they don't expect a direct hit.
	Additive	There's coffee in the pot. **And** there's tea if you prefer.
	Temporal	Brick tea is a blend that has been compressed into a cake. **First**, it is ground to a dust. **Then** it is usually cooked in milk.
	Causal	A: Why did you turn the TV off? B: **Because** I can't stand all those reality shows.
Lexical	Repetition	A: What sort of **novel** are you looking for? B: I'm looking for a **novel** that won't put me to sleep.
	Synonym	You could try reversing the car up the **slope**. The **incline** isn't all that great.
	Antonym	You say stop. I say go.
	Hyponym	A: Would you like some **papaya** or **mango**? B: Piece of each please. I love **tropical fruit**.
	Collocation	All that **plants** need for a healthy life are **sunlight**, **fertilizer** or other **nutrients**, and **water**.

of cohesion: **reference** (in the above text, *they* and *it* exemplify this category); **conjunctions** (also called **logical connectives**), which signal various kinds of logical relationships such as causality, temporality and concession (examples of conjunction in the above text include *however* and *but*), substitution, where a noun, verb or clause is replaced with a 'stand in' word such as do/does, one/ones, 'so', ellipsis, where an obligatory element is deleted because it is 'understood' from a previous sentence or utterance, and **lexical cohesion**, where the relationship is between semantically related items (exemplified here by *sunlight, plants, fertilizer, nutrients* and *water*.) These devices enable the writer (and speaker) to signal textual relationships in a cost-effective way.

When linguists first began exploring the question of what it is that differentiates random sentences from connected discourse, they pointed to these cohesive 'text forming devices' as the glue that holds a text together. Other linguists, however, argued that this is not the whole picture. It is possible to create texts that have no explicit links, but which, nonetheless, appear to be coherent. It is also possible to construct texts containing such linkages which do not hang together, as in the following 'text':

> When Anthony Burgess married for the second time, it was to a woman from Malta. Marriage as an institution reinforces traditional values. We have several institutions on our street. The street was recently closed in order for the cable television company to carry out much needed repairs. I don't have cable tv, but I'm thinking of getting it.

The fact is that while these linguistic resources provide helpful pointers to connectivity, they do not create or constitute the connectivity. So, where is the source of the coherence? If it does not reside in the language itself, it must reside in the individuals who process the language – you the reader and listener. In other words, while cohesion resides in the language, coherence resides in the person processing the text.

There is a school of linguistics that is devoted to **text structure** analysis. This approach looks at rhetorical patterns such as problem–solution and cause–effect patterns in written texts. (For an excellent introduction to text structure analysis, see Hoey 1983, 1991.)

Register

Register analysis explores the relationship between a text and the situational context that gave rise to the text in the first place. First developed by Halliday (1978, 1985), **register** looks at three aspects of language. These are 'field', 'tenor' and 'mode'. Field refers to the experiential content of the text. In other words, it's what the speakers or writers are 'on about'.

> Field refers to what is going on, where what is going on is interpreted institutionally, in terms of some culturally recognized activity (what people are doing with their lives, as it were). Examples of fields are activities such as tennis, opera, linguistics, cooking, building construction, farming, politics, education and so on. When people ask you what you do when first getting to know you, you tend to answer in terms of field (e.g. *Well, I'm a linguist. I play tennis. I'm interested in music* and so on.) (Martin, 2001: 152–3)

Tenor refers to the personal relationships between the individuals involved in an activity. It has to do with power. Such power relationships will be linguistically marked. (You wouldn't ask your boss or your professor to pass you a pencil in the same way as you would ask a child or a close relative).

Mode refers to the channel of communication. Is the text spoken or written? Is it a face-to-face conversation or a telephone conversation? Eggins (1994) provides a useful mode continuum which locates different channels according to the extent to which they allow for **feedback**.

In terms of meaning, field has to do with how the text hangs

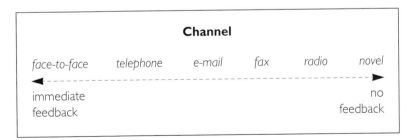

FIGURE 6.1 THE MODE CONTINUUM
Source: Eggins, 1994: 54

together experientially and logically, tenor has to do with how the text hangs together interpersonally, and mode has to do with how the text hangs together textually (Feez 1998: 72). These three register variables are summarized below.

Halliday (1973), the most significant figure in the field of systemic-functional linguistics, noted the parallel between these three aspects of register, and three dimensions of language choice. Martin (2001: 153–4) described the relationships in this way:

> As work on formalizing clause systems progressed, it became clear that [clause] systems tended to cluster into three main groups. One bundle of choices was referred to in his early work by Halliday as *transitivity*; this bundle of choices was concerned with the structure of clauses in terms of

TABLE 6.2 REGISTER VARIABLES

Register		
Field (what)	*Tenor (who)*	*Mode (how)*
■ topics ■ social activities (includes settings, situations language events) ■ skills and strategies to do with the representation of reality e.g. recognizing gist, identifying topic shifts	■ the relative status of those involved in text ■ the type a frequency of contact between people involved in text ■ interpersonal skills and strategies to do with roles and relationships e.g. politeness, increasing or reducing interpersonal distance or emotional intensity, gambits	■ distance in time between the language of the text and the social activity e.g. concrete language accompanying action, abstract language for reflection ■ distance in space and time between the interactants ■ skills and strategies for using the channel of communication e.g. face-to-face, telephone, letter

Source: Adapted from Feez, 1998: 73

the way they map reality – the difference between verbs of doing and happening, reacting, thinking and perceiving, saying, and describing and identifying, along with the *voice* (active/passive) potential associated with each. Another bundle he referred to as *mood*, and was concerned with distinguishing statements from questions, from commands, from exclamations as well as expressing the possibility, probability or certainty of some meaning. The third bundle, called **theme**, has to do with the way speakers order constituents in a clause, putting first a theme which connects with the overall development of a paragraph or text and last something that contains information which is new to the listener. Later, Halliday was to use more semantically oriented terms to generalize these three broad areas of meaning potential: **ideational** for meaning about the world, **interpersonal** for intersubjective meaning between speakers, and '**textual**' for meanings relating pieces of text to each other and to their context.

In any communicative situation, if any one of these variables changes, the resulting discourse will change. Consider the following communicative event:

Event
As they sit watching television, a sixteen-year-old girl is discussing with her mother what to buy her father for his birthday.
     Here the field is 'buying a gift'. The tenor is mother and daughter. The mode is face-to-face.

Let's now change each of the variables in turn. Imagine how the nature of the conversation will change as a result of changing one of the register variables.

Variation 1
A sixteen-year-old girl calls her mother to discuss what to buy her father for his birthday.
     Here the field and tenor remain the same, but the mode has changed from face-to-face to telephone conversation.

Variation 2
A sixteen-year-old girl is chatting with her boyfriend about what to buy his father for his birthday.
     The field remains the same, the mode returns to face-to-face, but the tenor changes from daughter/mother to girlfriend/boyfriend.

We could go on. Sixteen-year-old breaks news of pregnancy to mother over a cup of tea; sixteen-year-old breaks news of pregnancy to mother over the phone; sixteen-year-old breaks news of pregnancy to boyfriend but I'm sure you get the point. Changing any one of these register variables will change the discourse that results from the interaction.

Genre

Earlier in the book, I mentioned a group of linguists who are trying to develop a 'grammar' of discourse; that is, an approach to discourse mirroring that of sentence-level grammarians. The aim of the grammarian is to describe the rules that specify what is and is not a well-formed sentence (that is, they want to identify rules for grammaticality). We saw, in relation to spoken language, that the attempt by these 'super-sentence' linguists to specify the obligatory and optional elements for determining the 'well-formedness' of discourse has not been particularly successful. The position I have taken in this book is that the lack of success is due to the fact that discourse does not constitute a fourth, higher-order linguistic 'layer' over and above sounds, words and sentences; that there are, essentially, only three systems for creating messages.

There is one approach to **text analysis** that appears to offer some promise in identifying patterns in texts that go beyond the sentence. This is known as genre analysis. The practice of genre analysis is an ancient one, going back to the Greeks who studied the recurring patterns in literary texts, and who were able to show how epics differed systematically from lyrics and so on. The approach can be applied to the analysis of both spoken and written language, but for the sake of convenience, I have chosen to introduce it in relation to written language.

In recent years, the term has been used to refer to the analysis of every day, non-literary texts. The starting point for genre analysts is the overall purpose or function for the creation of a text. The purpose will determine the internal generic structure of the text as well as its key grammatical features. Questions such as 'What is the purpose of this instruction booklet, narrative account, or argumentative text?' and 'How is the purpose reflected in the overall structure of the text and the grammatical features that appear within it?' form the point of departure for the analysis.

Common texts include recounts, narratives, procedures, reports, explanations, expositions and discussions. The particular function of each of these texts is as follows:

Recount to tell what happened, to document a sequence of events and evaluate their significance in some way
Narrative to create a sequence of events culminating in a problem or crisis and a solution or resolution
Procedure to instruct the reader on how to make or do something
Report to present information on an event or circumstance
Explanation to explain how and why something occurs
Exposition to present an argument in favour of a proposition
Discussion to looks at an issue from a number of different perspectives before reaching a conclusion.

Cornbleet and Carter (2001) provide an amusing account of the extent to which we absorb the characteristics of different kinds of genres in our daily lives. A group of students was asked to rewrite the nursery rhyme *Incey Wincey Spider* as a police statement. Here is the rhyme and the statement.

Rhyme

Incey Wincey spider
Climbed up the water spout.
Down came the rain
And washed poor spider out.
Out came the sun
And dried up all the rain.
Incey Wincey spider
Climbed up the spout again.

Statement

The here-accused spider was witnessed climbing the aforementioned drainage system. At 3 p.m. it began to downpour which therefore led to the subsequent expulsion from the said drainpipe. At 3.15 p.m. precisely the rain ceased giving the accused the opportunity to re-ascend.

Cornbleet and Carter (2001: 54–5) comment:

Never mind how faithfully accurate this is or is not. The point is that it now seems right. What's going on here? The original, a children's verse, has end-line rhyme, is mostly monosyllabic and sounds childlike with the name, Incey Wincey, which not only rhymes but has the diminutive -y ending (like *doggy*, *bunny*). The sentences are single clauses or involve simple co-ordination ('*and*'). It is simple entertainment, written to accompany basic actions such as finger climbing and tickling. The police report is written to convey facts with absolute clarity. It is detailed and precise and logically sequenced. The vocabulary, grammar, register all fit the text.

vocabulary – legal lexis ('accused', 'witnessed', 'aforementioned', 'subsequent', 'said');
grammar – piling up of adjectives before nouns, often formed from verb participles: ('here-accused spider', 'aforementioned drainage system'); impersonal structures: passive ('was witnessed'), impersonal causal agent ('the rain ceased giving . . .');
the writer has invented 'downpour' as a verb, which only exists in noun form in standard English, presumably because it seemed to fit the formal tone;
register – vocabulary and grammar combine with factual precision, front positioning in the sentence of time elements ('At 3 p.m.', 'At 3.15 p.m. precisely') and formality ('ceased', 're-ascend') to produce the expected register of a stereotypical police statement.

Here is another genre. This one is a narrative, a genre that is familiar to all of us. The extract describes the death of a celebrated war correspondent and cameraman Neil Davis who covered regional wars and conflicts in the Asia-Pacific region, most notably the Vietnam War and the civil war in Cambodia. Davis was based in Bangkok. From here he travelled around the region covering topical stories for an international news service based in Tokyo. Unfortunately for Davis, he happened to be in Bangkok one September morning when a series of events occurred that resulted in his death:

Early on the morning of Monday 9 September, Davis's soundman Bill Latch was taking his daughter to school when he noticed tanks on the streets. Thailand was about to experience another coup d'etat – something that veteran correspondents regarded as part of the cycle of life in Bangkok, like the wet and dry seasons. Latch called the head of their news service, Bruce MacDonnell, in Tokyo. MacDonnell, an experienced newsman, was not overly excited by the news, but he appreciated the early tip-off on what could develop into a major story. He called Davis and, with some apologies, put paid to his plans for a relaxing day. In Bangkok, Davis and Latch filmed military activity in the street and made arrangements to have the early footage shipped out to Hong Kong to be sent to New York by satellite. Suddenly they came under direct tank and machine gun fire, and took cover behind a telephone junction box. The ground shuddered beneath them and shrapnel sprayed indiscriminately. The noise was stunning. A withering burst of fire was directed into the wall directly behind them, spewing out thousands of steel fragments. There was just time for Davis's brain to register that he had been mortally struck. He turned the camera on himself and filmed his own death. Through the crash of explosions could be heard his last words. They were not exclamation and expletive, but monumental irritation as he registered the futility of it all 'Oh . . . shit!'

This passage, adapted from Tim Bowden's dramatic account of the incident in the biography of Davis entitled *One Crowded Hour*, displays the essential stages of a narrative: orientation, event, event, event, crisis, resolution, coda. Grammatically, it consists of a series of events reported in the simple past tense.

A cursory glance through the daily newspaper or a favourite magazine will reveal numerous genres from letters to the editor to obituaries, from classified advertisements to editorials. Each of these will have their own characteristic 'shape' and linguistic features, as the two following examples demonstrate.

Example 1

> **200 grammes spaghetti**
> **45 grammes unsalted butter**
> **1 medium clove of garlic, sliced thinly**
> **Grated parmesan cheese**
> **Chopped parsley [optional]**
> **Roughly flaked sea salt and freshly ground**
> **Black pepper**

> Heat a large pot of water, add lots of salt and boil the pasta until it is *al dente*.
> Melt the butter in a small saucepan. Add the garlic and cook until softened and just starting to turn golden, then remove and discard the garlic.
> Continue to cook the butter until it turns brown and has a nutty aroma. Remove from heat until the pasta is ready.

> As soon as the pasta is *al dente*, put the butter
> back over a flame to heat until sizzling. Drain the
> pasta and place in a large serving bowl. Drizzle with
> the hot butter, add a big handful of grated
> parmesan, sprinkle with salt, pepper and parsley (if
> using) then toss quickly to combine. Divide between
> two bowls and serve with more parmesan.

This is clearly a recipe. Even someone with severely impaired sight would recognize the genre from the font and physical layout of the text. It also has an instantly recognizable overall generic 'shape', consisting of a list of ingredients followed by a set of instructions in the imperative ('Heat a large pot!' 'Add lots of salt!'). It also has a number of other linguistic features that identify it as a 'recipe'. These include the practice of leaving out redundant function words such as **articles** and prepositions. Interestingly the author of this recipe is inconsistent in this regard. Note that the first two ingredients (200 grammes spaghetti, 45 grammes unsalted butter) omit the preposition 'of', while the next one includes it. Despite the inconsistency, the recipe is not 'ungrammatical' because, as I have asserted repeatedly in this book, textual 'grammaticality' is defined in the head, not on the page.

Lexically, the text contains numerous items drawn from the world of cookery: '*al dente*', 'sizzling', 'drain' as well as names of food items – salt, pepper, parsley, parmesan, garlic. And, as already indicated, most sentences in the body of the text are couched in the imperative, which it typical of a procedural text.

The next example is a very different type of text.

Example 2

> S.T. Wu was one of Hong Kong's best-kept secrets. A private man who shunned publicity, he co-founded Maxim's – a company name that is as well-known as he was low-profile throughout his life. Such was his aversion to the limelight that only upon his passing, on 17 August, aged 92, did many realize he had lived so long.
>
> An unobtrusive man, Wu had many admirers as was evidenced by visitors to his funeral at the Hong Kong Funeral Home in North Point on Wednesday and Thursday. Paying their respects were tycoons such as Li Ka-shing, and politicians including Martin Lee Chu-ming and David Li Kwok-po. Those who expressed their sadness most openly, however,

were some of his 12,000 employees. Many sobbed as they approached his coffin for a final farewell. To me he still looked like a tough business-man prepared for another challenge.

This is part of an article on a recently deceased prominent member of the business community. It is an 'appreciation piece' rather than an obituary. (Obituaries have their own generic structure.) Linguistically, there are many interesting features to the text. One that is particularly worth noting is the amount of information that is packaged into each sentence. Consider, for example, the amount of information presented to the reader in the second sentence of the piece:

A private man who shunned publicity, he co-founded Maxim's – a company name that is as well-known as he was low-profile throughout his life

Here, we learn that Wu was a private man. That he shunned publicity. That he founded Maxim's. That Maxim's is a well-known company name. That Wu's name was not well-known. That this contrasts with the name of the company he founded. That he adopted a low profile throughout his life.

Another recognizable genre, and one that permeates our lives, is the advertisement. Advertisements seem to irritate, annoy or bore us as often as they inform. Many people find television advertisements so distracting and irritating that they record their favourite shows and watch them later without having to sit through the advertisements. Although ads typically consist of some kind of visual images (photos, graphics, diagrams, as well as language), it is language that I want to focus on here.

A basic function of advertisements, in fact, probably THE basic function, is to sell something. In order to do this, they need to make their product desirable to the potential purchaser. As we all know, sex sells, and it is therefore hardly surprising that sex is pressed in to service for selling everything from cars to aftershave lotion.

To illustrate the point, here are three advertisements taken from several different print sources. Each is an advertisement for a car, and each plays the sex angle to attract the reader. Now, there is no logical reason why sex should be selected to provide the advertising angle to sell cars. The associations are entirely metaphorical, based on the fact that cars, like people, have bodies.

SAFE SEX

Pleasure seekers take note. The Volvo C70 was recently voted one of the world's sexiest cars. And it comes with WHIPS as standard. (Calm down, it stands for Whiplash Protection System.)

YOU TOO COULD HAVE A BODY JUST LIKE THIS ... THE CURVY BODY WE'LL BE USING TO DRAW ATTENTION TO THE NEW ALMERA WON'T BE SITTING PROVOCATIVELY ON THE CAR. IT IS THE CAR.

VOLUPTUOUS
IS BACK
Think 'ideal weight distribution',
'Curves in all the right places'
And the vital statistics?
3.0 litre V6
240 bhp
For more information call 0800 708060
www.jaguar.com

Glamour is another essential ingredient in making a product desirable. Consider the names of the following products. What do you think they are selling?

Allure, Envy, Romance, Desire, Animale, Joy, Indecent, Tabu, Egoiste, Oui, Desirade, Hot.

If you guessed perfume, then you guessed right. Each of these is the name of a perfume.

Guy Cook, in his book on the language of advertising, suggests that there are fourteen features that distinguish advertisements as a separate genre in their own right. These include the use of visuals and music as well as language, the use of short, powerful imagistic and metaphorical language, and the use of language designed to provoke social, moral and aesthetic judgements (Cook, 2001: 219–20).

Summary and conclusion

In this chapter, I have looked at some of the characteristics of written language and drawn points of contrast between written language and spoken language. I have tried to show that written language is not 'talk written down', but that it has its own unique characteristics, grammatical features and genres. Humankind has evolved many unnatural practices. Writing is one of them. As I noted earlier in the chapter, all humans have a need to speak: not all humans have the need (or the wherewithal) to write. Without writing systems, however, most cultures would be impoverished, both materially and spiritually.

Here are the main points covered in the chapter:

■ Written and spoken language exhibit different characteristics, although all texts can be placed on a continuum from 'more like spoken' to 'more like written'
■ Writing evolved to preserve and transmit messages across time and space
■ Cohesion is a system of linguistic devices for marking relationships between entities and events in a text
■ Coherence exists in the head, not on the page; it is the ability to recognize that a spoken or written text 'hangs together'
■ Register analysis is concerned with the key textual variables: field (the subject matter of the text), tenor (the relationship between those involved in the communication) and mode (the means of communication: spoken/written; face-to-face/remote)
■ Genre analysis is concerned with the overall 'shape' of a text, and the grammatical and lexical features that characterize the text.

Questions and tasks

1 Reorder these sentences (Carver, 1993: 14) to make a coherent paragraph. Then identify the cohesive devices that enabled you to do this.

He remembered when Harriet had come home with the clock, how she had crossed the hall to show it to Arlene cradling the brass case in her arms and talking to it through the tissue paper as if it were an infant.
The air was already heavy and it was vaguely sweet.
Bill took a deep breath and entered the Stones' apartment.
The sunburst clock over the television said half past eight.

2 Identify and name the cohesive devices in the following extracts.

Peace in the Middle-East is a cherished dream. However, few people expect to see this in their lifetime. Conflict appears to be a sad reality in the region.

Two special Miro exhibitions were held in Barcelona recently. The first exhibition is of his early work. The other exhibition is of his later work. Most viewers prefer the later one, as do most of the critics. However, a minority of Miro critics prefer the former. This is causing something of a controversy in art circles.

3 Make a list of the ways in which the following interactions would differ linguistically.

A student in his final year at school is discussing his poor grades in a formal meeting with his teacher.
A husband and wife are discussing the poor grades of their son in an email exchange.
A student is discussing his poor grades with his girlfriend on the telephone.

4 Analyse several advertisements for a particular product (for example, cars, watches, holidays abroad). What similarities/differences are there between the products? How many of the features identified by Cook can you find in the advertisements?

Further reading

Burns, A. and C. Coffin (eds) (2001) *Analysing English in a Global Context* (London: Routledge).
This edited collection contains several papers that are relevant to this chapter, including:
Coffin, C., 'Theoretical approaches to written language'
Martin, J., 'Language, register and genre'
Halliday, M.A.K., 'Literacy and linguistics: relationships between spoken and written language'

Carter, R., A. Goddard, D. Reah, K. Sanger and M. Bowering (2001) *Working with Texts: A Core Introduction to Language Analysis*, 2nd edn (London: Routledge), Unit four: text and context: written discourse.
Unit four presents a hands-on introduction to written language with lots of authentic textual extracts and practical exercises.

7 A first language

Introduction and overview

The birth of a child is quite miraculous, particularly when it happens to be your own. The acquisition of language by that child is an additional miracle, and one which psychologists and linguists have struggled for many years to explain. Think about it. By the age of about four, most children have their **first language** pretty-well acquired. They are able to use sophisticated grammatical forms that grown adults with Ph.D.s are hard-pressed to explain. They have also acquired a rich and complex vocabulary at a remarkable rate. By the age of four, a first language speaker of English has acquired a vocabulary of over ten thousand words. This represents the acquisition of more than ten words a day; an astonishing feat of learning and memory. As older learners, acquiring a second language, we often struggle to acquire that many words in years. We have all achieved this miracle of acquiring a language, but none of us remembers how we managed to do it.

Some extraordinary children even manage more than one language. Children who acquire more than one language, perhaps because their parents speak different language to them are known as **bilingual**. The process of developing a second language after the first has been acquired is known as **second language acquisition**. I will not be dealing with second language acquisition in this chapter, although I have dealt with it extensively elsewhere (see, for example, Nunan, 1999).

In this chapter, we will look at:

- The behaviourist approach to language acquisition
- A critique of the behaviourist approach
- The mentalist approach
- The functional approach.

The behaviourist approach to language acquisition

It seems that the necessary and sufficient condition for the acquisition of a first language is exposure to that language at an early age. Beveridge (cited in Crystal 1997a) tells of a rather macabre experiment reportedly conducted by a sixteenth century Mogul Emperor of India, Akbar the Great. Akbar sought support for the hypothesis that children who were deprived of human contact would never learn to speak.

> As some who heard this (Akbar's hypothesis) appeared to deny it, he, in order to convince them, had a *serai* [mansion] built in a place which civilized sound did not reach. The newly born were put into that place of experience, and honest and active guards were put over them. For a time, tongue-tied wet nurses were admitted there. As they had closed the door of speech, the place was called the Gang Mahal (the dumb-house). On the 9th August 1582 he went out to hunt. That night he stayed in Faizabad, and the next day he went with a few special attendants to the house of experiment. No cry came from that house of silence, nor was any speech heard there. In spite of their four years, they had no part of the talisman of speech, and nothing came out except the noise of the dumb.

Other, more recent anecdotes support the notion that exposure to language is necessary for acquisition. These include children raised by animals, who, when returned to human contact after a certain age, never acquire the ability to speak.

Although child language acquisition has been of interest for thousands of years, the first comprehensive theory of language acquisition wasn't published until 1957. In that year, the psychologist Skinner published a book called *Verbal Behavior*. In it, he argued that language was acquired in the same way as all other forms of human behaviour; that is, through a process of imitation and habit formation. Basically, children learned how to speak by imitating their parents or whoever happened to be significant in their lives in their first few years of life.

A critique of the behaviourist approach

Unfortunately for Skinner, not long after his book was published, one of the most brilliant linguistic minds of the century appeared on the academic scene. The person was Noam Chomsky, who was to shake the linguistic universe to its very foundations. One of his first acts was to write a critique of *Verbal Behavior* that comprehensively demolished behaviourism as a credible theory of language acquisition.

These days, Chomsky's celebrity is not confined to linguistic and psychological circles. He is also well known among the general public.

Although he is a brilliant thinker who has transformed the field of linguistics with his radical theories on language and language acquisition, his present public celebrity stems more from his pronouncements as a left-wing critic of the political right in the United States and elsewhere.

The first problem for Skinner's behaviourist theory that languages are acquired through imitation and habit formation is the fact that the vast majority of utterances produced by an individual are one-off events that that are spoken once and only once and then disappear into the ether forever. While young children use formulae (that is, everyday, often-repeated, chunks of language such as *I want spoon* and *Where's dolly?*) they also generate unique utterances from an early age. This creative construction process is simply beyond the reach of behaviourist theory.

Another challenging problem for the behaviourist argument is the fact that children produce language that they could not possibly have learned through imitation because these utterances would never have been produced by an adult. A commonly cited example is that of the 'overregularized' past tense with verbs that do not follow the *-ed* rule (words like *go, run* and *see*). An example of this violation would be when children say *I goed to Billy's party yesterday* rather than *I went to Billy's party yesterday*. This is an act of creativity rather than imitation because to my knowledge no adult says *goed, runned* or *seed*.

What is interesting about this example is that initially children do use the correct past tense form of the verb. Then, at a certain point, they start using the incorrect form. In other words, when they start to talk, they use *went, saw* and *ran*, but then switch to *goed, seed* and *runned*. It is almost as if, at this point, they say to themselves *Oh, Ok, I get it, when I want to talk about something that happened in the past, I have to stick -ed onto the end of the verb.*

When I was collecting samples of language from my first daughter Jenny, I noticed something interesting. Like all kids, she went through the overgeneralizing process. Eventually she 'got it' however, and started using the adult forms of irregular verbs; that is, she started off using *went, saw* and *ran*, switched to *goed, seed* and *runned*, and then switched back again. However, at that time her best friend was about six months behind Jenny in terms of her linguistic development. When she was talking to her friend, Jenny would use the over-regularized forms, and then, when talking to adults, revert to the correct forms, often within the same conversation. In other words, she engaged in the sophisticated linguistic process of code switching.

Another compelling argument against the behaviourist position is the sheer quantity of utterances that people produce, and the simple impossibility of acquiring these through a process of stimulus-response, or memorization. During the few short years of language acquisition, language growth is nothing short of explosive.

The mentalist approach

As we saw in Chapter 1, Chomsky's solution to the language acquisition conundrum was to assert that children acquire language because they have no choice. Language is hard-wired into the human brain. To acquire it, all you need is to be born human. In the words of Chomsky's student Steven Pinker, language is an instinct. Spiders spin webs, birds fly south, humans speak. According to Chomskyites, if children were not born with a language instinct, they could never acquire it from their parents or significant others. For one thing, the language they hear around them is fragmentary, imprecise, and sometimes even ungrammatical.

Although many aspects of Chomsky's position are compelling, there are some holes in his argument. For a start, input to babies is much less 'junky' than might be imagined. When it comes to speaking to their babies, Mums and Dads clean up their act considerably. They speak more slowly, enunciate more clearly, and generally speak in complete, grammatically correct sentences.

Secondly, as they begin to develop, children get huge amounts of practice. Two-year-olds have been recorded uttering over 20,000 words over a twelve hour period, and a three-year-old has been recorded producing almost twice that number. (For a critique of the Chomsky theory, see Cziko 1995, 2000.)

There is also evidence to show that parents DO direct their infants' attention to aspects of language. Here is an example of a mother–child language focused interaction. Admittedly, the mother is not giving a grammar lesson, but she is drawing an aspect of language to the attention of the child – in this case the fact that written marks mean something, and that the marks are systematically related to the oral language that the child is acquiring. The interaction occurred at the end of a meal. The child was in her high chair playing with her plastic mug, which she turned over to reveal some letters printed on masking tape on the bottom.

Mother: *What's that say?* (Pointing to the name 'Becca' written on the bottom of a child's plastic mug.)
Rebecca: *P-A Me!*
Mother: *P-A Me! Ha! That says B-E-C-C-A. Becca. You're a funny duck!*

A little later, during the same interaction, a curious piece of miscommunication occurs. The child nominates a new topic, and the following interaction ensures.

Rebecca: *Me a a me a me a sec a Lawrie a dancing.*
Mother: *You and me and Lawrie dancing?*
Rebecca: *Me, a you a, a, Jenny, Lawrie a dancing.*
Mother: *Dancing?*
Rebecca: *Yeah.* (Begins shouting) *No. No. (No.) No. Ahh.*
Mother: *Jumping? (No.) Dancing?*
Rebecca: *Ah, ah guck.*
Mother: *You're stuck. Well don't have a fit because I didn't understand you. All right, you try and say it again, Darling. You, and me and Jennie and Lawrie.*
Rebecca: *Dancing. Dancing.*
Mother: (Tries to pronounce the word in different ways, but each time Rebecca cries out '*No*'). *Where do we do it? (No.) Oh, try again. Say it again. Say it again. (Ahhh!) Don't have a fit – you'll get stuck. You mustn't slide down like that. I'm sorry I didn't understand your word.*

In this interaction, Rebecca has something to say, but does not have the linguistic means to do so. This drives her into a major temper tantrum. Unable to get her meaning across, she is confronted with the limits to her **communicative competence**. This is at once a source of huge frustration, but also a powerful stimulus to acquisition.

There is another problem for the proponents of the hard-wired hypothesis. The problem presents itself in the form of children who are born without any linguistic wiring at all. If language is a defining characteristic of humanity, then these individuals are hard-pressed to claim membership of the human race.

The story of one such child, Whitney, was told recently by his mother Cheri Florance. Whitney was born without the power of speech, and, in fact, did not speak for the first six years of his life. Doctors diagnosed him as autistic and urged his mother to commit him to an institution. Luckily for Whitney, Cheri was not only his mother, she was also a celebrated brain specialist and expert in communication disorders. Rather than giving up on Whitney, she was determined to use her expertise to give him the power of speech.

The story of how she did this is powerfully and touchingly told in *A Boy Beyond Reach* (2003) written by Florance. Whitney eluded her best efforts until one day when he was five she heard him laugh at a Disney movie. She knew then that there was nothing wrong with his vocal chords. This and other behaviour convinced her that he processed the world visually, not verbally. He lacked the linguistic wiring to turn his perceptions into speech.

Florance set about wiring Whitney linguistically by working from the visual to the verbal. In other words, she taught him language through the eyes rather than the ears. For example, if she wanted him to go to bed, she would show him a picture of one of them by a bed. The next step was to help him to associate the words 'Go to bed, Whitney' with the visual representation. In this way, he was gradually able to differentiate human speech from all of the other noise that surrounded him, and then to make meaningful associations between the sounds and phenomena they represented. Gradually, Whitney learned to speak, to read and to write. His first words were uttered when he was seven. By the time that he was sixteen, he was a happy, healthy and normal high-school student. His IQ, which was originally assessed as 49, was reassessed as 150. This in itself is interesting. Conventional psychology has it that we are allocated a certain intelligence level or quotient at birth and that level is impervious to change through instruction or any other means. Traditional psychometry argues that IQ levels are inviolate, and we have to live and work with what we have been given at birth. Whitney would appear to call this assumption in to question.

Chomsky is an 'armchair' linguist. His paradigm-shifting theories and conjectures were spun out of introspection, creative thinking, and brilliant reasoning. He sees no need to venture forth and study children as they go through the process of actually acquiring language. Other linguists and child language specialists did see the need to conduct closely observed and meticulously documented studies of children in the process of acquiring language. Roger Brown, a Harvard psychologist, was one of these. His best known work, *A First Language* (1973), which quickly established itself as a classic in the field, is a longitudinal case study of the linguistic development of three children: Adam, Eve and Sarah. Although the children were unrelated and, indeed, unacquainted, Brown found that there was remarkable consistency in the development of each child's language. In particular, he found that the children acquired grammar items in the same order, although the rate at which their language developed varied radically. (Brown studied the acquisition of some of the bound morphemes that we looked at in Chapter 4 including third person -s, the -ing form of verbs, plural -s and so on.) Surprisingly, and this was yet another nail in the coffin of behaviourism which offered some support for Chomsky's theory, the frequency with which the children encountered morphemes was not a good predictor of their acquisition. Brown concluded from his investigations that:

> For the 14 English grammatical morphemes, there is no evidence whatever that frequency of any sort is a significant determinant of order of acquisition. [Although] some marginal role for frequency is really guaranteed; children will not learn constructions they never hear. (Brown, 1973: 409)

The functionalist approach to language acquisition

The work of the functional linguist Halliday has informed all aspects of this book. Although he is one of the most influential and important linguists of his generation, he is less well known in North America than he should be. For the purposes of this book, I would put him ahead of Chomsky because his work speaks directly to the concerns of language as a tool for communication – the major theme of the book.

Halliday made an important contribution to research into child language development with a case study of his son Nigel. He showed that at the beginning of the acquisition process the child develops a 'proto-language' in which there is a one-to-one correspondence between an utterance and its corresponding meaning. There is no grammar, nor any words, as we know them, in the child's proto-language. There are only sounds and meanings, and these are yoked together in a one-to-one relationship. When Nigel said *nananana*, it meant *Give me that thing now*. When he said *do*, it meant *Look, a dog*. At this point, child language is functioning rather like the road signs that we looked at in Chapter 1. There, if you recall, we saw that the difference between a system of road signs and human language is that the signs are not generative, like language, but are bound into a one-to-one relationship between the image and the things that they are meant to represent. Sign systems and animal communication systems have sounds and meanings but no grammar. Child proto-languages are the same.

In the early stages of language acquisition, children also wildly over-generalize. *Daddy* is not just the nice man who sleeps with Mommy. He is also Uncle Theo, the milkman, and the lady down the street who wears pants and cuts her hair extremely short. Little Ricky does not refer to the milkman as *Da-da* in order to embarrass him, but because in proto-language *da-da* represents 'large male-looking adult'.

In Chapter 5, we discussed speech acts, and looked at examples of the hundreds of things that an adult can do with language. However, based on his research, Halliday argued that children at the initial stages of learning can do just six things. They can satisfy material needs This is the 'I want' function. They can get others to do things. (The 'do as I tell you' function.) They can interact socially (the 'me and you' function). They can express their own uniqueness (the 'here I come' function). They can explore the world (the 'tell me why' function). Finally, they can use language imaginatively (the 'let's pretend' function). A little later, a seventh function, the informative or 'I've got something to tell you' function is added.

Halliday also noticed that a child's first utterances are not imitations of adult language. At this initial stage, their sounds are nothing like adult language at all. In pointing this out, Halliday is, implicitly at least, disclaiming any role for behaviourist learning in language development. He also explicitly rejected the hard-wired theory, arguing that

> Despite a commonly held belief to the contrary, the speech which the child hears around him is, in the typical instance, coherent, well-formed and contextually relevant … He has abundant evidence with which to construct the grammatical system of his language. (Halliday, 1973: 45)

Halliday describes the multiple stages that children grow through linguistically, as their language comes to approximate that of an adult. Most dramatic are the appearance of words, and then grammar. When words first appear, prior to the development of grammar, they serve multiple purposes. For example, 'Cat' can mean 'Hello cat', 'I want the cat', 'Look, there's a cat' and so on.

The two bits of conversation that follow, between a small boy Mark, and his mother, were documented by Gordon Wells, another child language specialist. Like Halliday, Wells takes a functionalist orientation. In the first extract, we see that despite the fact that Mark does not have much in the way of grammar and vocabulary, he is quite adept as a conversationalist. He knows how to take turns appropriately, and is able to nominate a topic ('birds' in the first conversation, and 'the disappearance of the man' in the second) and maintain the topics over several turns.

Mark: *Birds, Mummy.*
Mother: *Mm.*
Mark: *Jubs.* (birds)
Mother: *What are they doing?*
Mark: *Jubs bread.*
Mother: *Oh, look. They're eating berries aren't they?*
Mark: *Yeah.*
Mother: *That's their food. They have berries for dinner.*
Mark: *Oh.* (Wells, 1981:102)

This second conversation took place about six months after the 'birds' conversation. In it, we can see that Mark's conversation has developed. His contributions to the conversation are longer and grammatically more complex. He is also able to talk about something that is no longer physically present.

Mark: *Where man gone? Where man gone?*
Mother: *I don't know. I expect he's gone inside because it's snowing.*
Mark: *Where man gone?*
Mother: *In the house.*
Mark: *Uh?*
Mother: *Into his house.*
Mark: *No. No. Gone to shop Mummy.*
Mother: *Gone where?*
Mark: *Gone shop.*
Mother: *To the shop?*
Mark: *Yeah.*
Mother: *What's he going to buy?*
Mark: *Er – biscuits.*
Mother: *Biscuits mm.*
Mark: *Uh? Mm.*
Mother: *What else?*
Mark: *Er – meat.*
Mother: *Mm.*
Mark: *Meat. Er – sweeties. Buy a big bag.*
Mother: *Buy sweets?*
Mark: *Yeh. M – er – man – buy the man buy sweets.*
Mother: *Will he?*

Mark: *Yeah. Daddy buy sweets. Daddy buy sweets.*
Mother: *Why?*
Mark: *Oh er – shop. Mark do buy some sweets – sweeties. Mark buy some – um. Mark buy some – um. I did.* (Wells, 1981: 107)

In this conversation, it is not just Mark's language that is interesting, but also his Mother's. Here, she does a great deal of work in creating and maintaining a framework for the fantasy that Mark wishes to spin (that the man has not, in fact, gone inside, but has gone shopping). Wells calls this parental process 'leading from behind', which neatly captures the way in which primary caregivers scaffold the learning process for their children.

From discourse to grammar

Evidence from interactions between children and their parents such as the ones we looked at in the preceding section have convinced some linguists and psychologists that children do not learn how to form sentences and then subsequently use these to take part in conversations. Rather, they learn to 'do' conversations, and it is out of these social interactions with their parents and other significant people in their lives that they learn how to make grammatically correct utterances. The following story illustrates this process of an adult expanding on the child's one or two word utterances, and helping him to build a narrative.

[At eighteen months of age] Nigel was taken to the zoo. He had been stroking a goat when the goat tried to eat a plastic jam jar lid he had in his hand. The keeper took the lid away, explaining it was not good for the goat to eat. About four hours later, at home, Nigel says to his father, 'Try eat lid.' His father replies, 'What tried to eat the lid?' Nigel repeats, 'Try eat lid.' So his father repeats his question. This time Nigel responds 'Goat'. Then he puts the information together and says 'Goat try eat lid'. When he is encouraged to continue the story, he says, 'Man said no.' And having got his little narrative off the ground, he repeats, 'Goat try eat lid . . . man say no' several times. Later he brings up the story again, still in this form. This time his mother says, 'Why did the man say no?' and Nigel says, 'Goat shouldn't eat lid . . . [shaking head] good for it.' This is the final version, and it is repeated verbatim and ad nauseum for months afterwards. 'Goat try eat lid . . . man said no . . . goat shouldn't eat lid . . . [shaking head] good for it. (Halliday, 1978: 86)

Summary and conclusion

At the beginning of this chapter, I made the point that the acquisition of our first language is a mysterious, even miraculous business. Although the mystery remains, researchers have made some important advances in building an understanding of the processes involved. In the course of the chapter, I have tried to articulate some of the insights that have been generated by this research.

In the chapter, I reported on three very different approaches to the study of child language acquisition and development. The first of these is based on a behaviourist view of learning. The second looks at the work of cognitive scientists who believe that language is hard-wired into the human brain. For these researchers, language is what defines us as human beings. The third approach draws on the work of linguists who take a functional perspective, and who argue that language is a tool that is acquired by humans in order to fulfil particular needs. From the perspective of this group, 'language is what language does'. Ultimately, it may transpire that all three perspectives have something to offer as we try to build an understanding of language acquisition. At present, however, we do not have anything like a 'unified' theory of language acquisition.

The main points raised in the chapter are:

■ Acquiring a first language is probably the greatest of all human achievements; language may also be the defining characteristic of the species
■ There are several competing theories of language acquisition; these include (the now largely discredited) behaviourism, mentalism and functionalism
■ Behaviourists argue that language is acquired through a process of imitation and habit formation
■ Mentalists believe that language is part of our genetic makeup
■ Functionalists assert that language acquisition is stimulated by our drive to meet physical and emotional needs, including the need to affiliate with other members of the human race.

Questions and tasks

1 Summarize the arguments for and against the behaviourist and mentalist approaches to language acquisition.

2 What criticisms would you make of the functionalist approach?

3 The dramatic growth in a child's language between their second and third years is illustrated in the following box. The language samples here are taken from the same child at 27 and 37 months. Study the extracts and make a summary of the changes that have occurred over the ten months.

Samples of Rebecca's language

at 27 months	at 37 months
Mm. Wash it.	Think I need a bit help.
A bump.	Where?
Ah.	Know what one.
A bobble (bottle)	I don't want it outside.
A Lawrie a bobble as same	You hear that slurpy noise?
a me.	
P-A-me.	I am. I love ice block.
Got.	O . . . on a bench.
Num-num.	Yeah.
Yeah.	Baby crying.
Go sleep.	Why crying?
A mummy.	Wants Mummy.
Huh, bub, bub, bly.	Cause I want a drink.
A duff.	Not really.
Cream on a mozzie.	Cause I want a book.
Get me. Oh! Oh!	Cause I want a . . . I want a ice block.
Sore.	Why?
Bzzz! Yuk!	I can't rember.
Yeah. Poo, poo, a, a got uuk, yuk.	Mmm. Hope you can't do that.
Hate bees.	I don't know.
A ding, a Jenny, a mozzie a	A chicken's man coming?
sting a hard a	
Mummy cuddle.	Mmm, I think I have some spaghetti from last night.

Further reading

Foster, S. (1990) *The Communicative Competence of Young Children* (London: Longman).
The book draws on the fields of linguistics, psychology and anthropology in accounting for child language acquisition.

Peccei, J. (1994) *Child Language* (London: Routledge).
A practical introduction to the study of child language containing many examples and practical exercises.

8 Language at play

Introduction and overview

The last chapter on language acquisition contained fairly serious content and presented some complex concepts, although I hope that it was as interesting to read as it was to write. The data samples, interpretation and analysis in the chapter demonstrate that the journey children take as they acquire their first language is a truly remarkable one, and the language they produce along the way can be astonishing. From their very first words, children demonstrate a remarkable versatility and creativity, even with relatively limited resources.

In this chapter, I want to look at some of the more light-hearted aspects of language, although I will also make the point that language play can be a serious business. In the next few pages, we will explore ways in which people bend it, play with it, and sometimes even break the rules in their quest to communicate.

I also want to take a brief look at the language of laughter, focusing on forms of humour such as puns and plays on words where the essence of the humour is linguistic in nature. Finally, although we have already looked at advertisements in Chapter 6, I will revisit them here looking at the fertile ground they provide wordsmiths and advertising agencies with, for language play.

One important linguistic tool that I want to look at in some detail is **metaphor**. We are surrounded by metaphors (metaphorically speaking!), and use dozens of them every day. They are such an integral part of our language that we do not even know that we are using them most of the time.

Issues and concepts covered in this chapter include:

■ Playing with language
■ Language as humour
■ Limericks
■ Rhyming slang and other forms of word play
■ Metaphor
■ The language of advertising.

Playing with language

Most of the discourse samples and extracts in this book have been taken from transactional encounters in which the focus is on exchanging goods and services. However, as I have pointed out several times, there are two other important functions of language: the interpersonal and the aesthetic. The principal focus on this chapter is on these two functions.

David Crystal begins his book on language play with an extract from a dinner party conversation between four people: Janet, John, Peter and Jane. Janet is recounting the story of what happened when their respective cats met in the street. The conversation illustrates what Crystal calls 'ping-pong punning':

Janet: . . . *And so there was a sort of confrontation between Crumble and Splash –*
Jane: *Catfrontation you mean,* (Laughs)
Janet: *Well, all right, catfrontation if you insist – and they stood by the –*
Peter: *Near cat-astrophe if you ask me* (Groans all round)
Janet: *I wasn't asking you, Peter.*
Peter: *Sorry, I didn't mean to be categorical.* (More groans all round)
Jane: *This sounds like it's becoming a catalogue of disasters.* (Peals of laughter)
Peter: *I don't think John approves of all this jocularity, when Janet's trying to tell us a perfectly serious story.*
Jane: *You know what John's being though, don't you.*
Janet: *What?*
Jane: *A catalyst.* (More laughter all round)
Peter: *I thought that's what happened to moggies when they'd drunk too much.* (Further groans)
Janet: *Oh that's Christmas-cracker standard.*
Peter: *Of course, you know what Splash would get if he stayed outside for too long?*
Jane: *What?*
Susan [sic]: *Catarrh.* (More laughter all round)
Janet: *Anyway, to get back to the point . . .*
John: *Yes, get back to your catechism, Janet.* (More laughter)
(Crystal, 1998: 2–3)

Ping-pong punning illustrates the interpersonal function of language. No goods or services result from the interaction. No new knowledge is being generated or traded. The interaction is for social purposes only.

Not all jokes have a linguistic basis, although many of them do. Consider the following jokes. In which is the source of humour is a play on words?

Q: *What do you get if you cross a kangaroo with an elephant?*
A: *Bloody big holes all over Australia.*

Q: *What do you get if you cross a kangaroo with a sheep?*
A: *A woolly jumper.*

It's the second of these jokes that has a linguistic basis, achieving its humour through a play on words. As we will see, great deal of humour had a linguistic basis, relying on ambiguity of meaning and plays on words. For example, a pun is a form of verbal humour in which words that are alike in sound but different in meaning are interchanged. Many use the 'garden-path technique', leading us to embrace one particular meaning of a key word in the joke before switching to an alternative meaning in the punchline.

In London, in the 1970s, when graffiti art was in its infancy, someone (presumably a devoted Christian) scrawled 'Jesus saves' on buildings, billboards, and underground tube station walls. He (or she) was followed by someone less enamoured of the Christian faith, who scrawled beneath the religious exhortation, 'And Moses scores on the rebound.' (We can only wonder at whether the respondent was totally lacking in Biblical knowledge in putting players from the Old and the New Testaments in the same match, or whether this was a celestial game, in which time was irrelevant.)

As I have already said, a great deal of humour is linguistic, depending on plays on words and, as we saw in the case of newspaper headlines, grammatical ambiguity. It is possible that most jokes depend at least in part on linguistic means for their humour.

Other linguistic effects are achieved by playing around with the grammar. Many jokes are created through the use of the displaced phrase. (You might recall, from Chapter 3, the girl who was followed by a small poodle wearing jeans.) The same linguistic device of phrase displacement is used to create the humour in the following exchanges:

A: *I have a friend with a wooden leg called Pete.*
B: *Oh, yeah? What's his other leg called?*

(Wife to husband who is cleaning out the garden shed.)
Wife: *What are you doing?*
Husband: *I'm getting rid of the junk from the garden shed.*
Wife: *Are you wearing gloves?*
Husband: *No, I'm not.*
Wife: *What about the spiders?*
Husband: *They're not wearing gloves either!*

An insightful analysis of humour was provided years ago by Arthur Koestler in his book, *The Act of Creation.* Koestler was a popular thinker and writer whose best known book, *Darkness at Noon*, is a fictionalized account of the Moscow show trials of 1936–8 in which Stalin arrested and executed almost every important living Bolshevik from the Russian Revolution. *The Act of Creation* is a treatise on creativity, and in it Koestler builds a 'theory' of humour which, as you might imagine, is illustrated by many jokes whose humour swings on linguistic ambiguity. Here is one of them:

> In the happy days of *La Ronde*, a dashing but penniless young Austrian officer tried to obtain the favors of a fashionable courtesan. To shake off this unwanted suitor, she explained to him that her heart was no longer free. He replied politely: 'Madam, I never aimed as high as that.' (p. 36)

Here we have two metaphors ('my heart is not free', and 'I never aimed as high as that'). The metaphorical and physical meanings of freedom and height collide, and the humour is neatly established.

Koestler contends that all jokes, linguistic and otherwise, come about when two frames of reference intersect, and we as readers and listeners are forced to shuttle between the two. In linguistic jokes, such as the ones recounted here, the frames of reference are the two different meanings or interpretations of words. Koestler goes on to argue that all creative acts, from the greatest artistic and aesthetic creations to paradigm-shifting scientific discoveries, rest on the intersection of two frames of reference which bring together at a single point two otherwise separate, and often incompatible worlds.

Humour, intentional and otherwise can be found in environmental print – the notices and signs that surround us as we go about our daily lives. Each day, on my way to work in Hong Kong, I pass the 'Hop On Bicycle Shop', and nod to the proprietor, Mr Hop On, who sits on a stool in the doorway. I have often wondered whether his choice of merchandise had anything to do with his name.

While I deliberately set out to give this chapter a lighter tone, select-ing illustrative extracts from jokes, limericks and the like, I should point out, that language play has a serious aspect as well. The ways in which everyday talk is both serious and fun is beautifully illustrated by Ron Carter in his book on language and creativity. Drawing on a wide range of conversational extracts he shows that everyday speech is richly creative, and that such creativity 'is not the exclusive preserve of the individual genius, that, fundamentally, creativity is also a matter of dialogue with others' (Carter, 2004: 11). In the conclusion to his book he makes the point that 'Creative language is not a capacity of special people but a special capacity of all people' (Carter, 2004: 215).

The lure of the limerick

When I was an undergraduate, a favourite way of spending an idle evening was to sit in a pub or wine bar composing limericks. One person would propose a first line, and the next person had to complete it. This often happened late at night after a few drinks, and the results were rarely publishable or even (thank god) remembered next day. A limerick is a five-line rhyme in which the first, second and fifth lines rhyme, as do the shorter third and fourth lines. Very often the author of the limerick is forced to utilize eccentric or obscure place names in order to meet their rhyming obligations (the Lady from Riga, the plumber from Torrington Lea). They also often involve clever manipu-lations of the phonological, lexical and grammatical systems to achieve their ends. Many eminent poets sought relief from more weighty liter-ary concerns by penning limericks. Alfred Lord Tennyson apparently had a huge collection which, unfortunately, was destroyed by the heirs to his estate after his death.

Limericks are meant to be silly. As the author Norman Douglas said 'Limericks are jovial things' (cited in Baring-Gould, 1970):

> There was an old man of Dundee
> Who molested an ape in a tree
> The result was most horrid
> All ass and no forehead
> Three balls and a purple goatee

Baring-Gould, whose history of the limerick contains all of the classics, also points out that, when a limerick appears, sex is not far behind:

It is impossible to write of the limerick, its life and high times, without on occasion approaching the indelicate. As the limerick itself has it:

The limerick's an art form complex
Whose contents run chiefly to sex;
It's famous for virgins
And masculine urgins
And vulgar erotic effects. (Baring-Gould, 1970: 16)

The masculine urges of the plumber from Torrington Lea gave rise to the following well-known verse. With its plays on words, ambiguity and double entendres, it embodies all of the characteristic features of the 'vulgar' rhyme.

A plumber from Torrington Lea
Was plumbing his girl by the sea
Said the girl, 'Stop your plumbing,
There's somebody coming.'
Said the plumber still plumbing, 'It's me.'

In the introduction to his book, Baring-Gould asks why anyone should want to produce such an indecorous form of verse as the limerick. My answer would be that they appeal to the adolescent residing in all of us. His response is more considered. According to Baring-Gould, most people treasure at least one limerick, proper or improper, and chances are that the limerick was acquired through hearsay, word of mouth, rather than through books or magazines. The limerick is a part of our oral tradition, it is authentic folklore, a part of our heritage.

Other forms of word play: rhyming slang, spoonerisms, slips of the tongue and more

Another form of word play that uses rhyme and alliteration to achieve its effect is rhyming slang, which originated in Cockney London, although indigenous offspring can be found in working class areas in other parts of the world such as Australia. In rhyming slang, one or more words in an utterance are replaced with other words which often have no connection other than that they rhyme with the deleted words. For example, *Take off yer tit-for-tat and put up your plates of meat. (Take off your hat and put up your feet.*). More often than not, the expressions would become totally impenetrable to the outsider when the word that actually rhymed with the original was elided. So, in fact, what users of rhyming slang are likely to say is, *Take off yer titfer and put up your plates.*

Other rhyming slang expressions that peppered the speech of people in the mining community where I grew up included: *Trouble and strife*, meaning *wife* as in *How's the trouble and strife? Frog 'n toad* meaning *road* as in *I'm just going down the frog 'n toad.* To complicate matters even more for the uninitiated, *frog 'n toad* was a euphemism for going to the pub. Putting these expressions together with *pig's ear* (*beer*) resulted in statements such as the following: *I'm taking the trouble to the frog and toad for a few pigs ears*, meaning *I'm taking my wife to the pub for a few beers.*

Spoonerisms are slips of the tongue in which sounds and words are transposed to humorous (and usually unintended) effect. They are attributed to the Reverend William Spooner, an Anglican priest and scholar at Oxford University. Famous for going to London on the 'town drain', he reprimanded one student for 'fighting a liar in the quadrangle', another for 'hissing my mystery lecture', and a third for 'tasting two worms'.

Malapropisms are another form of unintended verbal word play. Named after Mrs. Malaprop, a character in the play *The Rivals* by Sheridan, malapropisms involve the substitution of one word for another that sounds similar. Here are some examples:

They had to use a distinguisher to put out the fire.
My best friend has extra-century perception.
It's just a pigment of your imagination.

The following samples from van Lier (1995: 76) exemplify the types of word play discussed so far in this chapter.

Spoonerism: *Please remain in your seats until the fasten turnbelt seat is signed off.* (Flight attendant)
Metaphor: *Congress piling up the pork, critics say.* (Newspaper headline about pork-barrel politics.)
Euphemism: *He was let go.* (Commenting on someone who was fired from his job.)
Pun: *Hair today, spray tomorrow?* (Attributed to newspaper columnist Dave Barry)

Oxymoron: *There was a certain amount of controlled chaos.* (Newspaper report about a riot in Germany.) (See page 171 for a discussion of oxymorons.)

Malapropism: *Let me divert for a moment here.* (President George H. Bush)

In his 1995 book van Lier makes the point that lexical phenomena such as these are more than just amusing diversions. They can give researchers insights into the mental processing of language, and they

> give a glimpse of how language is organised in the brain. For example, if people say *pice of peep* or *piece of pipe*, instead of *pipe of peace*, this must mean that they had the second word in mind already before they uttered the first. Studies of so-called slips of the tongue suggest that language is produced not word by word, but in chunks of various kinds and lengths (collocations, idioms, phrases etc.) At the moment of phonological production, certain sounds later in a unit can interfere with (for example, replace) sounds earlier in a unit. For this to be possible, a chunk of speech must be 'in mind' at the moment of producing the slip. (van Lier, 1995: 73).

Figures of speech represent a special kind of word play, and one that causes no end of trouble for second language learners because the link between the original and current meaning is lost in the mists of time, or because they simply defy logic. A student once asked me why *hit the bottle* means drink to excess, while *kick the bottle* means to give up drinking to excess. Another asked about the origins of the expression a *red herring*. I had an explanation for the latter term, but could only guess at the former.

Advertising revisited

As we saw in Chapter 6, nothing demonstrates the way that adults love to play around with language better than the world of advertising. While the majority of advertisements are pretty pedestrian, some display considerable creativity. Consider the following:

Newspaper ad for Guinness beer
'We've poured through the Reign'

TV commercial for Bolle sunglasses
Scene of two beautiful people in a steamy embrace on a tropical beach.
Girl: Do you have protection?
Boy: I do! (pulls out and dons a pair of sunglasses)

In this day and age, it is impossible to get through the day without being bombarded by advertisements of every kind. They are plastered on shop front hoardings, billboards, underground stations, and bus stops as well as buses and trains. Switching on the radio or television is an invitation to be assailed by advertisements at regular intervals. And with the explosion in Internet usage, along with electronic mail and unparalleled access to information, has come pop-up advertisements and spam: unasked for emails advertising everything from pornography to cheap mortgage loans.

Of course, as we have already seen, advertisements are much more than words. Most print advertisements consist of images as well as words. Television advertisements are also usually accompanied by sounds and music. The sounds and images, along with the design of the advertisement, the type of fonts used and so on are all important parts of the message (part of the *genre* of advertisements). In fact, one of the trends in advertising is for the number of words to be reduced and for the visual elements of the advertisement to do more and more of the work in carrying the message.

A linguistic feature of many advertisements that is common to the genre is that of comparison. In most cases, the comparison is implicit. (*Quicker than whom? More value than what?*) This is typical of many advertising texts. Note the implicit comparisons in the following advertisements:

MORE PEOPLE PREFER IT
FOR A SEXIER ALTERNATIVE
THE SPICIER CHILLI SAUCE
FOR A MORE FULFILLING CAREER
BE HEALTHY – LIVE LONGER
A MORE ENVIRONMENTALLY FRIENDLY ALTERNATIVE
KINDER TO OUR HANDS
A MORE AUTHENTIC DINING EXPERIENCE
MORE POWER – LESS FUEL

Figurative language

So far, I have looked at some of the more light hearted aspects of language play. I now want to get a little more serious (although, hopefully not TOO serious.) In this section, I will look at figurative language; principally metaphors. I will also take a passing look at literary language.

Figurative language represents a more serious approach to language play than puns and plays on words, although there can be a great deal of fun (often unintended by the speaker or writer) in the use of metaphors (mixed and otherwise) and oxymorons.

If you have had a fairly 'traditional' school experience, you may have endured English lessons in which you had to memorize definitions and find examples of 'metaphors', 'similes' and 'figures of speech' in the poems, plays and novels that had been set for study. I remember agonizing over which example belonged to which category. Was *I drifted lonely as a cloud* a figure of speech, a metaphor or a simile? If I got it wrong and the teacher called me an *imbecilic moron*, which he often did, was he speaking metaphorically or literally? When, at the end of the game, a footballer says *I'm knackered* does it really mean that he slipped off at half-time for a little operation?

A **metaphor** is a linguistic device through which a person, process, entity or state-of-affairs is represented as something it does not literally resemble. Like many other aspects of language, we use metaphors without even being aware that we are doing so. Once they become widely and automatically used, they become clichés. As Lakoff and Johnson (1980:3) note in their classic book on metaphor:

> Metaphor is for most people a device of the poetic imagination and the rhetorical flourish . . . For this reason, most people think that they can get along perfectly well without metaphor. We have found, on the contrary, that metaphor is pervasive in everyday life, not just in language but in thought and action.

Why do we use metaphors? In educational contexts, they can help to clarify difficult concepts by expressing an unfamiliar idea in terms of a familiar one. In addition, they can add colour and drama to our language. The best metaphorical language is both creative and arresting.

One place to observe the imaginative use of metaphor is in bars or at sporting or other social events (see, for example, Fox, 2004). Bar talk is often extremely inventive and rich, although many regular pub-goers would probably object to the notion that their use of language was poetic. Just note how many figurative pieces of language are used in the following brief conversation.

A: *How was that dinner thing you had to go to last night, Harry?*
B: *Terrible. It was a buffet, so everyone made pigs of themselves. I ended up at the foot of the table with the kids, and then had to foot the bill.*

Years ago, the linguist George Lakoff and his collaborator Mark Turner wrote a memorable book on metaphor. They also gave it a memorable title: *More than Cool Reason*. Here is what they have to say about the use of metaphor in everyday speech.

> It is commonly thought that poetic language is beyond ordinary language – that it is something essentially different, special, higher, with extraordinary tools and techniques like metaphor and metonymy, instruments beyond the reach of someone who just talks. But great poets, as master craftsmen, use basically the same tools we use; what makes them different is their talent for using these tools, and their skill in using them, which they acquire from sustained attention, study and practice. . . . Metaphor is a tool so ordinary that we use it unconsciously and automatically, with so little effort that we hardly notice it. It is omnipresent: metaphor suffuses our thoughts, no matter what we are thinking about. It is accessible to everyone: as children, we automatically, as a matter of course, acquire a mastery of everyday metaphor. It is conventional: metaphor is an integral part of our ordinary everyday thought and language. And it is irreplaceable: metaphor allows us to understand our selves and our world in ways that no other modes of thought can. (Lakoff and Turner, 1989: xi)

If you open a book or magazine at random, you are almost certain to find metaphors sprinkled through the prose, regardless of whether you have picked up a work of fiction or non-fiction. I just tried the test myself, opening a copy of *Newsweek* that happened to be lying on my desk. Here is the first sentence that hit me in the eye (metaphorically speaking, of course).

> Latin America is like a mouse sleeping next to an elephant. Let the United States roll over, and you run the risk of being crushed. America is a dangerous and unpredictable animal. (Carlos Fuentes, 'After I told you so', *Newsweek*, December 2003–February 2004: 23)

Writers of all kinds employ metaphors as a matter of course. In fact, my use of the word 'employ' in the preceding sentence is used metaphorically. Writers do not advertise for, interview, and subsequently pay metaphors a salary! Well used, metaphors enliven prose: overused and clichéd, they can have the opposite effect.

In the following passage, the author Bill Bryson is trying to turn his readers on to the topic of atmospheric temperature? How many metaphors can you identify? Are they all equally effective, or are some rather clichéd?

Sunlight energizes atoms. It increases the rate at which they jiggle and jounce, and in their enlivened state they crash into one another, releasing heat. When you feel the sun warm your back on a summer's day, it's really excited atoms you feel. The higher you climb, the fewer molecules there are, and so the fewer collisions between them. Air is deceptive stuff. Even at sea level, we tend to think of the air as being ethereal and all but weightless. In fact, it has plenty of bulk, and that bulk often exerts itself. (Bryson, 2003: 317).

Through the clever use of metaphor, Bryson is able to enliven what would, for most readers, be a fairly unexciting subject.

In fiction, metaphors are used to add poetic effect, and make an idea or sentiment more striking. This is its principle role in poetry. Reread your favourite poem, focusing particularly on the use of metaphor, and you will see what I mean. Here is an example which captures the desolation and hopelessness of being a prisoner.

I never saw a man who looked
With such a wistful eye
Upon that little tent of blue
Which prisoners call the sky (Oscar Wilde, 'The Ballad of Reading Gaol')

In my opinion, of all the poets who have bent and twisted language to suit their own ends, none, with the possible exception of the mystical Jesuit Gerard Manley Hopkins, comes close to the Welsh poet Dylan Thomas. In addition to his ability to manipulate syntax for poetic effect, his use of metaphor is little short of frenetic. Just consider the jumble of metaphors that are jammed into the first verse of his highly idiosyncratic account of the Creation.

In the beginning was the three-pointed star,
One smile of light across the empty face;
One bough of bone across the rooting air,
The substance forked that marrowed the first sun;
And, burning ciphers on the round of space,
Heaven and hell mixed as they spun. (Dylan Thomas, 'In the beginning')

While readers are often unsure exactly what Thomas is getting at, for me his ways with words and metaphors set off powerful experiential resonances and images. He is one of those poets whose words don't so much 'mean' as 'be': the poems are their own justification, and they appeal to our senses at an emotional rather than rational level.

Lyricists also make great use of metaphor. Think of the many ways in which love is portrayed in popular songs. *Love is blue. Love is bleeding, love is fleeting. Love is a red, red rose. Love's not an evil thing. Love hurts.*

Metaphor is also used to avoid making direct reference to embarrassing subjects or those that make us squeamish. Used euphemistically, they add to the complexity of a concept, or even add humour to serious subjects. Consider the multiple resources for referring to death in English: 'pass away', 'shuffle off', 'pass on', 'at peace', 'fall off the perch', 'go upstairs', 'suffer a loss', 'turn up one's toes'.

Comedians constantly exploit our squeamishness over death. In one of the most celebrated skits in the cult British comedy series *Monty Python's Flying Circus*, our squeamishness over using the word 'death' is parodied in the following description of a dead parrot:

> This parrot is no more. It has ceased to be. It's expired and gone to meet its maker. This is a late parrot. It's a stiff. Bereft of life, it rests in peace. If you hadn't nailed it to the perch, it would be pushing up daisies. It's rung down the curtain and joined the choir invisible. This is an ex-parrot. (www.davidpbrown.co.uk/jokes/)

Lakoff and Turner begin their book on metaphor with a discussion on the rich variety of metaphors for death and the fact these are not arbitrary.

> The euphemism 'He passed away' is not an arbitrary one. When someone dies, we don't say 'He drank a glass of milk' or 'He had an idea' or 'He upholstered his couch.' Instead we say things like 'He's gone,' 'He's left us,' 'He's no longer with us,' 'He's passed on,' 'He's been taken from us,' 'He's gone to the great beyond,' and 'He's among the dear departed.' (Lakoff and Turner, 1989: 1)

These metaphorical expressions all share the unifying notion of departure, and the end of a journey, just as metaphors for birth share the notion of arrival and the beginning of a journey. *Henrietta and Charles are thrilled to announce the arrival of their little bundle of joy, Clementine Adele.* Metaphors are thus culturally and linguistically bound, and a study of the metaphors favoured by a culture provide important insights into that culture.

Mixed metaphors are created when two contradictory or unlikely images are brought together. *Let's get this ship on the road. You tried to run before you could walk, but now your wings are well and truly clipped!*

Mixing metaphors is an affliction to which newspaper headline writers appear particularly prone:

SHIP OF STATE OFF THE RAILS
FOOTBALLER KEEPS INJURED LEG CLOSE TO HIS CHEST
TREASURER POURS COLD WATER ON SUGGESTION THAT
ECONOMY IS OFF THE BOIL
KEEP POSTED ON LATEST POSTAL STRIKE
FITNESS CLUB GOES BELLY UP

Thompson (1996: 165) defines this as 'the expression of a meaning through a lexico-grammatical form which originally evolved to express a different kind of meaning. The expression of the meaning is metaphorical in relation to a different way of expressing the "same" meaning which would be more congruent. The process is also known as **nominalization**.

In linguistic analysis, a special type of metaphor is the **grammatical metaphor**. Thompson (1996: 165), provides as extended discussion of grammatical metaphor in his book on functional grammar. He presents the following example to illustrate the concept of grammatical metaphor:

> The north [of Britain] emerges from every statistical comparison that can be made as significantly poorer than the south.

So where is the metaphor in this sentence? According to Thompson, the word 'comparison' is being used metaphorically. The sentence is reporting something that happened, a process, in which statisticians compared data from the north and the south of Britain. The original process may have been represented by a sentence such as the following: *Whenever people compare statistics about the north and the south, they find that the north is significantly poorer than the south.* However, the process, represented by a verb 'to compare', is turned into a 'thing', 'a comparison', in the sentence that finally appears. It is this process of turning processes into things that gives a metaphorical sense.

Oxymorons are self-contradictory figures of speech in which two contrary concepts collide. They can be created intentionally *To make haste slowly*, unintentionally, or out of an attempt at humour or sarcasm *British gastronomy, American diplomacy, Australian culture*. Like mixed metaphors, they are particularly favoured by newspaper writers. Of course, in some cases the oxymoronic nature of the expression might be in the eye or the ear of the beholder. To me *business ethics*, a subject one of my daughters is currently studying as part of her law/business degree, is oxymoronic, although I'm sure this is something that her professor would dispute.

When metaphors, similes and other kinds of figurative language are overused they cease being metaphors and become clichés. For most people who advise others on the art and craft of writing, clichés are to be avoided at all costs. In his advice to would-be writers, here is what one of the most successful authors in the world (in terms of book sales at least) had to say about clichés:

> The most common [potential pitfall of figurative writing] is the use of clichéd similes, metaphors and images. He ran **like a madman**, she was pretty **as a summer day**, the guy was **a hot ticket**, Bob fought **like a tiger** . . . don't waste my time (or anyone's) with such chestnuts. It makes you look either lazy or ignorant. Neither description will do your reputation as a writer much good. (King, 2000: 209)

King goes on to suggest that 'the key to good writing begins with clear seeing and ends with clear writing, the kind of writing that employs fresh images and simple metaphors'. This is a good general principal, although not one that is universally observed by all published writers, not even by King himself. (In his book on writing, King has his nose to the grindstone, he leans heavily on his intuition, has plots with holes big enough to drive a truck through, and thinks the themes of his novels are no big deal!)

While the overuse of clichés often reveals laziness and sloppy thinking on the part of the author, clichés are not necessarily all bad. While King's admonitions are well-taken, he overstates the case against them. The occasional cliché can actually ease that reader's burden. Because of their frequency, clichés are familiar. They therefore serve as easily processed formulae that smooth the processing demands on the reader. The main thing that writers need to be aware of is their choice of metaphorical, and even clichéd language, and their possible effect on the reader. Are they going to facilitate the reading process or get in the way?

Summary and conclusion

At the beginning of this book, we saw that there are three major functions of language: the transactional, the interpersonal, and the aesthetic. Most of the book has been devoted to an exploration of transactional and interpersonal functions. We have seen that language helps us to fulfil the basic needs of obtaining food, shelter and clothing when these necessities are not there simply for the taking, and that it also enables us to socialize. All creatures socialize, of course. Chimps do it by plucking nits from the head of those they care for. Dogs do it by licking one another. While some humans also demonstrate social contact through physical grooming, most prefer to use language.

The major focus of this chapter has been the third macrofunction; that is, the aesthetic. In the chapter, I have demonstrated that language is more than a utilitarian and social tool. Put to play, it can also engender laughter, tears, wonder and joy. In his book on language play (1998), Crystal makes the point that language play fulfils an important role socially. It helps people establish rapport, facilitates the bonding process, and fosters the growth of intimacy. For Crystal, it is language play that actually makes us human.

In this chapter, the following points are made:

- Language play is mainly concerned with the interpersonal and aesthetic macrofunctions of language
- A great deal of humour is linguistic in nature
- Linguistic humour involves bringing together two otherwise disconnected images or frames of reference
- Metaphors are important linguistic devices for representing experience in both literary contexts and everyday life
- Language play has a serious side.

Questions and tasks

1 In which of the following, is the humour linguistically-based? Explain the source of the humour.

   (a) Two peanuts walk into a bar, and one was a salted.
   (b) A jumper cable walks into a bar. The bartender says 'I'll serve you, but don't start anything.'
   (c) A school friend asks 'Where are you from Julie?' 'New York.' 'Which part?' 'All of me.'

(d)   A sandwich walks into a bar. The bartender says, 'Sorry we don't serve food in here.'

(e)   A dyslexic man walks into a bra.

(f)   A man walks into a bar with a slab of asphalt under his arm and says: 'A beer please, and one for the road.'

(g)   A woman walks into a clothing store and orders a fur coat. 'What fur?' asks the assistant. 'To keep me warm.'

(h)   Two aerial antennas meet on a roof, fall in love and get married. The ceremony wasn't much, but the reception was excellent.

(i)   Two cannibals are eating a clown. One says to the other: 'Does this taste funny to you?'

(j)   An invisible man marries an invisible woman. The kids were nothing to look at, either.

(k)   Two hydrogen atoms walk into a bar. One says, 'I've lost my electron.' The other says, 'Are you sure?' The first replies, 'Yes, I'm positive . . .'

(l)   I went to buy some camouflage trousers the other day but I couldn't find any.

(m)   I went to the butcher's the other day and I bet him 50 bucks that he couldn't reach the meat off the top shelf. He said, 'No, the steaks are too high.'

(n)   I went to a seafood disco last week . . . and pulled a mussel.

(o)   Two Eskimos sitting in a kayak were chilly; but when they lit a fire in the craft, it sank, proving that you can't have your kayak and heat it too.

2   Collect 6–10 advertisements that have slogans whose effectiveness rests on puns or plays on words. Analyse the advertisements and identify how the authors achieve their effects.

3   Find or invent examples of spoonerisms, metaphors, euphemisms, puns, oxymorons, and malapropisms.

Further reading

Carter, R. (2004) *Language and Creativity* (London: Routledge).
Explores the richness and creativity that abounds in everyday speech.

Cook, G. (2000) *Language Play, Language Learning* (Oxford: Oxford University Press).
Provides many entertaining and illuminating examples of language at play which show the centrality of language play to everyday life.

Crystal, D. (1998) *Language Play* (London: Penguin).
A comprehensive introduction to the ways in which humans play with language. Not only does Crystal show us the light-hearted side of language play, he also demonstrates it importance to social and personal life.

Lakoff, G. and M. Johnson (1980) *Metaphors We Live By* (Chicago: University of Chicago Press).
Although this book has been around for over twenty-five years, it is still widely referred to and provides an accessible introduction to the place of metaphor in everyday life.

9 Looking ahead: the future of language

Introduction and overview

The issue that I would like to take up in this concluding chapter is not whether language has a future but what form it will take. Will English, as the world's language, gobble up smaller languages, and then larger languages, until its global dominance is complete? Some linguists believe that this is already happening, while others have their doubts. In this chapter, I will look at the cases for and against the emergence and promotion of English as a global language. I will also look at linguistic varieties, and at native-speaker diversity.

In order to evaluate the impact of English on other languages, we need to estimate how many languages there are in the world. This is an even more difficult question to answer than one we considered earlier: How many words are there in any given language such as English? Most estimates put the number of language in the world today at around 4,000, although I have seen other estimates as high as 10,000. A major complicating factor here is deciding what counts as a language. Another is that languages are constantly being born as well as dying. Both of these factors are looked at later in this chapter.

Questions and issues looked at in the chapter include:

- Is English the world language?
- Language variation: pidgins and creoles
- Linguistic diversity among native speakers
- Language death.

Is English the 'world language'?

On the question of whether or not English is a world language and how it came about, there are believers and doubters. Crystal (1997b: ix) is a believer:

It all happened so quickly. In 1950, any notion of English as a true world language was but a dim, shadowy, theoretical possibility, surrounded by the uncertainties of the Cold War, and lacking any clear definition or sense of direction. Fifty years on, and World English exists as a political and cultural reality. How could such a dramatic linguistic shift have taken place in less than a lifetime? And why has English, and not some other language, achieved such a status?

Crystal goes on to devote much of his excellent little book on global English to an exploration of this question.

Not all agree with Crystal, however. Writing in the *Atlantic Monthly*, Barbara Wallraff is clearly a doubter:

English is not sweeping all before it, not even in the United States. Ten years ago about one in seven people in this country spoke a language other than English at home – and since then the proportion of immigrants in the population has grown and grown. Ever-wider swathes of Florida, California and the Southwest are heavily Spanish-speaking. Hispanic people make up 30 percent of the population of New York City, and a television station there that is affiliated with a Spanish-language network has been known to draw a larger daily audience than at least one of the city's English-language network affiliates. Even Sioux City, Iowa, now has a Spanish language newspaper ... From 1980 to 1990 the number of Spanish-speakers in the United States grew by 50 percent. (Wallraff, 2000: 21)

So, where does the truth lie? The short answer is that no one knows for sure – probably somewhere in the middle as it does with most things. As tools for communication, languages are constantly appearing, evolving, mutating, and disappearing. Just as English is gobbling up smaller languages and marching imperiously all over the globe, so too is it breaking down into barely comprehensible dialects, attaching itself to other languages that subsequently morph into forms of communication that are unrecognizable as English.

When academics, newspaper columnists and politicians want to know about the future of English, many of them go to a publication entitled . . . *THE FUTURE of english* (this is not a typographical error, it is how the title appears on the cover). This slim volume, by British academic David Graddol, is about 'the English language in the 21st century, about who will speak it, and for what purposes'. Although slim, it is an entertaining, impressive and informative volume. It even has an introduction by Charles, the Prince of Wales and heir to the throne of England, Australia, and probably a few other places as well.

The publication, which was commissioned by the British Council as part of its brief to promote Britain and the English language globally, is based on a survey of 2,000 English language professionals around the world. (I have vague memories of being one of those 2,000 who were surveyed, although I doubt that I would have claimed, either then or now, to be able to speak with authority on the future of English.)

The book attempts to whet our appetite by opening with a series of questions. They are not the kinds of questions likely to keep us awake at night ('Jurassic Park grossed $6m in India in 1994. But in what language?' 'What have been the heroic failures of the past to predict the number of English speakers?'). However, they give Graddol a useful framing device for laying out some fascinating facts and figures. (For the record, Jurassic Park in India was dubbed into Hindi!).

Graddol uses an esoteric-sounding instrument called the *engco model* to make predictions about the future number of speakers of English and other languages. According to this model, in 2050, English will not be the number one language in the world according to the number of people who use it as a first language. Then, as now, Chinese will beat it by many millions. (Graddol does not say which Chinese language he is referring to, but we must assume that he means Mandarin, or Putonghua.) Hindi/Urdu beat English into third place, and Spanish and Arabic are hot on its heels.

Does this mean that Chinese and Hindi will assume greater importance than English? The answer is almost certainly no. English is, and will probably remain, the dominant global language for at least the next fifty years because of its pre-eminent position as the language of science, technology, tourism, entertainment and the media. There is no evidence at the moment that the dominance of English in these areas will not continue.

The real measure of the reach of a language is to count the number of people who speak the language, not the number who are born into the language. When we do this for English, we get some indication of its importance, and why, at this point in time, it can rightly claim to be *the* global language. If we add to the number of native speakers the number of second language speakers of the language, then the number more than doubles and English begins to rival Chinese in terms of raw numbers. At about the time that I was writing this book, for the first time, the number of second language speakers around the globe using English as a second language surpassed those speaking English as a first language. If we add to the first and second language speakers, the number who have some competence in English as a foreign language, then English is clearly the world's dominant language.

The difference between English as a second language and English as a foreign language is worth a comment. The traditional distinction is that if someone is learning English in communities where it is the language of communication, as in Canada, the United States, Australia, the United Kingdom and New Zealand, then they are learning English as a second language. If they are learning English in countries such as Japan, Brazil or Morocco, where English is not the medium of communication, then they are learning English as a foreign language. Like most binary distinctions, this one is very crude. For example, the context and practice of teaching English in Brazil is very different from Japan. In addition, there are many thousands of people living in second language contexts who rarely if ever encounter English. They mix exclusively with their own ethnic communities, watch their own television programmes, and read their own ethnic newspapers.

However, it is not just the number of first and second language users that determines dominance, it is also how, where, when and why a language is used that determines its prestige. Here, English wins hands down. In Northern Thailand, at a meeting between a group of Chinese engineering consultants and their Thai counterparts to discuss a large dam construction project, the language of communication is neither Chinese not Thai, but English. When the Pope goes abroad, he is more likely to deliver his sermons and speeches in English than in one of the other numerous languages that he speaks. He knows that English will maximize the power of his message. In academia, over fifty per cent of the millions of academic papers published each year are written in English, and the percentage is growing year by year. If a German physicist working in Bonn or Hamburg, wants his work to see the light of day, he has no choice but to publish in English as over 90 per cent of all papers on physics are published in English.

This march of English across the globe has not been universally welcomed. In fact, a term has been coined to capture the phenomenon: *linguistic imperialism*. In postcolonial times, *imperialism* is considered to be highly undesirable, implying subjugation and exploitation. For those who see the global English phenomenon in terms of linguistic imperialism, the spread of English is to be condemned (Phillipson, 1992). Invading forces (with certain notable exceptions), may no longer use physical weapons, but their effect on local languages and cultures in no less destructive, according to those who see the spread of English in terms of linguistic imperialism.

This leads us on to the question of who owns English, and who has the right to decide how it should be shaped in the future. Patricia Friedrich, a linguist and non-native speaker of English provides the following perspective on this question:

> When I was an elementary school student, I remember doing exercises of the following type: 'In China, people speak Chinese, in Japan they speak Japanese; and in Great Britain and the US they speak English'. Indirectly, these exercises led me to believe that not only did these people speak those languages, but to some degree they also owned them. Languages do not have borders and yet many of us, especially those who do not speak English as a first language still believe that we do not have the same linguistic rights upon English that native-speakers do. (Friedrich, 2000)

We have already noted that English has been spectacularly successful in incorporating words from other languages into its lexicon. However, with its emergence as a global language, the direction has reversed, and it is now feeding other languages. According to Bragg (2003: 306), Russian has appropriated, adopted and adapted many words from English, including the following: 'futbol', 'chempion', 'kemping' (camping), 'khobbi' (hobby), 'klub', 'striptiz', 'ralli', 'boykot', 'lider' (leader), 'pamflet', 'bifshteks', 'grog', 'keks', 'puding', 'myuzikl', 'kompyuter', 'mobilny telefon', 'faks', 'konsultant', 'broker', 'sponsor', 'kornfleks', 'parlament', 'prezident', 'spiker' (speaker), 'elektorat', 'konsensus', 'ofis', 'supermarket', 'loozer' (failure).

Similarly, Japanese has, thanks to English, thousands of new additions to its lexicon: 'basukettobo-ru' (basketball), 'rajio' (radio), 'konpyu-ta' (computer), 'kare raisu' (curry rice), 'supootsu' (sports), 'sumu-zu' (smooth), 'sutoresu' (stress), 'insentibu' (incentive), 'haikingu' (hiking), 'ranchi' (lunch), 'kissu' (kiss). So prominent is English, that there is an entire dictionary of Japanese words that have been derived from English.

This trend to appropriate English words has not been universally applauded in official circles. In 1994, the French government banned the use of English words where a French equivalent existed. Apparently, transgressors, if identified and apprehended, face a hefty fine. It remains to be seen whether fining people for using words that might have originated in another language is a feasible proposition. I have my doubts. The spread and evolution of languages is an organic process, and one that has, in the past at least, defied legislation.

My own view is that English is the world language, that it has been for some time, and that its will remain so for the foreseeable future. The number of people who use the language for some form of communication in everyday life supports this assertion. Equally important, as we saw earlier in the chapter, is the scope of English. While its position as the language of international business may be challenged in certain contexts by other languages, particularly Chinese, its dominance in other domains such technology and entertainment is likely to go unchallenged for many years to come.

Language variation

We have already looked at accents and dialects, and we saw that dialects are variants of a particular language with differences of sound, vocabulary and grammar. These differences do not generally result in unintelligibility, although occasionally they do. This is particularly the case when the variations involve a blending of one language, such as English, with another, such as Chinese or Malay.

The other day, I overheard two Chinese people talking. While I am not in the habit of eavesdropping on conversations (unless I happen to be collecting data for books such as this), the sounds that the two speakers were making attracted my attention. They were using a language that seemed vaguely familiar, but it was one I didn't recognize. After they had finished their conversation, one of them walked away. I asked the other one what language they had been speaking. He gave me a quizzical look and replied *English, of course!*

Take a look at the following utterances, and decide whether or not you think the speakers are using English.

Wah lau you maken yet?
So kiasu one.
Hey he talk cock lah.

These utterances are a variety of English used in Singapore known as *Singlish*. The 'regular' English meanings of the utterances are, respectively *Have you eaten yet?*, *He's really aggressive* and *He talks a lot of nonsense*. So concerned has the Singaporean government become at the emergence of this variety of English that they are determined to stamp it out, arguing that it will cost Singapore dearly in terms of jobs and money. These, the government believes, will migrate to other countries in the region which are rapidly catching up in the English-speaking stakes. They now have a 'Speak Good English' campaign, to improve the quality of English and stamp out Singlish. I wish them luck. If we have learned anything at all about language and the way it spreads and mutates it's this: language, like wayward teenagers will not be controlled. It pays little heed to purveyors of purity, and when used as an instrument of communication in foreign and second language situations will intermingle and cohabit with local languages. In Singapore, the languages rubbing shoulders with English are Chinese, Tamil and Malay, and it is out of these languages that Singlish has been born.

The samples of Singlish provided above prompt the question: At what point does a language cease being English, or Spanish or Chinese and become something else? Another question is: What degree of diversity can we tolerate before a particular language breaks down? These questions are pertinent, not just for English, but for other languages as well. Adelaide Parson (personal communication), who teaches at the University of Missouri, says that in her state immigrant communities from Latin America these days speak a language that they claim to be Spanish, but which is largely incomprehensible to native speakers of Spanish.

Languages are in a constant state of flux: an inevitable consequence of the fact that they are practical tools for communication. As living organisms, they are constantly coming into being, evolving and dying. Minority languages are under threat, and are dying out in increasing numbers. Majority languages such as English, Spanish and Chinese are mutating into forms that are incomprehensible to native speakers.

This process of diversification results in what are called pidgins and creoles. **Pidgins** are hybrid languages used for communication between people who do not share a common language. A **creole** is a pidgin that has evolved into a language in its own right. In other words, it is a pidgin that has become the first language for a particular speech community. Creolization is thus a two stage process that occurs over a couple of generations.

Here is an example of New Guinean Tok Pisin, a language that is recognized by the country's constitution. As you read it, see how much of it you can figure out.

TOK BILOG GAVMAN
Sipos yu painim sompela Japan i les long pait, yu gifim dispela pas. Sipos i
savi walkabout, i kan kam ontaim yupela nau painim soldia bilong yumi.
Im i sik tumas, orait, yu brinim tok.
Toki m gut, mipela nokan kilim ol, kalabus dasol, nau salim ol iko long
Astralia, na weitim pait I pinis.
WOK BILOG GAVMAN. I GAT PEI.

The message was written on a piece of paper I discovered in a box belonging to my father. I was cleaning out his possessions after he died and it was clearly a document that had originated during the Second World War. It was accompanied by two drawings. The first of these showed a wounded Japanese soldier slumped under a tree. A New Guinea highlander native peers around the tree at him. The second illustration shows the highlander, holding the piece of paper, leading three Australian soldiers through the jungle. One the other side of the piece of paper is a message written in Japanese.

Here is a literal translation of the Tok Pisin message completed by Philip Aratiso, a speaker of New Guinea Tok Pisin:

GOVERNMENT'S MESSAGE
If you find some Japanese who refuse to fight, you give them this letter. If he is able to walk and come on time you (plural) must look for our soldiers. If he is very sick, OK, you bring the message.
Tell them clearly that we cannot kill them but (we will) take them as prisoners only and send them to Australia, and (they will) wait for the war to end.
GOVERNMENT'S WORK (JOB) HAS A WAGE (REWARD)

The message, a relic from the jungle warfare in New Guinea during the Second World War, was intended for New Guinea Highlanders who frequently came across sick or wounded Japanese soldiers. How successful it was, and whether any of these natives were actually literate is doubtful.

The sample shows how far English travelled as it mutated into Talk Pisin. Although there are vestiges of the original language in sounds, words and structure, the new language is largely incomprehensible to native speakers of English.

Linguistic diversity among native speakers

The anecdotes in the preceding section illustrate the fact that, just like living organisms, languages transform themselves and mutate as they spread across the globe – witness the astonishing diversity of accents, dialects and forms of vocabulary across relatively small geographical areas in tiny England. Travel north, cross the border into Scotland and you will find many speakers of the language who are barely comprehensible to speakers of other dialects.

In England, in addition to geographical variations, there are also social class differences in pronunciation, vocabulary and grammar. Class distinctions in the way that people speak have provided novelists and playwrights with themes for many years. Perhaps the best known example is George Bernard Shaw's *Pygmalion* (later turned into the musical and a film, *My Fair Lady*) in which a professor of phonetics bets that he can transform the language of a working class girl and pass her off as a member of the upper class. (It was also Shaw who said that it was impossible for an Englishman to open his mouth without making some other Englishman despise him.)

In the 1950s, class-based distinctions in speech were captured by A.S. Ross (cited in Crystal, 1997a), who coined the terms 'U' and 'non-U'. U stood for 'upper class', non-U stood for the rest of the population. Here are some of the lexical differences of both classes as proposed by Ross:

U	non-U
have a bath	take a bath
luncheon	dinner
sick	ill
jam	preserve
wireless	radio
napkin	serviette
rich	wealthy
vegetables	greens

More recently, Fox (2004) has reported on her investigation into class-based linguistic differences in England. These exist in the three linguistics systems that we have looked at in this book, the phonological, the lexical and the grammatical, and they reveal that the binary U/non-U distinction is a gross oversimplification. Fox claims to have a linguistic basis for identifying working, upper-working, lower-middle, middle-middle, upper-middle, and upper classes.

Lexically, she suggests that there are seven words that can unerringly place a person in their social class. These are 'pardon', 'toilet', 'serviette', 'dinner', 'settee', 'lounge' and 'sweet'. Here's what she has to say about 'pardon':

This word is the most notorious pet hate of the upper and upper-middle classes. Jilly Cooper recalls overhearing her son telling a friend 'Mummy says that "pardon" is a much worse word than "fuck"'. He was quite right:

to the upper and upper-middles, using such an unmistakably lower-class term would be worse than swearing. Some even refer to lower-middle class suburbs as 'Pardonia'. Here is a good class-test you can try: when talking to an English person, deliberately say something too quietly for them to hear you properly. A lower-middle or middle-middle person will say 'Pardon?'; and upper-middle will say 'Sorry?' (or perhaps 'Sorry – what?' or 'What – sorry?'); but an upper-class and a working-class person will both just say 'What?' The working class person may drop the 't' – 'Wha'?' – but this will be the only difference. Some upper-working-class people with middle-class aspirations may say 'pardon', in a misguided attempt to sound posh. (Fox, 2004: 76)

Not surprisingly, global distance has also affected varieties of English. Canadian English is different from American English, although the differences are not as marked as those between Canadian English and New Zealand English. Surprisingly, however, the differences are not as pronounced as one might expect given the distances involved, and we have to assume that these varieties of English emerged at a time when transportation enabled readier contact between speakers of different varieties. Although some regional variations are evident across countries as vast as Canada and Australia, these differences are minimal.

A great deal has been written about the differences between the two systems that dominate international English: American English and British English, and there has been much conjecture as to the origin of these differences. Some linguists believe that most American dialects represent a kinds of 'fossilized' Shakespearean English, and that the 'darker', 'richer' tones of American English reflect the more 'macho' ethos of the younger society.

Burgess (1992: 225), writing about differences in the sound systems of both languages adduces examples such as the following:

Another highly noticeable difference between British and American usage is to be found in words like 'do' and 'dew'. The semi-vowel /j/ makes one different from another in most varieties of British English – /du:/ versus /dju:/. In America there has been a merger. The /j/ after labials and velars so that 'music' and 'cute' are pronounced in the British manner, but initial dental sounds /t/, /d/, /n/ permit the loss of the semi-vowel. Americans sing toons and eat stu while reading Toosday's noospaper with doo reserve. In Britain there is a certain dubiety about whether to wear a suit or a soot, or string a lute or a loot. America shows no such dubiety.

Another area of evident difference is that of vocabulary. Americans walk on 'sidewalks' not 'pavements'. They don't go to the 'toilet', 'lavatory' or 'loo', they visit the 'rest room' or the 'wash room' or the 'men's/ladies' room'. And they ascend in 'elevators' rather than 'lifts'. Most differences such as these are innocuous enough, but not all are benign. According to Burgess:

> British hearers of the song 'Walking my Baby Back Home' were uncomfortable with the line 'I get her powder all over my vest', seeing the latter as an undershirt when it was merely a waistcoat. 'Knickers' has a powerful erotic charge for the British, but the word, coming from the American 'knickerbockers', is quite suitable for what one wears on a Florida golf course. 'Pecker' as in 'Keep your pecker up', is a dangerous expression for a British visitor to the United States to use, since pecker is a penis. And the 'knock someone up', meaning in Britain to awaken, is in American to impregnate. Sex often makes language a minefield, and Anglophones visiting France who use *baiser* meaning 'to kiss' frequently discover. (Burgess, 1992: 229)

The other obvious difference between British and American English is that of spelling. 'Centre', becomes 'center', 'programme' loses its last two letters to be rendered as 'program'. 'Behaviour' becomes 'behavior'. Although the great majority of these differences are breathtakingly trivial, the two dominant varieties generate irritation at best and outrage, at worst on both sides of the Atlantic. 'Get your hands (or your tongue) off our language', cry the English. 'We're just cleaning up the mess you made', retort their transatlantic cousins. So which variety is superior? Well, as a speaker of a variety that is neither British nor American, the answer is neither. The differences only become a problem when they stand in the way of effective communication. (Which, on occasion, they do, as witnessed by the jibe that the two nations are divided by a common language.)

In addition to American English, there are several other variations that have gone their own way as they and the countries to which they belong have drifted away from the motherland. The best known of these are Canadian, New Zealand, Australian and South African English, each of which has its own peculiarities of vocabulary and pronunciation which, at their most extreme, render them incomprehensible to speakers of the mother tongue, a fact which has given rise, both to mutual irritation and humor. Here is an example of the latter:

A group of English cabinet makers were in Australia looking for interesting timbers. At a timber mill in Victoria they were inspecting some newly sawn timbers and asking for information.

Now this, said the Australian, *is hardwood, and it's used for makin' kegs for beer.*

He means barrels for ale, a posh voice announced from the back of the group.

And this one is hard, hardwood, and it's used for makin' coffins for stiffs.

He means caskets for corpses, said the posh voice at the back.

The Aussie let the remark pass and pointed to a third example of local timber.

And this one is hard, hard, hardwood and it's used for makin' piles for piers. And for the benefit of the bloke up the back, I don't mean haemorrhoids for aristocrats.

Language death

As I mentioned at the beginning of this chapter, one phenomenon that has been written about extensively by anthropologists and linguists is the propensity of dominant languages to gobble up smaller ones. And one of the most omnivorous of killer languages is English. In the course of considering the future of language then, we should spare some thought for languages that have no future.

Making estimates of the number of languages still in existence is no easy matter. In fact, it is just about as difficult as predicting the future. The consensus seems to be that there are currently around 6,000 languages. Experts seem convinced that about half of these will die in the next 100 years. Of the 6,000 languages, less than 300 are spoken by more than one million people, the critical mass for long-term survival.

Does this matter? I think that it matters desperately. Languages are the most significant manifestation of the cultures that gave them birth, and the death of a language signifies the death of the culture. As a species, we are impoverished by the death of each and every language. Linguistic and cultural diversity are as significant for the survival of the species as physiological and biological diversity. The alarms that have been ringing over the dangers to diversity of human cloning should be ringing just as loudly for linguistic and cultural cloning.

It has been claimed that the global spread of English represents a form of linguistic imperialism. This is a controversial issue, but there is some evidence to support the notion that the spread of English is symptomatic of economic and cultural imperialism. Multinational corporations in numerous parts of the world are mandating English as the official corporate language for reasons of control. Head office needs to know what is being discussed and what policy directions are being taken by regional offices. The only way to do this effectively is to insist that all communication happens in a language that those at head office understand. Increasingly, that language is English. The 'English as the official language of the corporation' policy is given teeth through promotion and preferment for those who achieve high levels of competence in the language.

Summary and conclusion

In this chapter, I looked at the emergence of English as a global language and the diversification of English amongst native speakers in different parts of the world. I also looked at language variation, and the ways in which languages evolve from one form to another through processes of pidginization and creolization. In the final section of the chapter, I looked briefly at the demise of certain languages as they fall victim to globalization and the dominance of majority languages such as English, Chinese and Spanish.

The main points covered in the chapter include the following:

- Although not completely unchallenged, English has emerged as the language of global communication
- As English has become a tool for communicating in diverse contexts around the world, it has fragmented into a wide range of dialects, some of which are approaching mutual incomprehensibility
- Language variation reflects differences of geographical location, education and class
- Numerous languages are under threat from the regional and global spread of languages such as English and Mandarin Chinese.

Questions and tasks

1 Carry out a websearch activity and find how many speakers there are of the following languages.

Language   *As a first language*   *As a second language*
British English
American English
Mandarin (Chinese)
Spanish
Hindi

2 Brainstorm and come up with your own list of differences between British and American English. Which of these are likely to cause embarrassment or difficulty to speakers of the other variety?

Further reading

Crystal, D. (1997) *English as a Global Language* (Cambridge: Cambridge University Press).
A readable and widely cited account of the emergence of English as a global language.

Graddol, D. (1997) *The Future of english* (London: British Council).
Although this survey was conducted some years ago now, it contains important and useful data about the status of English as a global language.

Postscript

As I said in the introduction, language is the stuff that surrounds us. Many of us spend a great deal of our lives listening, speaking, reading, and, with the advent of the Internet, writing. Despite this, most of us remain ignorant (blissfully or otherwise) of this phenomenon that defines us as humans – language. I hope that having made it this far, you are now somewhat more enlightened on the nature of the subject, and that you have renewed respect for yourself on the significance of your own achievement in mastering your mother tongue – even though you had very little choice in the matter!

A major theme of this book is that while meaning is central to language, 'meaning' itself does not constitute a linguistic system. Why is this so? I have hinted at an answer to this question at various points. In Chapter 1, we saw that systems are complex wholes, sets of connected things or parts, organized bodies of entities. The problem for language is that as far as meaning is concerned, the connections are made in the mind. While we can't know what the future might bring, at present, the largest linguistic unit of analysis is the sentence. As an applied linguist, I may well be in the minority in this view, but I can take comfort in the fact that I am not alone.

> Of course, this is not to say that there are no 'larger' linguistic objects which are worth studying. Such larger objects as *conversations, discourse, stories* and *texts* are, without doubt, structured, and, indeed, research into these areas has often assumed that some notion of 'grammar' is applicable to them. This may be so, but we believe that any such 'grammar' will have a very different form ... and will have to take account of a wide range of factors which extend beyond the knowledge of language. (Radford *et al.* 1999: 279)

There are of course exceptions. We have already looked at formulaic language and certain adjacency pairs – a greeting demands a greeting in reply, so in a sense, these fit the definition of a system. However, even here things are far from straightforward.

> Greetings and introductions are such an awkward business for the English. The problem has become particularly acute since the decline of 'How do

you do?' as the standard, all purpose greeting. The 'How do you do?' greeting – where the correct response is not to answer the question, but to repeat it back, 'How do you do?' like an echo of a well-trained parrot – is still in use in upper-class and upper-middle circles, but the rest are left floundering, never knowing quite what to say. (Fox, 2004: 37)

The simple fact is that many if not most utterances can be followed by practically any other, and usually, with a little ingenuity, we can make a connection. The operative word here is 'make' or 'create'. Creating the connection occurs, not on the page but in the mind.

Take the utterance *John's flight arrives at one*. The response, *So does ours* is both cohesive (utterance and response contain linguistic connectives) and coherent (we instantly recognize them as being 'on about' the same thing. However, consider the following comment and response:

A: *John's flight arrives at one.*
B: *I work at HappyMart.*

Here, there are no overt linguistic connectors. However, if we recognize A's utterance as a request, *John's flight arrives at one. Can you pick him up*. And B's as an excuse for not being able to comply with the request. *I work at HappyMart and can't get off till three.* We can establish a functional connection.

Here is a more problematic pairing.

A: *John's flight arrives at one.*
B: *The Pope died yesterday.*

Although it demands a greater degree of ingenuity, we can still create a connection.

A: *John is flying to Rome to be there for the passing of the Pope. His flight arrives at one.*
B: *Hmm the Pope died yesterday. He'll be disappointed.*

While I have generally avoided invented examples in this book, the ones above do illustrate the point that connectivity, or, as I've called it, coherence, exists in the mind. The words themselves provide signposts to meaning, they do not constitute the meanings between the speakers.

*   *   *   *   *

This book has been about a thing called language. Not only does language define us as humans, it also provides many of us with a livelihood. Have you ever paused to consider how many people make their living from crafting spoken and written language? Novelists and actors do of course. But then there is an almost endless list of others who do very well through creating and manipulating language in order to provide information, sell you things, and move you spiritually or emotionally in some way: journalists, politicians, songwriters, scriptwriters, poets, lawyers, academics, speechwriters, admen, secretaries, newsreaders, authors of instructional manuals, translators, designers . . . The list goes on and on. In my own case, I have been a newspaper columnist, speechwriter (for the Thai Minister for Education among others, no less), author of books on language and language learning, and writer of textbooks for learning English as a foreign language.

So, you'd like to try your hand at writing, but don't know where to start? You'd like to share your ideas, or move people with the limpidity of your prose or even verse. But you just don't know how to get that finger to the keyboard? There is only one way to start, and that's by writing. Just as we learn to talk by talking, we learn to write by writing. And, as with the development of most skills, a little practice carried out consistently over a period of time will do more to hone your skills than a frenzied forty-eight hours of writing followed by months of inactivity. Sure, it's good to get guidance and help. Just don't fill your shelves with books on how to do it. If these people could, they would. If they're making millions from the writing trade, why should they cut you in?

I try to write 1,000 words a day. I do this regardless of where I am and what my other commitments are that day. Those 1,000 words are my linguistic treadmill. My target used to be 2,000 words a day, but I'm slowing up in my old age! Often many of those 1,000 words are subsequently discarded, but that doesn't matter. What counts is getting those words down in the first place. So, if you want to be a writer, the only advice I have to give you is – write. Set yourself a daily word limit and try to meet that limit regardless of what else you have to do.

That reminds me that I had better get on with it. It's seven-thirty, almost time to go to my day job, and I have only written 700 words!

Key figures

In this section, I have provided a 'potted' biography of some of the key figures in the field of language study and linguistic analysis. It is a highly selective and personal list, and makes no attempt to be exhaustive. I have included the figures that have had a significant influence on my own thinking. I have also highlighted those aspects of their work that have influenced the ideas presented in this book.

I would like to apologise in advance to anyone, living or dead, who feels they should have been included but were not. If you are interested in obtaining more detailed information on key figures in the field, I recommend the following:

Joseph, J., N. Love and T. Taylor (2001) *Landmarks in Linguistic Thought II. The Western Tradition in the Twentieth Century* (London: Routledge).

John Austin (1911–60)

Austin was a philosopher of language who changed the way we think about language. His output was not prolific, and he died relatively young. However, his influence has been considerable.

Linguistic philosophy places itself within philosophy rather than linguistics, although the boundaries are blurred. The same can be said for scholars who see themselves as anthropologists or sociologists rather than linguists. This highlights the hybrid nature of linguistics and the fact that the discipline draws nourishment from numerous other academic fields of inquiry. Philosophers of language have made significant contributions to how language is used to create and convey meaning. Insights and understanding from these scholars have informed many of the ideas presented in this book.

In 1962 a little book called *How to Do Things with Words* was published. This slim volume, which grew out of a series of lectures given by Austin, had a remarkable impact on the field, and its effects are still being felt today. Austin's argument was deceptively simple: that whenever we say something, we are also performing an action. Thus, when a preacher or some other suitably qualified individual utters the words *I pronounce you man and wife* he is not reporting a fact, he is performing an act – in this case the act of marriage. Acts such as these have no truth value. It would make no sense for someone to leap up and say *No you don't!*

Austin pointed out that there are three potentially different acts 'packaged' into any given utterance. The first is the locutionary act, which is the surface meaning of the utterance. *There's a big black dog at the back door* is a statement about two entities – a dog and a door and their proximity to each other.

According to Austin, however, we need to consider two other aspects of the utterance: what the speaker intended to achieve in making the statement, and how the listener interpreted the utterance. Was the speaker trying to warn the other person, to direct him or her to open the door, to order him or her to keep the door firmly closed? Austin called the speaker's intention the illocutionary act. The third dimension that needs to be considered is the interpretation of the utterance by the listener. Austin labelled this the perlocutionary act.

Leonard Bloomfield (1887–1949)

Leonard Bloomfield is considered to be one of the founding fathers of modern linguistics. His book, *Language*, published in 1933 is a seminal text. Like several other key figures in the field, he was an anthropologist by training. In order to study Native American cultures, it was necessary for him to learn the languages of these people. His approach to language analysis grew out of his experience in learning and documenting the Algonquian language.

Bloomfield found that the traditional tools of linguistic description and analysis that developed for analysing classical languages were inadequate for describing Native American languages, and so he developed his own – an approach that became known as structural linguistics. Rather than using the grammatical categories that had evolved for the analysis of classical languages, structuralists tried to analyse each new language in its own terms, maintaining that as each language is basically different, each demands its own form of structural analysis. They isolated significant linguistic structures and patterns which were segmented into smaller and smaller constituents. These were considered to be the basic building blocks of the language.

Bloomfield also had a great deal to say about how languages were learned. His approach to linguistic description and analysis fitted well with behaviourism, the dominant theory of learning at the time. The language teaching method known as audiolingualism represented a marriage of behaviourist psychology and structural linguistics. As a structuralist, Bloomfield was more interested in form than meaning, and this is reflected in audiolingualism which seeks to focus on inculcating language patterns rather than developing extensive vocabulary knowledge.

Noam Chomsky (1928–)

To the non-specialist, Chomsky is almost certainly the most celebrated figure in the field of linguistics. This has as much to do with his political views as his linguistic theory. He sprang to prominence as a political activist in the 1960s when he was a vociferous opponent of the Vietnam War. Since then he has continued to speak out against United States government policy and military action in different parts of the world.

Chomsky's model is known as transformational-generative grammar. The aim of TG was to devise a set of rules that would generate all grammatical but no ungrammatical utterances in the language. Chomsky famously and contro-versially argued that syntactic form and communicative meaning were totally separate. His celebrated sentence *Colorless green ideas sleep furiously* was intended to illustrate this assertion. Interestingly, Chomsky was a student of Zellig Harris, who first developed the concepts upon which Chomsky based his theory of language. Harris, in contrast to Chomsky, argued that form and meaning were inseparable.

Academically, Chomsky first came to prominence with a brilliant critique of B.F. Skinner's book *Verbal Behavior*, which proposed that language acqui-sition occurred through a process of stimulus and response. Chomsky showed that language acquisition and use cannot be accounted for as a process of habit formation.

Chomsky's theory gave rise to spin-off theories and models, including the notion that language is an inherited characteristic, and the concept of univer-sal grammar (UG). UG scholars believe that all human languages are based on a limited set of rules and principles that are shared by all languages.

David Crystal (1941–)

Readers who are familiar with the field may think it strange that I have put David Crystal on this list. Unlike most other members of the list, he is prob-ably not considered a seminal figure in the field. He has not created models or theories that have changed the way we think about linguistic theory and analy-sis. However, more than any other linguist in recent times, he has placed language and linguistics in the public eye. He has taken the theoretical and empirical output of others and made it accessible to the non-specialist.

Crystal was born in 1941, and spent his early years in Wales, before being educated in Liverpool and London. He taught in Wales before taking up a lecturership at the University of Reading where he eventually became a Professor. Here, he made significant contributions, particularly in the branches of speech and hearing science, before moving out of academia to work as a writer, lecturer and consultant.

J.R. Firth (1890–1960)

Firth is one of the founders of the modern 'British' tradition in linguistics which, loosely interpreted, is the tradition followed in this book. In fact, he occupied the very first Chair of General Linguistics in Britain at what is now London University's School of Oriental and African Studies. He was one of the first to recognize the potential of English to emerge as a global language, and he influenced many teachers and researchers, most notably M.A.K. Halliday (see below) who used Firth's ideas as the basis of his own model of language, which was to become known as systemic-functional linguistics.

Firth's approach to language description and analysis stood in stark contrast to the ideas being developed in North America by Leonard Bloomfield. Although, in terms of language acquisition both were influenced by the prevailing behaviourist tradition, Bloomfield was a structuralist who rejected the notion that form and meaning could be systematically related. Firth took a very different stance, arguing that meaning and context were fundamental to the study of language and should form the point of departure for linguistic analysis. He was influenced by the work of the anthropologist Malinowski (see below) from whom he borrowed the phrase 'context of situation'. (This term was subsequently embraced by Halliday as he began his own theories.)

Firth also bequeathed to linguistics the notion that all linguistic systems and subsystems are systematically interrelated. The position that I take in this book is thus very much a Firthian one. In his later work, he devoted considerable attention to the sound system, exploring the interrelationships between sound, meaning and context. The concepts and tools he developed for prosodic analysis were taken up by subsequent scholars and have become fundamentally important to phonology.

Michael Halliday (1925–)

Halliday is widely considered to be one of the most important linguists in the world today, although his influence is more pronounced in England, where he grew up, and Australia, where he has lived and worked for the last thirty years, than in North America.

Halliday began his academic life as a scholar of Chinese language and literature. At the conclusion of the Second World War, he studied in China at Peking and Lingnan Universities before returning to England to complete his PhD in Chinese linguistics at the University of Cambridge.

Halliday was influenced by his teacher J.R. Firth as well as by the Prague School of linguistics. He developed a model of language description and analysis known as systemic-functional linguistics. This approach attempted to establish a relationship between language form and language function. (One of Halliday's most celebrated quotes is *Language is what language does*.) It therefore contrasts with work being carried out in North America by Chomsky and others which sought to separate form and function.

Halliday published a seminal account of child language development based on a case study of his own child, Nigel. The study gave him an opportunity to develop and refine his model of systemic functional linguistics. As I have already indicated, this model is predicated on the assumption that systematic relationships exist between grammatical form and the communicative functions, and that the linguist's task is to tease out these relationships. The term 'systemic functional linguistics' captures the essence of the model. Language consists of interlocking subsystems which enable us to communicate meanings of different kinds. In his study of child language development, Halliday showed how a child's language evolves from a primitive 'protolanguage' into the fully-fledged form.

Halliday's model has been adapted and modified in ways that he would not necessarily embrace. Particularly influential in both first and second language education has been the 'genre' school, which has used insights from systemic-functional linguistics to develop a wide range of approaches to language teaching and assessment.

Zellig Harris (1909–92)

Harris, an immigrant from what is now Ukraine, came to the United States with his family at a young age. He was a brilliant linguist who completed his Ph.D. at the age of 25, by which time he had already published several important works. At the age of 35, he founded the linguistics department at the University of Pennsylvania, the first such department in North America. He spoke a wide range of languages, and was also a mathematician. Mathematics was to play an important part in his approach to linguistic analysis.

Harris made important contributions to all areas of linguistics from phonology, to morphology to syntax. He recognized the interconnections between the various linguistic subsystems and rejected the prevailing approach to linguistic analysis, which was that each subsystem should be investigated separately.

Interestingly, although he is considered one of the first linguists to see language in transformational and generative terms, he did not, as did later transformational-generative linguists such as Chomsky (who was a student of Harris), reject any connection between form and meaning: quite the opposite, in fact. Harris argued that form and meaning were two sides of the same coin. His interest in the relationship between language and social context led, in 1952, to a seminal paper published in the journal *Language* called 'Discourse Analysis'. With this paper, a new subdiscipline within in linguistics was born.

Shirly Brice Heath (1939–)

Shirly Brice Heath is an anthropologist, linguist, and social historian. She currently serves as Professor of Anthropology and Education at Brown University in the United States, having spent many years as Professor of English at Stanford. Most of her work has been carried out in the areas of oral and written language, youth development, race relations, and organizational learning, although more recently she has become more interested in arts education and language, and multi-media language development among older learners.

She is probably best known for using techniques from anthropology to study language learning and use in socially and culturally diverse contexts in the United States. The most important research was an investigation into the language development of black and white working class children in rural communities in the United States. Carried out over a ten-year period, her research showed what parents and teachers did to help children develop the language skills they need in order to succeed educationally. Her book, *Ways with Words*, in which she documents her research, has become a classic. It (somewhat controversially) argued that poor black communities provided a richer linguistic environment for their children to develop speaking and interactional skills than did their counterpart white communities.

Heath involved herself personally in the communities she studied, helping families with chores around the house and attending church and other social events. She based her research conclusions on observation and detailed qualitative analysis of conversations in the home and at school.

Roman Jakobson (1896–1982)

Jakobson was a Russian linguist who is widely considered one of the most important linguists of the twentieth century because of his research into the structural analysis of language. Influenced by Ferdinand de Saussure (see below), Jakobson sought to analyse the ways in which language structure serves communicative functional needs.

Following the Russian Revolution, he moved from Russia to Prague where he became one of the founders of the 'Prague School'. His emphasis on the role of context and the importance of form-function relationships marks him as one of the founding fathers of functional linguistics. However, he also influenced developments in transformation-generative linguistics with his work on linguistic universals. (Researchers in the field of linguistic universals seek to identify principles that are true for all languages such as 'All languages have nouns and verbs.')

William Labov (1927–)

Labov came to linguistics after beginning a career as an industrial chemist. (It seems that linguistics was a second career choice for many of the most influential figures in the field.) He spent most of his academic life at the University of Pennsylvania in the United States where he studied sociolinguistics and dialectology. One of his central theses is that people use certain speech features to affiliate with and mark their membership of particular social groups.

Labov is probably best known for his investigations into the relationship between race, class and dialect. In 1966, he published a study into the social stratification of English in New York City using, amongst other informants, shop assistants at Macy's Department Store. This work was of interest as much for the methods that Labov used to elicit speech samples from his informants as it was for the results. Labov is also known for his study into the speech of African Americans. He showed that Black Vernacular English (BVE, later changed to AAVE) was just as linguistically sophisticated as standard American English.

Labov's work is significant for this volume because of the insights it provides into the importance of context. He challenged the idea that there is a single 'ideal' model underlying any given language, and showed that variation in language use is systematic and is determined by context. This context can be situational or linguistic. Variety exists between different social and racial groups. It also exists within individuals. We change the way we speak according to the company we keep.

Bronislaw Malinowski (1884–1942)

Malinowski was born in what is now Poland, where he trained as a mathematician and scientist before developing an interest in anthropology. During the First World War, he studied primitive tribes in New Guinea and the South Pacific. After the War, he returned to Europe where he completed a doctorate in anthropology at the London School of Economics.

Malinowski is widely regarded as one of the most important anthropologists of the twentieth century. He pioneered techniques in ethnographic field work, such as participant observation, which are widely used today. Prior to Malinowski, anthropologists tended to keep their distance from their subjects, but Malinowski stressed the importance of developing an insider's perspective on the culture they were investigation.

Although not a linguist himself, Malinowski's perspectives and methods of investigation had a profound influence on many linguistic anthropologists who used his techniques, such as participant observation, to investigate language development and use within the cultural contexts in which they occurred.

Kenneth Pike (1912–2000)

Kenneth Pike was an American linguist, anthropologist and second language educator who studied under the great linguistic anthropologist Edward Sapir (see below). He spent most of his academic life at the University of Michigan, where he served as Professor of Linguistics and Director of the English Language Institute.

Pike's two major contributions to linguistics were his concepts of 'etic' and 'emic' analysis, and the theory of tagmemics. Pike applied the 'etic'/'emic' distinction to the study of speech sounds. An 'etic' perspective seeks to present an objective inventory of sounds. An 'emic' perspective distinguishes between sounds as they affect meaning (thus, the distinction between phon*etics* and phon*emics*). Pike argued that only 'insiders' – that is, native speakers – were in a position to make 'emic' judgements as these are essentially subjective. A native speaker knows instinctively which sound differences to ignore as they do not affect meaning, and which must be attended to. More recently, the concepts have been applied by cultural and anthropological linguists who distinguish between 'etic' (outside) and 'emic' (insider) description and analysis of societies and cultures.

Subsequent to his study of sounds, Pike sought to apply the etic/emic distinction to the study of grammar. While most descriptive grammarians took an 'etic' perspective, attempting to generate 'objective', context-free descriptions, 'etic' descriptions would attempt to account for form-function relationships and analyse how language functions in communicative contexts. In effect, he was one of the principal architects attempting to create a grammar of discourse by showing how, just as words are made up of sounds, and sentences are made up of words, so too is discourse constructed of sentences. (This is what I referred to in the book as the 'super sentence' approach to discourse analysis.)

Steven Pinker (1954–)

Anyone who can make the story of language acquisition read like a thriller deserves accolades, and Steven Pinker has had plenty of those. To my knowledge, he is the only linguist to have made it onto the *Time* list of the top 100 'people of the year'. Like some of the best American linguists, Pinker was a Canadian first. He grew up in Montreal, completing his bachelor's degree in psychology at McGill University, and then completed a doctorate in psychology at Harvard University. A disciple of Chomsky, Pinker worked at the Massachusetts Institute of Technology where Chomsky has held court for many years, before taking up a Chair in Psychology at Harvard University.

Pinker has achieved the extraordinary feat of making Chomsky's theory (or theories – when I was an undergraduate we used to joke that it didn't matter if you missed the latest theory of transformational grammar – there would be another one along any minute) comprehensible to non-linguists. His best known book is *The Language Instinct*, which sets out his theory of language acquisition. Pinker believes that language is a defining characteristic of humans, that the predisposition to language is part of our genetic code, built into our DNA in the same way as the ability to spin webs is built into the genetic code of spiders, and the ability to find pollen and bring it back to the hive is part of the genetic make-up of the bee.

Edward Sapir (1884–1939)

Sapir emigrated to the United States from Germany when he was a small child. His teacher Franz Boas was another German émigré. Both men were anthropological linguists whose main focus was the documentation of Native American languages.

Sapir's great contribution to linguistic thought lies in his linking of language and culture. While all languages share certain universal characteristics, there are aspects of language that are culturally specific. According to Sapir, the language and culture into which one is born shape the way one thinks. They create mental 'tracks' upon which our minds run. Sapir also argued that cultures sharing a language share a way of thinking, and that these ways of thinking constituted the psychology of the culture.

Ferdinand de Saussure (1857–1913)

Saussure, a Swiss/French academic, is widely regarded as the father of modern linguistics. However, had it not been for a group of enthusiastic students who collected and published his lectures, he may well have disappeared without trace.

Saussure introduced several key concepts into linguistics including *langue* and *parole* and the notion of syntagmatic and paradigmatic relationships in linguistic analysis. He pointed out that any word has a syntagmatic relationship with any other words that can follow it in a sentence, and a paradigmatic relationship that can replace it. In the sentence *The man yawned loudly*, *The* has a syntagmatic relationship with any word that can replace man (for example, woman, child, dog and so on) and a paradigmatic relationship with the indefinite article *a*.

Benjamin Lee Whorf (1897–1941)

Like many who have strayed into the world of language and stayed, Whorf began life as something else – a chemical engineer, to be exact. In fact, he continued to work as an engineer until his death at the comparatively early age of forty-four.

Along with Edward Sapir (see above), Whorf formulated the notion that that ability to make sense of the world is conditioned, if not determined, by the language that we speak. In his work as a fire-prevention officer for an insurance company, he was fascinated by the ways in which people constructed narrative accounts of their experiences of accidents caused by fires. These accounts said as much about the narrators and their cultural backgrounds as they did about the events themselves.

According to the strong version of the Sapir–Whorf hypothesis, we cannot see what we cannot name. Thus, the Hopi Indians, according to Whorf, have no conception of time because the Hopi language has no tenses or time expressions.

The notion that the way we talk conditions how we think, and, in fact, controls our perception of reality, has been hugely controversial. The linguistic determinism implicit in the Sapir–Whorf hypothesis has been largely discredited (are we REALLY incapable of seeing puce if our language lacks a label for that particular colour?), and is unfashionable these days. Nonetheless, it represents an important landmark in linguistic thought.

Ludwig Wittgenstein (1889–1951)

Wittgenstein was an extraordinary character who tried to live an ordinary life. He is widely regarded as one of the most important philosophers of the twentieth century. In 1929, he returned to Cambridge after an absence of many years. Among the celebrities who met him was John Maynard Keynes, himself regarded by many as one of the greatest economists of the century, who remarked to his wife, 'Well, God has arrived. I met him on the 5.15 train.'

Wittgenstein was born in Vienna into one of the wealthiest and best connected families in the Austrio-Hungarian Empire. He trained initially as an engineer, and travelled to England to pursue his engineering studies. There he fell under the spell of the philosophers Bertrand Russell and G.E. Moore, and switched his allegiance to philosophy. During the First World War, he fought with distinction against the Russians and the Italians, was decorated for bravery, and spent time as a prisoner of war in Italy.

Although a considerable body of Wittgenstein's work now exists in published form, the only book on philosophy that was published in his lifetime was *Tractatus Logico-Philosophicus*, which appeared in 1921. This work was considered so important that, in 1929, he was given a Cambridge doctorate and a lectureship on the strength of it. His other major work, considered by some to be his most significant, was *Philosophical Investigations* which was published after his death.

For Wittgenstein, philosophical problems are basically linguistic in nature. A central feature of his theory is that language is essentially creative in that we are able to recombine familiar elements in new ways to express propositions that have never been expressed before. This creativity, or generativity as it came to be called by tranformational-generative grammarians, was a central plank in Noam Chomsky's theory of language (see above.)

Glossary

abstract noun: a noun that represents an abstract concept or quality such as *interest, beauty, hope*. Abstract nouns contrast with concrete nouns (*father, doorstop, iPod*) and are often derived from verbs or adjectives. For example: *arrive – arrival; empty – emptiness.*

active voice: A sentence or utterance in which the doer of the action is the subject of the sentence.
Example: *The author finally finished the book.*

adjacency pair: A pair of utterances in a conversation produced by different speakers that are functionally related or that commonly co-occur.
Example: A: *Wanna see a movie?* (offer)
B: *OK.* (accept)

adjective: A major word class whose members modify or define more clearly a noun or pronoun.

adverb: An important class of words that modify or qualify *verbs, adjectives* or other *adverbs.*

affix: A bound *morpheme* that is added to the beginning (prefix) or the end (suffix) of a word.
Examples: *de*stress; vapor*ize.*

agreement: A grammatical relationship between two elements in a sentence or clause.
Example: third person 's'. *I live in Hong Kong but my brother lives in New York.*

allophone: Variations in the pronunciation of individual sounds that do not signal differences in meaning (in contrast with *phonemes* which do signal differences in meaning).

anaphora (*anaphoric reference*): Within a text, the reference to a person, object, place or event, in which the second and subsequent references are marked by some form of pronominalization.
Example: *In my opinion, the greatest movie of all time is* Casablanca. *I've seen* it *at least fifteen times.*

antecedent: The first element in a cohesive tie.
Example: *Could you pass me the* red wine. *I haven't tried it yet.*

antonym: A word having the opposite meaning of another word.
Example: *Stop* is the antonym of *go.*

article: The **determiners** *the, a/an* preceding a noun or noun phrase. Articles are complex and they perform a number of important discourse functions such as indicating temporality and speaker attitude.

authenticity: Spoken and written texts used in language teaching that came about in the course of communication rather than being specially written for language teaching purposes.

back-channel: Ways in which a listener gives feedback to a speaker. The purpose of the feedback is to let the speaker know that he or she is being listened to and has been understood, and to encourage him or her to continue.
Example: A: *I went to see that new movie at the Cyberport Cinema* . . .
B: *Uh-huh.*
A: *. . . yesterday, and it was a waste of money.*

background knowledge: The knowledge of the world that the reader or listener utilizes in interpreting a piece of spoken or written discourse.

bilingualism: The ability to speak two languages fluently.

bottom-up processing: Decoding the smallest elements (phonemes or graphemes) first, and using these to decode and interpret words, clauses, sentences and whole texts.

bound morpheme: A morpheme that does not have its own existence but must be attached to another morpheme.

cataphora (*cataphoric reference*): Within a text, the use of pronominalization to refer to a person, object, place or event that has yet to be identified. For example: *It was on Hyndford Street in East Belfast, in a small terraced house that had belonged to* his *mother's family since she was nine, that* George Ivan Morrison *was brought into the world* . . . (Heylin, 2002:3)

clarification request: A negotiation of meaning strategy in which an interlocutor asks his or her conversational partner for a more explicit reformulation of what has just been said.
Example: A: *I don't feel too hot today.*
B: *Sorry? What do you mean by that, exactly?*

classroom discourse: The distinctive type of discourse that occurs in classrooms. Special features of classroom discourse include unequal opportunities to speak, the use of display questions and the provision of corrective feedback.
Example: (The teacher circulates around the room asking questions about train departure and arrival times based on a timetable that the students have.)
T: *Now . . . back to the timetable. Where do you catch the train? Where do you catch the train?* (She points to a student in the front row.)

S: *Keswick.*
T: *Yeah . . . Now what time . . . What time does the train leave?*
S: *Nine. Nine o'clock. Nine pm. Nine pm. Nine pm.*
T: (leans over a student and checks the timetable.) *OK. Depart nine am.*

clause: A major grammatical building block containing a main verb. Independent clauses can stand alone as sentence in their own right. Dependent clauses, marked by *conjunctions*, must be attached to a main verb.
Example: *If I get home in time* (dependent clause), *I will give him a call* (independent clause).

cleft structure: A sentence in which the normal Subject + Verb + Object pattern is recast to give greater prominence to a particular element within the structure.
Example: *Catherine plays tennis.*
            It's tennis that Catherine plays. (Emphasizes that Catherine plays tennis not hockey or basketball.)
            It's Catherine who plays tennis. (Emphasizes that Catherine, not Sophie or Maria who plays tennis.)

coherence: The extent to which discourse is perceived to 'hang together' rather than being a set of unrelated sentences of utterances. Coherence is a psycholinguistic rather than a linguistic phenomenon. In other words, it exists in the mind of the listener or reader rather than on the page.

cohesion: Linguistic links existing between clauses and sentences that mark various types of relationships.

collocation: A form of lexical cohesion in which two or more words are related by virtue of belonging to the same semantic field.

communicative competence: The ability to use language effectively to communicate in particular contexts and for particular purposes. There are four dimensions to communicative competence: grammatical competence, sociolinguistic competence, discourse competence, and strategic competence.

complement: That part of a clause which provides additional information or defines the subject or object of a clause.

compound word: A word which is constructed from other words. Compound words usually begin life as two disconnected words (*first class*), then become joined by a hyphen (*first-hand*) and then merge into a single word (*aircraft*).

comprehension: Processes through which listeners and readers make sense of spoken and written texts.

comprehension check: A strategy used by a speaker to see whether the listener has understood correctly.

Example: A: *You need to fold the masking tape along the edge of the card-board. Know what I mean?*
B: *I think so.*

concordancing: Lexical analysis that draws on computerized databases of authentic language (called *corpora*) to identify patterns, principles, regularities and associations between words that would not be readily apparent from a casual inspection of language samples.

concrete noun: A noun describing a physical entity (*Jack, mountains, gold*). Concrete nouns contrast with **abstract nouns**.

conditional clause: A **dependent clause** expressing a condition and marked by a conjunction such as *if* or *unless*. There are three types of conditional clause which mark different types of attitudinal and temporal meanings.
Examples: *If you arrive on time, they'll let you in.*
If you arrived on time, they'd let you in.
If you had arrived on time, they'd have let you in.

confirmation request: A strategy used by listeners to confirm that what they think they heard is correct.
Example: A: *I saw a bank robbery a couple of weeks ago.*
B: *A robbery?*

conjunction: A word or a phrase such as *however, in addition, on the other hand*, that makes explicit the logical relationships between the ideas in two different sentences of clauses. There are four types of logical relationship in English: additive (marked by conjunctions such as *and* and *also*); adversative (marked by words such as *but* and *however*); causal (marked by words such as *because*); and temporal (marked by conjunctions such as *firstly, then, next* and *finally*).

connotation: A meaning implied by a word that goes beyond its literal meaning.

constituent structure: When one linguistic element is made up of lower-order elements, we say they have a constituent structure. For example, the constituent structure of the word *watched* is the morphemes *watch* and *-ed*.

content word: A word that refers to a thing, quality, state action or event. (Content words contrast with function words.) In the following example, the content words are emboldened.
In the **afternoon**, *I* **played tennis** *with* **Geoff.**

context: The linguistic and experiential environments in which a piece of language occurs. The linguistic environment refers to the surrounding words, utterances and sentences. The experiential environment refers to the real-world context in which the piece of language occurs.

contrastive analysis: Procedures for identifying and comparing similarities and differences between the linguistic systems of different languages.

conversation: A piece of oral interaction between two or more speakers.

conversation(al) analysis: A type of analysis that aims to identify the principles and procedures that facilitate or impede effective communication in conversations. The main aim of conversational analysts is to answer the question: 'How do conversations work?'

cooperative principle: This was formulated by the linguistic philosopher Grice as a way of accounting for how people interpret discourse. There are four maxims to the principle: 'Be true; be brief; be relevant; be clear.'

coordination: The joining of two different ideas with a coordinating conjunction. Use of coordination signals that the ideas have the same status within the discourse. It contrasts with **subordination** in which the ideas have unequal status.

countable noun: A noun that has both a singular and plural form. Countable nouns contrast with **uncountable nouns**.

creole: A pidgin that has evolved into a language in its own right.

culture: The (often implicit) norms and rules and practices that govern the interactional and personal behaviour of groups and individuals.

declarative knowledge: Knowledge that can be stated (or 'declared') such as a grammatical rule.

decoding: The process of determining the meaning of words by sounding out the individual phonemes making up the word.

deductive learning: The process of learning in which one begins with rules and principles and then applies the rules to particular examples and instances.

definite article: The word *the* which precedes a noun or noun phrase. In discourse terms, the word signals that the speaker or writer assumes that the listener or reader knows the specific entity being referred to. For example, if the speaker says *I'll see you at the concert* he/she assumes that the listener knows which concert is being referred to.

deixis: Word that 'point' the listener or reader to particular entities in space or time.
Example: *Could you please put my coffee over* there?

demonstrative: The words *this, that, these, those*, which indicate the proximity of objects to the speaker. These words are also referred to as a *deixis*.

descriptive grammar: A grammar that sets out to describe the way people use language without prescribing what is correct or incorrect.

determiner: Words that modify nouns to limit their meaning. Common determiners in English include articles (*a/an, the*), demonstratives (*this, that, these, those*), possessives (*his, their*), and quantifiers (*some, much, many*). Determiners are important elements in cohesion.

dialect: A variety of language, usually marked by pronunciation and vocabulary, that is associated with geographical regions or social classes.

direct object: An object that is directly affected by the main verb in a sentence. Direct objects contrast with *indirect objects*. In the sentence *I gave the book to John, the book* is the direct object, and *John* is the indirect object. Switching the direct and indirect object (for example, changing the above sentence to *I gave John the book*) has the discourse function on making *John* not *the book* the focus of the utterance.

discourse: Any stretch of spoken or written language viewed within the communicative context in which it occurred.

discourse analysis: The systematic study of language in context. Discourse analysis is sometimes contrasted with *text analysis*, which focuses on analysing the formal properties of language. In this book, discourse analysis is used as a blanket term to cover both discourse and text analysis because it includes an analysis of linguistic as well as contextual features.

display questions: Questions to which the person posing the question already knows (or *thinks* he/she knows) the answer. Display questions are typical of classroom discourse.
Example: Teacher: *What's this?* (Holds up a pen.)
Student: *It's a pen.*
Teacher: *Very good. It's a pen.*

ellipsis: The omission of clauses, words or phrases that, strictly speaking, are required to make an utterance grammatical, but that can be recovered from the preceding utterance.
Example: A: *Are you busy?*
B: *Yes, I am.*
(Here, B omits *busy*, which can be recovered from A's question.)

end focus: The principle of placing *new information* at the end of the sentence. Examples: *I gave my girlfriend the chocolates* versus *I gave the chocolates to my girlfriend*. In the first sentence, the new information is what the speaker gave his girlfriend, whereas in the second sentence it is who got the chocolates.

error: A piece of speech or writing that deviates from native speaker usage.

ethnomethodology: A branch of sociology which is concerned with the analysis and interpretation of everyday spoken interaction.

exchange: A basic interactional pattern in classroom discourse consisting of three functional moves: an opening move (initiation), an answering move (response) and a follow-up move (feedback).

Example: Teacher: *What's today, Jose?*
Student: *The 24th.*
Teacher: *The 24th. Very good.*

existential subject: (also known as *empty* or *dummy subject*) Use of *there* or *it* in existential statements.
Examples: *There will be a storm later.*
It's surprising how much time you take to get ready.

exophoric reference: Referring expressions such as *he, this* and *here*, which point to entities and events in the world outside the text.

face-saving: An important principle underlying a great deal of interpersonal interaction is the need for interlocutors to save face. This is most commonly achieved by using indirect speech acts. (For example, saying *Are you doing anything this evening?* rather than *Would you like to come to the movies with me?*)

feedback: Providing information to speakers about something they have just said. Neutral feedback simply informs the speaker that their message has been received. It may be verbal (*Uh-huh*) or non-verbal, such as a nod of the head. Evaluative feedback tells the speaker whether the message has been positively or negatively received.

first language: An individual's native tongue.

fluency: The ability to read or write without undue hesitation.

function: Another name for *speech act*: that is, the things people do through language such as apologizing, complaining, instructing.

function word: A 'grammatical' rather than 'content' word, belonging to one of the closed word classes such as *determiners*, prepositions, pronouns, modals and conjunctions.

genre: A purposeful, socially constructed oral or written text such as a narrative, a casual conversation, a poem, a recipe or a description. Each genre has its own characteristic structure and grammatical forms that reflect its social purpose.

given/new: Any utterance or sentence can be said to contain given (or assumed) and new information. Given information is that which the speaker or writer assumes is already known to the interlocutor. New information, on the other hand, is assumed to be unknown. Given and new information are reflected in the way information is distributed in a sentence or utterance. (Generally speaking, the new information comes at the end of the sentence or utterance.)
Example: *The rat was eaten by the cat.* (Given: Something ate the rat. New: The cat did the eating.)

> *What the cat did was eat the rat.* (Given: The cat did something. New: The cat ate the rat.)

grammar: The specification of how words are formed and combined to enable the communication of meaning.

grammar-translation: A language teaching method based on grammatical analysis and the translation of sentences and texts to and from the learners' first and target languages.

grammatical metaphor: The process of turning actions into things.
Example: *They are* constructing *a new building next to our school which has increased the amount of noise in the area considerably*, which becomes *The* construction *of the new building next to our school has increased noise in the area considerably*.

grammar word: A word belonging to a closed grammatical class such as prepositions or articles. They are also called *function words* or structural words.

grapheme: The smallest meaningful unit in the writing system of a language.

homonym: Words that are spelled or pronounced the same, but have different meanings.
Examples: *Club* (a social institution, golfing implement).

homophone: A word that sounds the same as another word.
Example: *Hair, hare.*

hyponym: A word that is the subordinate of a more general word.
Example: *Rose* and *geranium* are hyponyms of *flower.*

ideational meaning: That aspect of a text that relates to information about objects, entities and states of affairs. In other words, ideational meaning has to do with content. It contrasts with interpersonal meaning, which has to do with the attitudes and feeling of a speaker or writer towards that content.

illocutionary force: The illocutionary force of an utterance is the function that a speaker intends to perform in producing that utterance. In many cases, the illocutionary force of an utterance can only be understood if we know the context in which the utterance occurs.
Example: The statement *There's a dog at the back door* could, depending on the context, be a description, a warning, an explanation, an invitation or numerous other functions.

immersion: An approach in which learners acquire a language by studying other subjects such as science, history or mathematics through that language. (The approach is also known as content-based instruction.)

indefinite article: The word *a/an* used before singular count nouns or noun phrases to refer to an entity that is either unknown or has not previously

been mentioned. Use of the indefinite article can indicate the attitude of the speaker or writer towards the entity.
Example: A: *Who's Chris Patten?*
B: *Oh, he's a former governor of Hong Kong.*

indirect object: A noun phrase that usually comes between the main verb and *direct object* in a sentence or utterance.
Example: *I gave* my boyfriend *a really cool t-shirt for his birthday.*

inductive learning: The process by which a learner arrives at rules and principles by studying examples and instances. (Inductive learning contrasts with deductive learning, in which the rules are spelled out and learners subsequently apply the rules to samples of language.)

information structure: The ordering of information within sentences and utterances according to assumptions made by the speaker or writer about the listener or hearer's state of knowledge and the content that the speaker or writer wishes to emphasize. (See also *given/new*.)

insertion sequence: A sequence of utterances separating an *adjacency pair*. In the following example, the offer/refusal is separated by a clarification question/response that constitutes the insertion sequence.
Example: A: *Want to see that new movie at the Odeon tonight?*
B: *What time's it on at?*
A: *Six.*
B: *Sorry. I can't get away from work by then.*

instantial relationship/meaning: A meaning or relationship between entities, events or states-of-affairs that only makes sense within the spoken or written context in which it occurs.

interaction: Verbal communication between two or more people.

interjection: Words interpolated into a conversation to indicate the listener's attitude towards what he or she is being told.
Examples: *damn, hurrah, cool.*

interlanguage: The language system of a second language learner the develops in the course of second language acquisition. As they become more and more proficient, learners pass through a series of interlanguages, each of which has its own system of rules with their own internal consistency, although they deviate from the target language.

interlocutor: A conversational participant.

interlocutor effect: The effect that participants in a conversation have on the current speaker.

International Phonetic Alphabet: A system and set of symbols for representing spoken language in written form.

interpersonal function/meaning: That aspect of an utterance that reflects the speaker's feelings and attitudes towards the topic of the utterance. Interpersonal meanings are marked by grammatical features such as modal verbs, and phonological features such as intonation.

intonation: Raising or lowering voice pitch to convey aspects of meaning. Intonation is one of the *suprasegmental* aspects of the pronunciation.

language awareness: A conscious understanding of the nature of language, its components and its role in human life.

language transfer: The effect of a learner's first language on the acquisition of a second language. Transfer can be positive, when the first and second language items are similar and the first language facilitates the acquisition of the second, or negative, when they differ, and the first language interferes with the acquisition of the second language.

lexeme: A word as an abstract concept having different formal realizations.

lexicon: All of the words in a language.

lexical: To do with the words in a language.

lexical cohesion: Lexical cohesion occurs when two or more content words in a text are related. The two major categories of lexical cohesion are reiteration and collocation.
    Examples: Reiteration: Technology *has greatly facilitated the development of* animation. *Prior to the advent of* technology, animation *was a slow and laborious process.*
            Collocation: *Our* garden *looks best in* spring. *By* summer, *the* flowers *are past their best.*

lexical density: The ratio of content words to grammar/function words in a text. Generally speaking, written texts have a higher lexical density than spoken texts.

lexical relationship: The relationship between content words in a text. (See also *lexical cohesion*.)

lexicology: The study of words.

linguistics: The systematic study of language. Linguistics is divided into a series of subdisciplines, including *phonetics*, *phonology*, *morphology*, *syntax*, *semantics* and *pragmatics*.

literacy: The ability to read and write a language.

locutionary aspect: The propositional meaning of an utterance.

locutionary force: The propositional (as opposed to functional or illocutionary) meaning of an utterance.

logical connectives: Conjunctions such as *therefore, however, in addition, firstly, and* and *but* that mark textual relationships such as causality, temporality, and adversity.

metaphor: Words used to describe things they do not physically resemble.

minimal pair: Two words in a language whose meaning is signalled by differences in a single vowel or consonant.
Example: *ship – sheep*.

modal verb: A closed set of verbs (*can, could, have to, may, might, must shall, should, will, would*) that express attitudes such as certainty, permission and possibility.

modality: That aspect of a sentence or utterance that reveals the attitude of the writer or speaker towards the content of what has been said or written. The most common way of expressing modality is through modal verbs and adverbs.
Examples
Indicating attitude towards the propositional content:
Proposition: *The vicar did it.*
Modalized statements: *The vicar* may *have done it.* They say *the vicar did it. The vicar* must have *done it.* Obviously, *the vicar did it. The vicar* undoubtedly *did it.* I'm sure *the vicar did it.*
Indicating attitude towards illocutionary force:
Directive: *Clean the car.*
Modalized statements: I'd suggest *you clean the car.* You might like to *clean the car.* How about *cleaning the car?* I'd be grateful if you'd *clean the car.* Can *you clean the car this morning?*

morpheme: The smallest meaningful element into which a word can be analysed.
Example: The word *walked* consists of two morphemes: *walk* which signifies an action and *-ed* which signifies the fact that the action took place in the past.

morphology: The study of the internal structure of words.

morphosyntax: The combined study of the internal structure of words (morphology) and the rules that govern the arrangement of words into clauses and sentence (syntax).

move: A basic interactional unit in classroom discourse. Three-part exchanges consist of three moves: an initiating move, a responding move, and a follow-up move.
Example: Teacher: (points to a picture) *What's this?* (initiating)
            Student: *A dolphin.* (responding)
            Teacher: *A dolphin. Very good.* (follow-up)

natural order hypothesis: An hypothesis that grammatical items will be acquired in a predetermined order that cannot be changed by instruction.

negotiation of meaning: The interactional work done by speakers and listeners to ensure mutual understanding in interactions. Commonly used negotiation of meaning strategies include **comprehension checks, confirmation checks** and **clarification requests**.

nominalization: The process of turning verbs into nouns. (See also **grammatical metaphor**.) Nominalization has a number of purposes, including that of removing the doer of the action. It also allows for a process to be topicalized.
Example: *The home team won which excited the crowd*, which becomes *The team's win excited the crowd*.

notions: General concepts expressed through language such as time, duration and quantity.

nouns: Probably the largest class of content words in any language, nouns refer to persons, objects and entities. There are various ways of classifying nouns: for example, countable (*boys, computers, glasses*) versus uncountable (*music, silence, water*); concrete (*pavement, birds, CD*) versus abstract (*beauty, eternity, friendship*). New nouns are being created as quickly as new entities are entering our universe.

object: That part of a sentence or utterance that follows the main verb and is affected or 'acted upon' by the subject.

object complement: A word or phrase that describes or modifies the object of a sentence.
Example: *I used to call her **my best friend**.*

paralinguistics: Nonverbal forms of communication such as facial expressions and body language.

parse: To divide a sentence into its component parts and label these grammatically as subject, verb, object and so on.

passive voice: A sentence or utterance in which the result of an action rather than the performer of the action is made the subject. The passive voice contrasts with the **active voice** and has a number of important discourse functions, such as to emphasize or **thematize** an action or result of an action, or to refer to the result of an action where the doer is unknown.
Example: *The book was finally finished. The hotel room was totally trashed.*

performance: The actual use of language *transformation-generative linguistics* distinguishes between **competence** and performance.

perlocutionary effect: The effect that an utterance has on a listener, or the interpretation that the listener places on the utterance.

phoneme: The smallest meaningful unit of sound in a language.

phonetics: The description and analysis of the ways in which speech sounds are produced, transmitted and understood by speakers and hearers.

phonology: The description and analysis of the distinctive sounds in a language, and the relationship between sound and meaning.

pidgin: A hybrid language used for communication between people who do not share a common language.

polysemy: The property of a word having different but semantically related meanings.

politeness strategies: Discourse strategies that enable the *interlocutors* in a conversation to save face.

pragmatics: The study of the way language is used in particular contexts to achieve particular ends.

preposition: A grammatical word used to relate a noun or noun phrase to some other part of the sentence.

procedural knowledge: The ability to use knowledge to do things. It is sometimes informally known as 'how to' knowledge, and contrasts with declarative knowledge which has to do with the ability to declare rules and principles.

pronominalization: The process of substituting a pronoun for an entire noun phrase.
Example: *I went to the football match yesterday. It was better than I expected.*

pronoun: A word that substitutes for a noun or a noun phrase.

pronunciation: The ways in which sounds are produced. Features of pronunciation are divided into *segmental phonology* (individual sounds) and *suprasegmental phonology* (stress, rhythm and intonation).

proposition: A statement about some entity or event.

propositional meaning: The formal (*locutionary*) meaning of a sentence or utterance which takes no account of the *function* (*illocutionary* meaning) of the utterance within the discourse.
Example: Propositionally, the utterance *The window is open* is a statement about the disposition of an entity – that is, a window. The illocutionary or functional force of the utterance may be a request (*It's awfully cold in here – would you mind shutting the window?*); a suggestion (A: *I can't get out of the room – the door is stuck.* B: *The window is open – why don't you climb out?*) and so on.

psycholinguistics: The study of the mental processes underlying language acquisition and use.

received pronunciation: A British accent associated with public schools and the professions.

reciprocal listening: Listening situations in which the listener also takes part in the interaction as a speaker.

recount: A *genre* consisting of a sequence of events initiated by an introduction and orientation and ending with a comment and conclusion.

reference (cohesive): Those proforms (largely pronouns and demonstratives) in a text that refer to and can only be interpreted with reference to some other part of the text, or to some entity or event in the experiential world.

register: The kind of language used by discourse communities for particular communicative purposes. In systemic-functional linguistics, register is described in terms of field (the subject of the communication), tenor, (the relationship between the interactants) and mode (the means of communication; for example, written versus spoken).

reiteration: A form of lexical cohesion in which the two cohesive items refer to the same entity or event. Reiteration includes repetition, synonym or near synonym, superordinate, and general word. In the following example, the unitalicized words refer to the same entity, and are therefore an example of reiteration.
Example: My computer *has been playing up ever since I installed that new software*. The thing *has been driving me crazy*.

relative clause: A clause that modifies or provides additional information about the subject of a sentence. Relative clauses provide a level of 'delicacy' not possible with co-ordinate clauses because they can indicate the relative status of the additional information. For example, in *My brother, who lives in Tokyo, is visiting me in Hong Kong*, the important information (that is, that which is contained in the main clause) is that the speaker's brother is visiting Hong Kong. In *My brother, who is visiting Hong Kong, lives in New York*, the more important piece of information from the speaker's perspective is that his brother lives in New York.

repair: The correction of clarification of a speaker's utterance, either by the speaker (self-correction) or by someone else (other correction). These corrections serve to fix communication breakdowns in conversation.

reported speech (or *indirect speech*): Language used to report what someone else said. Reported speech involves a tense shift.
Examples: *I am sorry*. > Jake said that he was sorry.
          I finished my assignment early. > Jane said that she had finished her assignment early.
          I'll be there at six. > John said that he'd be there at six.
          I've seen that movie five times. > Wendy said that she had seen the movie five times.

schema theory: A theory of language processing based on the notion that past experiences lead to the creation of mental frameworks that help us make sense of new experiences.

second language acquisition: The psychological and social processes underlying the development of proficiency in a second language.

segmental phonology: The description and study of individual vowels and consonants in a target language. The description of minimal pairs (for example, /ship/ /sheep/), in which the difference in meaning between the two words depends on a single contrasting vowel or consonant, is a major focus of segmental phonology.

semantic network: A network of words in which individual words belong to a particular 'family'.
Example: *rose, petunia, gardenia, hyacinth, poppy*

semantics: The study of the formal meanings expressed in language without reference to the contexts in which the language is used.

sentence: A unit of language containing a subject and a finite verb. Sentences can be simple, containing a single clause, or complex, containing more than one clause. The basic elements of a sentence are ***subject, verb, object, complement*** and ***adverbial***.

sociolinguistics: The study of language in its social context.

speech act: The description of an utterance in terms of what it is doing functionally. There are two main dimensions to a speech act: its ***locutionary force*** which relates to its propositional meaning, and its ***illocutionary force*** which relates to its functional meaning.

stress: The emphasis placed on a syllable or word.

subject complement: A word or phrase that describes or modified the subject of a sentence.
Example: *I am really tired.*

subordinate clause: A clause that is part of another clause. Subordinate clauses are labelled according to the way the way they function in relation to the main clause.
(a) Nominal clauses take on functions associated with noun phrases; for example, subject or object in the main clause;
(b) Adverbial clauses take the function of adverbials;
(c) Relative clauses take an 'adjectival' function, as modifiers in a noun phrase;
(d) Comparative clauses take a modifying function in an adjective phrase, an adverb phrase, or a noun phrase, following a comparative word or construction. (Leech, 1992: 108)

subordination: The process of 'downgrading' one clause in a sentence in order to show that the information it contains is less significant than the information in the main clause.

substitution: A category of cohesive device in which proforms stand in for earlier mentioned nouns, verbs and clauses.
Examples
Nominal substitution:
That car is second hand. **This** one *is brand new.*
Verbal substitution:
A: *I like to take the subway to work.*
B: *So* do *I.*
Clausal substitution:
A: *Are you meeting us for lunch tomorrow?*
B: *I hope* so.

suprasegmental phonology: The study of the role of *stress*, *rhythm* and *intonation* in creating meaning. Suprasegmental features perform many important functions including highlighting important information, and indicating speaker attitude.
Examples
Highlighting important information:
That's *the one I want.*
(Word stress indicates the important information)
Indicating speaker attitude:
That's my drink, isn't it? (upward inflection)
(The upward inflection indicates the speaker's lack of certainty.)

syllable: A unit of pronunciation, usually containing one vowel sound.

synonymy: A special kind of lexical relationship in which two terms refer to the same entity.
Example: *After resisting the temptation for some time, I bought an* iPod *yesterday.* The thing *is now indispensable.*

syntax: The study of the rules that govern the formation of grammatical structures and the ordering of *words* into *sentences*. *Grammar* consists of syntax and *morphology*.

systemic-functional linguistics: A theory that sees language as sets of interrelated systems, that stresses its social nature, and that attempts to account for grammatical features in terms of their communicative functions.

tag question: A question added to a declarative statement. The verb in the tag question usually contrasts with the verb in the main clause in that if the latter is positive, then the former is negative and vice versa. However, this is not always the case. In addition, intonation carries important interpersonal meaning.
Examples: *She's Japanese, isn't she?*
She isn't French, is she?
She's Chinese, is she?

text: The written record of a communicative event which conveys a complete message. Texts may vary from single words (for example, 'EXIT') to books running to hundreds of pages.

text analysis: The analysis of textual features such as cohesion, text structure and information focus. The focus is on formal rather than functional features of language, and the analysis generally makes little reference to the extra-linguistic context that gave rise to the text in the first place.

text structure: Rhetorical patterns within texts such as problem-solution.

texture: The linguistic qualities and characteristics that differentiate a coherent text from a set of random sentences.

text-forming devices: The formal linguistic devices such as cohesion and text-sensitive grammatical choices that create ***texture***.

thematization: The process of giving prominence to certain elements within a sentence or utterance by placing them at the beginning of the sentence or utterance.

theme: The initial word or phrase in a sentence or utterance that forms its point of departure. The rest of the sentence is known as the ***rheme***.

Examples: Theme	Rheme
I	*will meet you at six o'clock at the video store.*
DILLON, Mavis	*dearly beloved sister of Doris and aunty of Michael*
It	*was a pity about the weather.*

top-down processing: The use of background knowledge, knowledge of text structures and so on to assist in the interpretation of discourse.

topic: The experiential subject of a text; that is, what the text is about.

topic selection and change: The interpersonal procedures through which ***interlocutors*** negotiate and agree on a conversational topic, and the procedures through which the topic is subsequently changed.

topicalization: Very closely related to the concept of ***thematization***, topicalization is the process of giving prominence to certain elements in a sentence or utterance by shifting them to the beginning. The following sentences express the same propositional content, but each is topicalized differently.
Examples: *I will finish this glossary tonight.*
This glossary will be finished tonight.
Tonight, I will finish this glossary.

transactional language: Language that is used to obtain goods and services. This use of language contrasts with ***interpersonal language*** where the purpose is primarily social.

transcription: The written record of a piece of spoken discourse.

transformational-generative grammar: A theory of linguistics that attempts to specify the rules underlying a language in the most parsimonious way.

turn: One person's speaking opportunity in a conversation that is bounded by one or more other speakers.

turn taking: The process by which opportunities to speak are distributed between two or more speakers. Rules for turn taking differ from culture to culture. Some allow overlaps and interruptions, while others don't.

utterance: The spoken equivalent of a written sentence.

verb: A word class denoting actions and states.

voice: There are two forms of voice, active and passive. Voice enables the speaker or writer to focus on the person performing the action or the result of the action.

word: A single meaningful unit consisting of one or more *morphemes*.

References

Austin, J. (1962) *How to Do Things with Words* (Oxford: Oxford University Press).

Baring-Gould, W. (1970) *The Lure of the Limerick* (London: Panther Paperback).

Barron, C. (1996) Review of Steven Pinker, *The Language Instinct*; Hong Kong *Journal of Applied Linguistics*, 1, 1, 163–7.

Blakemore, D. (1992) *Understanding Utterances* (Oxford: Blackwell).

Bowden, T. (1987) *One Crowded Hour: Neil Davis Combat Cameraman 1934–1985* (Sydney: William Collins).

Bragg, M. (2003) *The Adventure of English* (London: Hodder & Stoughton).

Brazil, D. (1997) *The Communicative Value of Intonation in English* (Cambridge: Cambridge University Press).

Brown, E.K. and J.E. Miller (1988) *Syntax: A Linguistic Introduction to Sentence Structure* (London: Hutchinson).

Brown, R. (1973) *A First Language* (Cambridge MA: Harvard University Press).

Bryson, B. (2003) *A Short History of Nearly Everything* (London: Doubleday).

Burgess, A. (1987) *Little Wilson and Big God* (London: Penguin).

Burgess, A. (1992) *A Mouthful of Air: Language and Languages, Especially English* (London: Hutchinson).

Carter, R. (2004) *Language and Creativity: The Art of Common Talk* (London: Routledge).

Carter, R., A. Goddard, D. Reah, K. Sanger and M. Bowering (2001) *Working with Texts: A Core Introduction to Language Analysis*, 2nd edn (London: Routledge).

Carter, R. and M. McCarthy (1997) *Exploring Spoken English* (Cambridge: Cambridge University Press).

Carter, R. and M. McCarthy (1997) *Exploring Spoken English* (Cambridge: Cambridge University Press).

Carver, R. (1993) *Short Cuts* (New York: Vintage Books).

Catford, J.C. (1988) *A Practical Introduction to Phonetics* (Oxford: Oxford University Press).

Celce-Murcia, M. and E. Olshtain (2000) *Discourse Analysis for Language Teachers* (Oxford: Oxford University Press).

Chomsky, N. (1957) *Syntactic Structures* (The Hague: Mouton).

Collins, B. and I. Mees (2003) *Practical Phonetics and Phonology* (London: Routledge).

Collins (1992) *Collins Cobuild English Usage* (London: HarperCollins Publishers).

Cook, G. (2000) *Language Play, Language Learning* (Oxford: Oxford University Press).

Cook, G. (2001) *The Discourse of Advertising* (London: Routledge).

Cornbleet, S. and R. Carter (2001) *The Language of Speech and Writing* (London: Routledge).

Crystal, D. (1997a) *The Cambridge Encyclopedia of Language* (Cambridge: Cambridge University Press).

Crystal, D. (1997b) *English as a Global Language* (Cambridge: Cambridge University Press).

Crystal, D. (1998) *Language Play* (London: Penguin).

Crystal, D. (2004) *The Stories of English* (London: Penguin).

Cziko, G. (1995) *Without Miracles: Universal Selection Theory and The Second Darwinian Revolution* (Cambridge, MA: MIT Press).

Cziko, G. (2000) *The Things We Do* (Cambridge, MA: MIT Press).

Donmall, B.G. (ed.) (1985) 'Language Awareness', NLCE Papers and Reports 6 (London: Centre for Information on Language Teaching and Research).

Economou, D. (1986) *Coffeebreak: The Language of Casual Conversation* (Sydney: National Centre for English Language Teaching and Research).

Eggins, S. (1994) *An Introduction to Systemic Functional Linguistics* (London: Pinter).

Feez, S. (1998) *Text-based Syllabus Design* (Sydney: National Centre for English Language Teaching and Research).

Finch, G. (2003) *Word of Mouth: A New Introduction to Language and Communication* (Basingstoke: Palgrave Macmillan).

Florance, C. (2003) *A Boy Beyond Reach* (New York: Simon & Schuster).

Forbes Global (2004) Review of Simon Winchester, *The Meaning of Everything*, February 2004.

Fox, K. (2004) *Watching the English* (London: Hodder & Stoughton).

Friedrich, P. (2000) 'Who owns English?', *New Routes*, July, Sao Paulo: Disal.

Fuentes, C. (2004) 'After I told you so', *Newsweek*, December 2003–February 2004.

Graddol, D. (1997) *THE FUTURE of english* (London: British Council).

Grice, H.P. (1975) 'Logic and conversation', in P. Cole and J.L. Morgan (eds) *Syntax and Semantics. Vol. 3. Speech Acts* (New York: Academic Press).

Halliday, M.A.K. (1973) *Explorations in the Functions of Language* (London: Arnold).

Halliday, M.A.K. (1975) *Learning How to Mean: Explorations in the Development of Language* (London: Arnold).

Halliday, M.A.K. (1978) *Language as Social Semiotic: The Social Interpretation of Language and Meaning* (London: Arnold).

Halliday, M.A.K. (1979) 'One child's protolanguage', in M. Bullows (ed.) *Before Speech: The Beginning of Interpersonal Communication* (Cambridge: Cambridge University Press).

Halliday, M.A.K. (1985) *An Introduction to Functional Grammar* (London: Arnold).

Halliday, M.A.K. and R. Hasan (1976) *Cohesion in English* (London: Longman).

Harmer, J. (1987) *The Practice of English Language Teaching* (London: Longman).

Hatch, E. (1992) *Discourse Analysis* (Cambridge: Cambridge University Press).

Heath, S.B. (1982) *Ways with Words* (New York: Cambridge University Press).

Heylin, C. (2002) *Can You Feel The Silence? Van Morrison: A New Biography* (Chicago: Chicago Review Press).

Hoey, M. (1983) *On The Surface of Discourse* (London: Allen & Unwin).

Hoey, M. (1991) *Patterns of Lexis in Text* (Oxford: Oxford University Press).

Humphrys, J. (2004) *Lost for Words: The Mangling and Manipulation of the English Language* (London: Hodder & Stoughton).

James, C. (2006) 'The continuing insult to the language', *The Monthly*, June.

Joseph, J., N. Love, and T. Taylor (2001) *Landmarks in Linguistic Thought II* (London: Routledge).

King, S. (2000) *On Writing: A Memoir of the Craft* (London: Hodder & Stoughton).

Koestler, A. (1940) *Darkness at Noon* (New York: Bantam Books).

Koestler, A. (1969) *The Act of Creation* (London: Pan Books).

Kuiper, K. and W. Scott Allan (2004) *An Introduction to English Language: Words, Sound and Sentence*, 2nd edn (London: Palgrave Macmillan).

Laing, R.D. (1970) *Knots* (London: Longman).

Lakoff, R. (1975) *Language and Woman's Place* (New York: HarperCollins).

Lakoff, G. and M. Johnson (1980) *Metaphors We Live By* (Chicago: University of Chicago Press).

Lakoff, G. and M. Turner (1989) *More Than Cool Reason* (Chicago: University of Chicago Press).

Leech, G. (1992) *Introducing English Grammar* (London: Penguin).

Lyons, J. (1981) *Language, Meaning and Context* (London: Fontana Paperbacks).

Lustig, M. and J. Koester (1993) *Intercultural Competence: Interpersonal Communication Across Cultures* (New York: HarperCollins).

Macintyre, B. (2004) 'Column on language', *The Times*, 19 June.

Martin, J. (2001) 'Language, register and genre', in A. Burns and C. Coffin (eds) *Analysing English in a Global Context* (London: Routledge).

Nation, P. (2003) 'Vocabulary', in D. Nunan (ed.) *Practical English Language Teaching* (New York: McGraw Hill).

Newbrook, C. (2005) *Ducks in a Row* (London: Short Books).

Noble, J. (1998) 'The evolution of animal communication systems', PhD thesis, School of Cognitive and Computational Science, University of Sussex.

Nunan, D. (1988) *The Learner-Centred Curriculum* (Cambridge: Cambridge University Press).

Nunan, D. (1992) *Research Methods in Language Learning* (Cambridge: Cambridge University Press).

Nunan, D. (1993) *Introducing Discourse Analysis* (London: Penguin).

Nunan, D. (1999) *Second Language Teaching and Learning* (Boston: Thomson/Heinle).

Phillipson, R. (1992) *Linguistic Imperialism* (Oxford: Oxford University Press).

Pinker, S. (1994) *The Language Instinct* (London: Penguin).

Radford, A., M. Atkins, D. Britain, H. Clahsen and A. Spenser (1999) *Linguistics: An Introduction* (Cambridge: Cambridge University Press).

Richards, J., J. Platt and H. Weber (1985) *Longman Dictionary of Applied Linguistics* (London: Longman).

Roach, P. (1991) *English Phonetics and Phonology*, 2nd edn (Cambridge: Cambridge University Press).

Roach, P. (1992) *Introducing Phonetics* (London: Penguin).

Ross, A.S. (1997) (cited in D. Crystal) *The Cambridge Encyclopedia of Language* (Cambridge: Cambridge University Press).

Schiffrin, D. (1994) *Approaches to Discourse* (Oxford: Blackwell).

Searle, J. (1969) *Speech Acts: An Essay in the Philosophy of Language* (Cambridge: Cambridge University Press).

Skapinker, M. (2003) Column, *Financial Times*, 30 July.

Skinner, B. (1957) *Verbal Behavior* (New York: Appleton Crofts).

Slade, D. and L. Norris (1990) *Casual Conversation* (Sydney: National Centre for English Language Teaching and Research).

Spiegl, F. (1965) *What the Papers Didn't Mean to Say* (Liverpool: Scouse Press).

Tannen, D. (1991) *You Just Don't Understand* (New York: Ballentine Books).

Thomas, D. (no date) 'In the beginning', *Miscellany II* (London: Faber).

Thomas, J. (1995) *Meaning in Interaction* (London: Longman).

Thompson, G. (1996) *Introducing Functional Grammar* (London: Arnold).

Truss, L. (2004) 'Why I'm hooked on Tiger's semantic antics', *The Times*, Game supplement, 12 July.

Ur, P. (1989) *Grammar Practice Activities* (Cambridge: Cambridge University Press).

van Lier, L. (1989) 'Reeling, writhing, drawling, stretching, and fainting in coils: proficiency interviews as conversation', *TESOL Quarterly*, 23, 489–508.

van Lier, L. (1995) *Introducing Language Awareness* (London: Penguin).

van Lier, L. (2001) 'Language awareness', in R. Carter and D. Nunan (eds) *The Cambridge Guide to Teaching Speakers of Other Languages* (Cambridge: Cambridge University Press).

Wallraff, B. (2000) 'What global language?', *The Atlantic Monthly*, November.

Wells, G. (1981) *Learning Through Interaction* (Cambridge: Cambridge University Press).

Widdowson, H.G. (1983) *Learning Purpose and Language Use* (Oxford: Oxford University Press).

Widdowson, H. (1990) *Aspects of Language Teaching* (Oxford: Oxford University Press).

Wilde, O. (1948) 'The Ballad of Reading Gaol', in *Complete Works of Oscar Wilde* (London: Collins).

Willing, K. (1989) *Workplace Communication* (Sydney: National Centre for English Language Teaching and Research).

Winchester, S. (2003) *The Meaning of Everything* (Oxford: Oxford University Press).

Yallop. C. (1995) *English Phonology* (Sydney: National Centre for English Language Teaching and Research).

Author index

Subject index